T0281695

Beyond jQuery

Ray Nicholus

Apress®

Beyond jQuery

Ray Nicholus
Johnson Creek
Wisconsin, USA

ISBN-13 (pbk): 978-1-4842-2234-8   ISBN-13 (electronic): 978-1-4842-2235-5
DOI 10.1007/978-1-4842-2235-5

Library of Congress Control Number: 2016953737

Copyright © 2016 by Ray Nicholus

This work is subject to copyright. All rights are reserved by the Publisher, whether the whole or part of the material is concerned, specifically the rights of translation, reprinting, reuse of illustrations, recitation, broadcasting, reproduction on microfilms or in any other physical way, and transmission or information storage and retrieval, electronic adaptation, computer software, or by similar or dissimilar methodology now known or hereafter developed.

Trademarked names, logos, and images may appear in this book. Rather than use a trademark symbol with every occurrence of a trademarked name, logo, or image we use the names, logos, and images only in an editorial fashion and to the benefit of the trademark owner, with no intention of infringement of the trademark.

The use in this publication of trade names, trademarks, service marks, and similar terms, even if they are not identified as such, is not to be taken as an expression of opinion as to whether or not they are subject to proprietary rights.

While the advice and information in this book are believed to be true and accurate at the date of publication, neither the authors nor the editors nor the publisher can accept any legal responsibility for any errors or omissions that may be made. The publisher makes no warranty, express or implied, with respect to the material contained herein.

Managing Director: Welmoed Spahr
Acquisitions Editor: Louise Corrigan
Development Editor: James Markham
Editorial Board: Steve Anglin, Pramila Balan, Laura Berendson, Aaron Black, Louise Corrigan,
    Jonathan Gennick, Todd Green, Robert Hutchinson, Celestin Suresh John, Nikhil Karkal,
    James Markham, Susan McDermott, Matthew Moodie, Natalie Pao, Gwenan Spearing
Coordinating Editor: Nancy Chen
Copy Editor: Corbin Collins
Compositor: SPi Global
Indexer: SPi Global
Cover Image: Courtesy of Freepik

Distributed to the book trade worldwide by Springer Science+Business Media New York, 233 Spring Street, 6th Floor, New York, NY 10013. Phone 1-800-SPRINGER, fax (201) 348-4505, e-mail orders-ny@springer-sbm.com, or visit www.springer.com. Apress Media, LLC is a California LLC and the sole member (owner) is Springer Science + Business Media Finance Inc (SSBM Finance Inc). SSBM Finance Inc is a Delaware corporation.

For information on translations, please e-mail rights@apress.com, or visit www.apress.com.

Apress and friends of ED books may be purchased in bulk for academic, corporate, or promotional use. eBook versions and licenses are also available for most titles. For more information, reference our Special Bulk Sales–eBook Licensing web page at www.apress.com/bulk-sales.

Any source code or other supplementary materials referenced by the author in this text are available to readers at www.apress.com. For detailed information about how to locate your book's source code, go to www.apress.com/source-code/. Readers can also access source code at SpringerLink in the Supplementary Material section for each chapter.

Printed on acid-free paper

Contents at a Glance

Contents

About the Author

Ray Nicholus is a software developer for Widen (www.widen.com) in Madison, Wisconsin, and has been heavily involved in web development for years. Although much of his code is closed source and not publicly available, he has spent a great deal of time contributing to the open source software movement, primary focusing on JavaScript, front-end library development, and developer education. His open source contributions range from large and popular open source projects, to small and focused libraries and educational code repositories. He is a true believer in FOSS, and has even written about the topic, such as in his post on Medium.com (https://medium.com/@RayNicholus/disrupting-open-source-the-story-of-fine-uploader-80160eb557d9#.63z1olm9d) that detailed his decision to release Fine Uploader, a popular commercially licensed JavaScript library, to the free open source software community.

Since 2012 he has been the lead developer and product manager of the Fine Uploader (http://fineuploader.com) organization, which is commonly known as for its uniquely featured cross-browser, no-dependency file upload JavaScript library. His involvement outside of Fine Uploader in the open source community has included creation of other popular software libraries dealing with web components, namely ajax-form (https://github.com/rnicholus/ajax-form) and file-input (https://github.com/rnicholus/file-input), video and image manipulation, such as frame-grab.js (https://github.com/rnicholus/frame-grab.js), and informative code collections, such as the notable fullstack-react project on GitHub (https://github.com/Widen/fullstack-react) and its associated articles on the Widen Engineering site (http://engineering.widen.com/blog/future-of-the-web-react-falcor/).

In addition to frequent coding outside of his day job, he also spends time speaking about web development topics (https://slides.com/raynicholus). He has presented to students at the University of Wisconsin and DePaul University regarding careers in software development. And he has prepared and delivered presentations to many professional developers regarding the mysteries of Cross Origin Resource Sharing, the importance of automated testing, the File API web specification, the web components specifications, agile software development, accessibility, and software architecture (among others). He organized and taught a JavaScript 101 class targeted at interested professionals and spoke about the usefulness of uploading files directly to Amazon's Simple Storage Service from the browser via Fine Uploader.

His writing also includes the precursor to this book, the "You Don't Need jQuery!" series of blog posts (http://blog.garstasio.com/you-dont-need-jquery/), articles on Google Glass (www.widen.com/blog/ray-nicholus), and a large number of other articles that help developers integrate file uploading capabilities into their web application or library (http://blog.fineuploader.com/author/rnicholus/). He was also featured in an article in *Fortune* magazine by Anne Fisher based on his experiences with Google Glass in the workplace (http://fortune.com/2014/09/30/google-glass-at-work/).

He currently lives in Johnson Creek, Wisconsin, with his wife Kat and his son Ray IV. They are known to spend long stretches of time in Thailand (especially in the Udon Thani area) where a portion of this book was written.

Preface

Back in 2010, I abruptly and unexpectedly moved into professional web application development. My background up to that point was almost exclusively dedicated to the server. User interfaces were developed using Java Applets or Swing. I spent most of my time writing Java code, without much interest in the Web. That all changed when I joined a project in Avid's broadcast division. It was to be our first web offering, a multi-role media production tool code-named "Jennings," now known as MediaCentral UX (`https://www.avid.com/US/products/MediaCentral-UX`).

Jennings was my first *real* web project. Sure, I had dabbled in the Web before, but never created anything particularly interesting or useful. I wasn't alone though—many others on the team came from a similar place. Jennings had some lofty goals, and there was little time to get up to speed on all things web. As a result, I spent a negligible amount of time brushing up on JavaScript, HTML, and CSS. An alternative, it seemed at the time, was to simply embrace jQuery. I managed to stumble though my tasks, leaning on jQuery the whole way through. But I can remember a number of instances where the warm blanket of jQuery was unexpectedly yanked off, and I was forced to deal directly with the web API and JavaScript. I doubt I even knew *what* the web API was at the time.

Over the course of the next year, it became clear that substantial gaps in my knowledge had formed as a result of the shortcuts I took. I (partially) learned a *library* instead of learning the fundamentals. I felt anchored to jQuery, as I didn't possess the knowledge to develop much of anything web-based without it. Perhaps I was just a bad developer. Surely other developers were smarter, and took the proper path. But my discussions with others through the years put this assumption to rest. Indeed, my experience was all too common. Even today, just browsing the jQuery questions on Stack Overflow suggests that this backwards approach is still the status quo.

Shortly before I left Avid in early 2011, I promised myself that I would never again be confounded by the browser or JavaScript. I pressed a figurative "reset" button and began to learn web development through a strict study of the fundamentals. I didn't abandon jQuery during this process. In fact, I studied jQuery just as closely, and not just its API, but its code, design, and purpose. I began to develop small libraries, first jQuery plug-ins, then small dependency-free libraries. And then, in 2012, I became the sole maintainer and developer of Fine Uploader, a large cross-browser, no-dependency file upload library. I spent years re-developing Fine Uploader, and other libraries, honing my understanding of the web API and JavaScript.

At some point, after helping a number of developers to better understand the browser *and* JavaScript, I decided to begin sharing my knowledge in the form of writing. My target audience mostly mirrored a younger me, early on in my web development career, but I aimed to educate more experienced developers as well. Out of this desire came a series of blog posts titled "You Don't Need jQuery!" (`http://dont-need-jquery.raynicholus.com`). In this six-post series, I covered element selectors, DOM manipulation, AJAX requests, event handling, and common utility functions. The overarching goal was to show developers how to solve a number of common problems without jQuery. Although "You Don't Need jQuery!" was popular, it was also a bit controversial. There were mostly positive responses to the information contained in my articles, though clearly some developers with heavy attachments to the library were offended. One even claimed that the title was "condescending." I had struck a nerve.

The heavy response to my blog meant that my message was important. It seemed clear that the web development community needed something like this. I even wished that I had come across something similar earlier in my career. Quite a few developers were excited at the possibilities of *Life After jQuery* (an early contender for this book's title). Their newfound knowledge empowered them, and this was ultimately my goal. My articles were translated into Chinese and Portuguese, so, clearly, the audience was not limited to my home country. The desire to learn about the Web outside of the lens of jQuery spanned the world.

I originally planned to create another series of articles, this time based on cross-domain browser-based communication, another field in which I posses a good deal of knowledge. But it occurred to me that I had more to say on the topic of jQuery, the web API, and JavaScript. Perhaps if I took some time to expand on this message, even more developers would benefit. Something long-form, perhaps a book, seemed like the next logical step, and *Beyond jQuery* was born.

Acknowledgments

So many people have helped make this book possible in one way or another, but I'd like to thank three people in particular for their advice and ideas. Annette Jensen (`www.linkedin.com/in/annettekayjensen`), the director of software development at Widen (`http://widen.com`), gave me the initial idea to turn my series of articles on transitioning away from jQuery into this book. Without her insight, *Beyond jQuery* would not exist. Matthew Gonnering offered quite a bit of guidance and advice on publishing and procedural decisions. He also was more than willing to listen to me gripe about the stress associated with writing a book, and provided a great amount of feedback that allowed me to pursue my goals as a writer. Phil Nash (`https://philna.sh/`), developer evangelist for Twilio, provided an amazingly comprehensive technical review of this book for me. Not only were his suggestions insightful and appropriate but they also prompted me to reexamine other areas of the book, which resulted in even more necessary changes before publishing. I can't express enough how grateful I am for his help. And finally, Widen (my employer) has contributed by providing a free environment (`www.marketwired.com/press-release/worldblu-certifies-widen-as-a-freedom-centered-workplace-2025603.htm`) where developers can be creative, productive, and happy in their pursuit of developing amazingly innovative marketing technology. Thank you to everyone who has assisted me in my work.

Introduction

This book is not about bashing jQuery. Although I am personally very much in favor of directly utilizing what the browser and the JavaScript language provide, the primary purpose of this book is not necessarily to compel developers to abandon all third-party solutions. This is not primarily a stage to host a competition between jQuery and the web API. I have a great amount of respect for those who have maintained and supported jQuery since its inception. I mean no disrespect to those associated with jQuery. In fact, similar arguments could be made about other libraries, such as underscore.js, lodash, or zepto.js. But the ubiquitousness of jQuery makes it the most appropriate reference for this book.

The purpose of this book is to teach you about the browser's native tools. Of course, if you want to continue using jQuery, you may do so (not that you need my permission). This book will hopefully give you the confidence and knowledge you need to remove this dependency from your future projects, if you so choose. At the very least, by reading all of this, you will gain a better understanding of the web API and JavaScript as a language, which is important to your evolution as a web developer, whether you use jQuery or not. Although I do stress use of the native web API and JavaScript sans jQuery, my intention is not to encourage JavaScript as a solution to all problems. JavaScript and the web API are simply tools that may be used to solve some problems. CSS and proper use of HTML may be more appropriate solutions to some of these problems, as you will see later on.

In addition to instilling confidence in new web developers and those a bit overwhelmed by the browser's native API, *Beyond jQuery* has many other goals. I intend to teach you about the fundamentals, pitfalls, and best practices that are otherwise masked by jQuery. You will learn to perform common operations and solve common problems without the use of jQuery. I will also reveal why jQuery may have been necessary in the past, but is no longer needed with the advent of modern browsers and more evolved web and JavaScript specifications.

When you finish this book, you will be able to write more efficient front-end code by examining some performance issues historically associated with jQuery. Native alternatives are described as well. You will learn more about the browser's API, JavaScript, and even jQuery through detailed explanation and code examples. I demonstrate how common operations are performed using jQuery, and then solve the same problems using the web API and "vanilla" JavaScript. *Beyond jQuery* contains copious amounts of code snippets, ranging from simple to complex, to help you understand how to develop something substantial without the crutch of a third-party library.

I have also created a companion exercise for readers of this book, hosted in a GitHub repository at `https://github.com/Beyond-jQuery/exercise`. This project demonstrates a number of the techniques and native APIs described throughout this book in a single comprehensive web application. Feel free to clone the exercise repository, run it yourself, and customize the code. Though the code itself is already annotated with helpful comments, you may also ask questions about the exercise in the project's issue tracker.

CHAPTER 1

■ ■ ■

The Oppressive Magic of jQuery

For many years, both amateur and professional web developers alike have made use of jQuery to ease the burden of bringing a library or web application to market. In a sense, jQuery has been an integral part of web development. Even at the time of writing, jQuery is referenced in the vast majority of public websites,[1] more so than any other library, by a wide margin.

Many developers seem to consider jQuery to be a default requirement. The common thought is: if you are developing a library or a web application, you *must* depend on jQuery. jQuery is seen as this magical black box that solves all of the woes of web development. It's a framework that is easy to understand and allows even novices to swiftly codify their ideas.

Professionals tend to be quite invested in jQuery as well. After all, this is what we used back when *we* were novices. It's comfortable. We understand it. We trust it. It has served us well over the years. You don't have to think (much) about the DOM, or browser bugs, or cross-browser behaviors. jQuery solves all of these problems for us . . . doesn't it?

There is no denying that jQuery *is* indeed a bit magical. In fact, it allows developers of almost any skill level to create something useful. But at what cost? Consider only understanding the web through rose-colored jQuery lenses. What if you encounter a low-level behavior that jQuery has not properly abstracted? What if you encounter a bug in jQuery? What if you are simply not able (allowed) to use jQuery? This is akin to a city dweller being dropped into the tundra of Siberia. Under these conditions, you are scared, disoriented, and ill-prepared.

Although the likelihood of being whisked away to a foreign land against your will is small, being without jQuery in the future is a much more realistic possibility. If you don't have a good grasp of the DOM, the web API, and JavaScript, you will eventually feel a *bit* like a cold and confused urbanite, trying to survive the unfamiliar conditions of the Siberian expanse.

One goal of *Beyond jQuery* is to demystify this seemingly ubiquitous front-end library. The benefits of shedding any blind dependence on jQuery will become clear. At the end of this book, you will have the power to grow further as a web developer given your newfound understanding of the browser's API *and* JavaScript.

This chapter explores reasons why developers have depended on jQuery, and why they continue to do so. You will see why relying entirely on one monolithic library creates gaps in your knowledge and prevents you from evolving as a developer. I will discuss why a filtered understanding of the web and JavaScript is a potentially hazardous predicament for developers. Given this knowledge, you will be able to better understand the benefits of depending more on your own solid understanding of the fundamentals.

---

[1]https://w3techs.com/technologies/history_overview/javascript_library/all/y

© Ray Nicholus 2016

R. Nicholus, *Beyond jQuery*, DOI 10.1007/978-1-4842-2235-5_1

Why Have We Been Using jQuery?

Before exploring how (and why) we should consider removing jQuery from our toolbox, we should first understand why jQuery even exists. Why have countless web developers over the years depended on this library? Why has it been such a central component of websites and applications? Why does it continue to be so ubiquitous? Why *have* we been using jQuery? We all have our reasons, and there are many reasons indeed. Above all else, jQuery has proven to offer a low barrier to entry. In other words, even amateur or occasional developers find that it allows them to implement a concept or idea with little resistance.

Simplicity

The assumption is that, if you are reading this book, you are already somewhat familiar with jQuery. You have likely already used it in some project, regardless of the size. So let's explore *why* this library is so easy for developers of all skills levels to use.

Above all else, jQuery's API is intuitive. Want to add a CSS class to an element? Just use the addClass() method. Need to send a POST request? Just use the post() method. And hiding an element is as simple as passing it as a parameter into jQuery's hide() method.

The magic of jQuery is evident in its dirt-simple API. It allows those who have little prior knowledge of the browser or JavaScript to create something intriguing and useful. This is quite appealing and arguably even most appropriate for those who only dabble in web development. Conversely, the simplicity of jQuery is also a potential hazard for professional web developers. If you do not already believe this to be true, we will explore this theory a bit more later on.

Community

On Stack Overflow (at the writing of this book), 1.2 million questions are tagged as JavaScript questions, and 750,000 are tagged as *jQuery* questions. jQuery is the 6th-most popular tag on Stack Overflow. The next most popular front end library is AngularJS in a distant 21st place, which only has 200,000 tagged questions. Interestingly, 200,000 questions are tagged as jQuery and *not* JavaScript. In many cases, jQuery is not seen as a JavaScript library. In fact, it is seen as an alternative to JavaScript. A way to address the browser without having to ever deal with the underlying language or API. While the relation to JavaScript may not be clear to some, jQuery has no shortage of developers willing and ready to offer advice on the library. Of the 750,000 jQuery-tagged questions on Stack Overflow, 550,000 (74%) contained at least one upvoted answer.

As of mid-2016, jQuery is still the most used JavaScript library in public websites. In fact, 70% of all public websites depend on jQuery in some way.[2] The next most popular library is Bootstrap, which is only used in 13% of all public sites. With this impressive market share, there is certainly a fair share of users with some working knowledge of the topic.

In addition to the jQuery tag on Stack Overflow and the wealth of different forums and sites dedicated to advising those invested in the technology, jQuery's site has its own active user forums. Help is easy to find, and any problem you may run into has likely already been solved and discussed at length. The reality of a large and mature community is an appealing reason to depend on any software library.

Habit

The large number of examples, blog posts, and forums aimed at jQuery beginners is one of the reasons why those new to web development choose this library to assist with their project. But what about seasoned developers? Why do they *continue* to use jQuery in *their* projects? A polished, experienced developer was once an amateur. As amateurs, they may very well have embraced jQuery. Now, with multiple projects under

---

[2]http://w3techs.com/technologies/history_overview/javascript_library/all/y

their belt, jQuery has proven itself. And even if some of the flaws in the library have been noticed, they are well understood.

To a seasoned developer, jQuery is consistent and reliable enough. It has become part of the development process. A strong community is a benefit realized by experienced developers as well, and this is yet another reason to stick with such a trustworthy tool.

jQuery has been a prerequisite for everything we write. We mindlessly import it, partially because we have been trained, out of habit, to do so. We have been trained to think that this is a vital component of every web application. Habits are hard to break, especially those that have produced positive results.

Software development can be stressful and frustrating. A typical developer wrestles with a seemingly infinite number of variables on a daily basis. No problem, it seems, is simple to solve. Consistency and predictability of a tool, process, or outcome is highly desired and rare. Can you blame the web development community for relying on a consistent and reliable tool like jQuery for so long?

Elegance

Have you ever heard anyone claim that the DOM is ugly or JavaScript is flawed and riddled with time bombs? Perhaps you think this yourself. While beauty is mostly subjective, this seems to be a surprisingly common thought, especially among more seasoned developers who continue to use jQuery late into their web development career.

The oft-perceived lack of elegance in the native browser API and JavaScript ostensibly drives developers to this library, among other things. The thought is that simple problems are difficult to solve without the aid of jQuery. Don't believe me? Ask some of the developers you work with. Why do they use jQuery? Expect to hear about how simple it is to create elegant and terse code in response to common problems. As discussed earlier in this section, the API itself is intuitive and elegant.

But the elegance of jQuery is more than simply a predictable API. The usability considerations surrounding the design of the API further this claim of elegance.

Take method chaining, for example, which allows a developer to very easily tie together a number of operations on the same element or elements without the burden of repetition or temporary variable creation. Suppose you want to select a set of elements, then add a class to all of them, and finally add a class to an even more specific subset of the initial set of elements. You can do all of this very easily by harnessing the elegance of method chaining provided by jQuery's API. Listing 1-1 demonstrates this by adding a class of "underline" to all elements that contain a class of "alphabet". It then selects only child elements of "alphabet" elements that contain a class of "vowels" and finally annotates them with a class of "bold" while hiding any child of "vowels" elements that themselves also contain a class of "a":

Listing 1-1. jQuery method chaining

```
1  $('.alphabet').addClass('underline')
2    .find('.vowels').addClass('bold')
3      .find('.a').hide();
```

I have found that many developers tend to struggle with asynchronous operations in JavaScript, such as AJAX requests. Making these requests is not difficult, but dealing with the result, given the asynchronous nature of the call, proves to be frustrating for some. jQuery simplifies this a bit by allowing a response handling function to be elegantly tied to the function call that sends the underlying request. Listing 1-2 sends a request to retrieve a user's name, providing simple access to the result from the server's response.

Listing 1-2. jQuery GET request

```
1  $.get('name/123', function(theName) {
2    console.log(theName);
3  });
```

■ **Note**   The console object is not available in Internet Explorer 9 and older unless the developer tools are open. Also, the preceding example does not handle error responses, only success.

With all this "beauty," it's easy to forget about other attributes of our efforts, such as performance. Are there potential efficiency land mines in the previous examples? Yes, but these may be tough to identify initially. I discuss this more in a later chapter.

Fear

jQuery makes everything easier—web development is hard. You can't develop a solid web application or library without some help. It's far too difficult to ensure your app will work properly in all browsers without jQuery. The web API implementation varies wildly between browsers. All the good plug-ins you need depend on jQuery anyway. These are all common excuses for blindly depending on jQuery, and they are all based on fear. We have all relied on jQuery due to fear of the unknown. We see the DOM as a mysterious and unpredictable black box, littered with serious bugs. We fear cross-browser implementation variances.

The creator of jQuery, John Resig, famously concluded that "The DOM is a mess" back in 2009.[3] At that moment in web history, Internet Explorer 6 and 7 accounted for almost 60% of the browser market.[4] With this in mind, it's hard to argue with Mr. Resig's statement at the time. The DOM was indeed a scary and fickle beast, and the most popular browsers of the day had very poor and limited built-in tools. What if we look even further back, to August 2006, when jQuery was created and first released? At that time, the newest version of Internet Explorer was version 6. IE6 (and older) accounted for an incredible 83% of all browsers in use.[5] At this point, the web API was exceptionally immature, stability of browsers was much lower than we have come to expect in the current era, and standards compliance was quite inconsistent across the browsers of the time.

In addition to immature developer tools, varying web API implementations, and the unintuitive DOM, browsers can certainly be buggy. Similar to any other complex bundle of code, browsers are not immune from bugs. jQuery has historically promised a wide range of browser bug workarounds.[6] For many years, the web seemed to be akin to the Wild West in terms of standards observance and quality control. It's not hard to see why a library that aims to normalize the browser landscape was so popular. No need to fear cross-browser support anymore. No need to even worry about cross-browser testing. jQuery will do all of the heavy lifting for you, so you can focus entirely on developing intriguing and useful web applications and libraries. Or can you? While the hope is that jQuery will free you from all of the problems and complexities baked into the browser, the reality is a bit different.

A Crutch Is Only Temporary

JavaScript libraries are often useful tools. They assist in your efforts to architect a useful and reliable web application, or perhaps even *another* library. They save you time and keystrokes. They serve as a buffer between you, your code, and the browser, filling in the gaps and normalizing behavior. In another sense, these libraries can function as crutches. They help inexperienced and uneducated developers, without actually teaching them anything about the underlying complexity. Even though the tone of this book may at times suggest otherwise, libraries like jQuery are not inherently bad. They are only limiting if your learning does not progress beyond the library.

---

[3]http://ejohn.org/blog/the-dom-is-a-mess/
[4]www.w3counter.com/globalstats.php?year=2009&month=1
[5]www.onestat.com/html/aboutus_pressbox44-mozilla-firefox-has-slightly-increased.html
[6]https://docs.google.com/document/d/1LPaPA3ObLUB_publLIMFORlhdnPx_ePXm7oWO2iiT6o/
preview?sle=true#heading=h.fumxprdxo2gn

Does jQuery *always* save you time? Is it *always* making your web development experience easier? Are the conventions associated with the core library or its plug-ins intuitive? Does it really solve all of your problems, or does it perhaps create some new ones? Have you taken the time to ponder the syntax and conventions that come with the library? Is there a better solution, or does jQuery really patch all of the usability holes that developers often fall into? Mostly, jQuery's API is pleasing to the eye and remarkably intuitive. But of course this is not true *all* of the time. There are certainly parts of the library that are unpleasant. Let us example the elegance and necessity of jQuery a bit.

jQuery does not completely shield you from the browser's quirks. This is not a realistic goal of any library. Aside from this, jQuery is simply a library, a tool, an aid. It isn't meant to replace the *entire browser stack*. Some problems are even best solved with CSS or static HTML. But to the developer using jQuery as a crutch, it is the only way to interface with the browser. To the uninformed developer, it is perfectly reasonable to write minimal HTML and make any and all adjustments to markup using jQuery's API. Or perhaps it would be even easier to generate all markup using jQuery. You can create elements with jQuery, and then easily insert them onto the page.

Instead of declaring styles in CSS files, the inclination is to use `$(element).css('fontWeight', 'bold')`. While very convenient, this is a horribly unmaintainable method of generating inline styles. The importance of separation of concerns may not be readily apparent to the new developer. The magical all-encompassing API of jQuery makes it easy to ignore the native tools available to us. The appropriate roles of HTML, CSS, and JavaScript do not always enter into the equation when you are blindly depending on a monolithic abstraction. This library is not just a tool for some, it is *the* tool. It is the be-all and end-all of web development. You'll see why this is a dangerous line of thinking, especially for professional and aspiring developers.

Indeed, jQuery is a crutch for many. It is not fused to the browser and merely acts as a supplement. Experienced and knowledgeable developers may actually prefer to use jQuery, and there is certainly nothing wrong with that. But for others, it serves as a prop. Those new to the world of web development often pick up this crutch and hobble along for quite some time. But eventually, the crutch is pulled out from under them, and they fall.

You Are a Mechanic, Not a Driver

A popular question on Stack Overflow asks "Is it a good idea to learn JavaScript before learning jQuery?"[7] One particular answer to this question provides some curious advice. The contributor goes on to say in his answer "You really don't need to focus too much on learning the ins and outs of the HTML DOM if you are going to use a framework like jQuery. Just do things the 'jQuery way' and then pick up as much HTML DOM as is necessary along the way."[8] Though this line of thinking is apparently *not* common among others who contributed answers to this question (perhaps more experienced developers). I myself was a new and inexperienced web developer at one point and remember how this train of thought was embraced by those entering the confusing world of browser-based front-end coding.

In a series of blog posts I wrote entitled "You Don't Need jQuery",[9] a commenter provided a striking analogy that outlined one of the goals of the blog (and this book).

"One of the things I try to guide my peers on is the fact that you don't put up walls on a foundation before you pour the foundation. In fact you should level the ground, lie the plumbing for functionality (testing) and then pour the foundation before you begin building the structure. This comes into understanding the core of your tools (HTML, CSS, JS) when building for any endpoint (browsers)",[10] Lawrence Francell).

In other words, for a stable, long-lasting application or library, you must have a good understanding of exactly how your tools work. Short of this, you are not a developer. You are, in fact, a *library integrator*.

---

[7]http://stackoverflow.com/questions/668642/
is-it-a-good-idea-to-learn-javascript-before-learning-jquery
[8]http://stackoverflow.com/a/841292/486979
[9]http://blog.garstasio.com/you-dont-need-jquery/
[10]http://blog.garstasio.com/you-dont-need-jquery/why-not/#comment-1799026169

It's difficult to argue with the sound advice of the commenter, but the stunning magic of jQuery seems to blind us sometimes. This does not make us "bad" developers. In fact, it may not even be our fault. We are wired to take the path of least resistance. This is actually a well-studied and documented psychological theory, known as the "principle of least effort" (from *Human Behavior and the Principle of Least Effort* by George Kingsley Zipf (Addison-Wesley Press, 1949).

Playing devil's advocate, perhaps we could refute the previously quoted analogy with another. Most of us probably drive a car on a daily basis. But how many of us are able to diagnose an issue with a typical internal combustion engine? How many of are even capable of anything beyond changing a flat tire? The answer to these questions is likely "very few."

Do we really need to be competent auto mechanics to drive a car? No, of course not. For many of us, driving is not a profession. Instead, it's a convenience that we rely on. We don't have the time to understand every minute detail of our cars, and we shouldn't have to. Cars exist to simplify our lives and save us time. Car manufacturers don't expect their customers to be auto mechanics. They design their products with the average person in mind in order to ensure their cars are usable by as many people as possible, for obvious reasons.

Can we compare driving a car to driving the browser? As software developers, do we really need to understand the underpinnings of the web? As you saw in the above Stack Overflow answer, some may say no. But it's important to understand that we are *not* drivers. We are mechanics and designers, *not* users.

Stunted Growth

What happens when you are thrust onto a new project without jQuery, without your crutch? If your capabilities stop at the edge of the library's API, your options are limited. You're very much invested in this abstraction, jeopardizing your ability to grow beyond it. Do you really want to be dependent on a single chunk of code for all of your projects? In the short term, this doesn't seem like a problem. Looking forward, the feasibility of this path becomes questionable.

The landscape of software development, and technology in general, is constantly changing. As developers, we not only understand this, we embrace it. This makes our jobs both challenging and interesting. There's nothing wrong with using jQuery, or any other library. But by using these as a crutch, we cease to be software developers. We are jQuery programmers.

As a new developer, your goals shouldn't necessarily revolve around agility. Learning the fundamentals at this early stage is paramount. By becoming comfortable with your environment—the browser—you put yourself in a better position to make good decisions as your project and career evolves. Only after you have a firm grasp of the fundamentals and a better understanding of web development in its most basic form should you focus on choosing and learning a tool to speed up your development process.

This advice is really not specific to software development. Do you remember back when you were first learning math? All the exercises you completed could have easily be solved using a calculator. Most likely, you were strictly forbidden from using a calculator, though (I know I was). Why? Calculators are faster and more accurate. Simply put, in this stage, the aim is not speed. A thorough understanding of the fundamentals—of math—is most important. Once you understand *how* the calculator performs these tasks, you can choose to use one, or not, as you solve more complex problems in the future. Understanding the fundamentals ensures you are not chained to a tool.

When our library of choice fades into obsolescence or is otherwise pulled out from under us, our blind reliance prevents us from moving forward. Examples of this unfortunate situation are readily available. In a fairly recent article in JavaWorld,[11] the author cites "6 reasons you should be using jQuery." The reasons are questionable as the author clearly is missing even a basic understanding of the browser stack. This is particularly evident in claims such as "jQuery is a major component of HTML5," conflating JavaScript with

---

[11]www.javaworld.com/article/2078613/java-web-development/6-reasons-you-should-be-using-jquery.html

a document markup specification. Another troubling quote from this article: "jQuery pages load faster." It's this type of oversimplification that leads us, as developers, to take the complexity of our jobs for granted. By pretending that a beast like the browser can be tamed with a single library just opens us up to a frustrating struggle that we will eventually lose.

The Price of Shortcuts (a True Story)

What follows is a real story of a real web developer who took real shortcuts (really). He only focused on the short term, on making his job easier. His main concern was pleasing project managers. Learning the fundamentals was a waste of time to him. Churning out code and plowing through a long list of features as quickly as possible was his goal. That developer was *me*.

jQuery makes everything easier. You can't develop a solid web app without it. It's far too difficult to ensure your app will work properly in all browsers without jQuery. The DOM API implementation varies wildly between browsers. All the good plug-ins you need depend on jQuery anyway. I bought into all of these excuses, and more. Some of them were even good excuses at one time.

A New Direction, a New Web Developer

Back in the very early days of my web development career, I was transitioning from exclusive server-side work. I was assigned to Jennings, a web-based journalist production tool. I had no professional HTML, CSS, or JavaScript experience. My front-end skills were lacking, to say the least.

No one on the team was comfortable with web development. We were all rookies, former back-end developers struggling in vain to make sense of our knowledge in this new context. The deadlines were strict, the goals lofty. It seemed that we all needed some help—perhaps a tool to make our jobs a bit easier. There was no time to learn. We had an application to write!

Shortcuts and My Own Stunted Growth

My first exposure to JavaScript and the web was filtered through jQuery. In fact, I didn't even bother to learn proper JavaScript. I didn't have a clue what the web API looked like, or how to deal with the DOM directly. jQuery did everything for me. This huge gap in my knowledge caught up with me when I later ended up on a project without my jQuery crutch. I was forced to learn proper web development, and I never looked back.

After Jennings, jQuery was a requirement (for me) in all future projects. It was a must, because I didn't know any other way to tame the browser. This didn't seem unusual at the time. In fact, it wasn't. jQuery was an expected dependency in most applications and libraries. My blind faith was not an obvious hinderance.

Some of the issues of this blind dependency became apparent, to some degree, as I searched for plug-ins to solve common problems in my projects. jQuery is a useful library by itself, but it only addresses core, low-level concerns. If you want to support higher-level features, such as a modal dialog, you need to either write this yourself or find a plug-in that has already solved the problem for you.

Naturally, I looked *exclusively* for jQuery plug-ins to fill the holes in my projects. In fact, I shied away from anything that didn't depend on it. I didn't trust any plug-in that *didn't* make use of this wonderful magic box. jQuery solved all my problems and made cross-browser development easy for me. Why should I trust the work of a developer who hadn't achieved this same level of enlightenment?

After a short while, it became apparent that the quality of many of these jQuery plug-ins was surprisingly low. The reality is, the low barrier to entry of jQuery is a double-edged sword. Sometimes it's easy to quickly write something useful. But it's even easier to write unmaintainable bug-prone spaghetti code, quickly! I found that a lot of these plug-ins were very poorly written. My novice knowledge of web development made it tough to sort through and work around the issues I encountered with these jQuery plug-in libraries. Frustration set in, and cracks in my foundation as a developer began to appear.

But bugs and inefficiencies in poorly written libraries only exposed the tip of the iceberg. Leaky abstractions in these plug-ins and even jQuery core were rampant and nearly impossible for me to make sense of. Why can't I trigger a custom event handler created outside of jQuery with jQuery? jQuery supports custom events—why doesn't this work? This was a specific issue I ran into when working on a project that relied both on jQuery and Prototype, an alternate JavaScript web framework with similar goals. I naively thought I could easily trigger custom event handlers bound with Prototype using jQuery—no such luck.

Take file uploading as another example. One would think that uploading files using jQuery is as simple as including the file as the data in the request. Not so. If you do that, jQuery will attempt to URL-encode the file. After a frustrating amount of reading and experimentation, I learned that two obscure properties must be set to false to ensure that jQuery does not attempt to modify the file before the request is sent.

Yet another issue developers run into when blindly relying on this library: sending cross-domain requests in older browsers is unintuitive with jQuery. This is a surprising realization to make when working with a library that is supposed to iron out web API differences and allow older browsers to be managed with ease. I discuss all of this and much more in Chapter 9.

jQuery's attribute handling utility function changed in drastic ways over the course of the library's life. Let's consider a common task as an example: determining the state of a checkbox. In older versions of jQuery, the correct approach via jQuery was to make use of the attr() method. If the checkbox is checked, a simple invocation of $(checkboxEl).attr('checked') would return true. Otherwise, it would return false. For a seasoned JavaScript developer, this is an odd behavior in itself, but we'll save those details for Chapter 5.

For a narrowly focused jQuery developer, the story of this portion of jQuery's API gets worse. In later versions of jQuery, the same call would return the value of the checkbox element's checked attribute (which does not naturally change as the checkbox is checked and unchecked). Although this is actually the correct behavior, as it properly mirrors the element's actual attribute, it was confusing for me after the breaking change. I didn't have a proper grasp of HTML due to my over-reliance on jQuery. I didn't understand why I later had to rely on jQuery's prop() method to obtain the current state of the checkbox, even though the old behavior or the attr() method was technically incorrect.

I fell into a trap, and this is a trap that many new, occasional, and hobbyist web developers fall into. Had I taken the time to understand JavaScript and the API provided by the browser first, I would have saved myself a lot of trouble. The proper sequence of events is this:

1. Learn JavaScript.

2. Learn the browser's API.

3. Learn jQuery (or any other framework/library that you may need across projects).

Many start with #3, delaying #1 and #2 to a much later date (or *never*). If you don't understand what jQuery is actually doing for you, there will be many frustrating days ahead as the leaky abstractions come out of the woodwork. This is a trap you must avoid if you want to effectively grow as a web developer—a trap that stunted my career as a web developer for longer than I would have liked.

A Challenge: No jQuery Allowed!

In early 2012, I began to replace the Java Applet uploader in Widen Collective,[12] Widen's flagship digital asset management SaaS offering. Dealing with Java in the browser turned out to be a nightmare, and we were eager to move to a native JavaScript/HTML solution. I first looked into jQuery File Upload (the most popular upload library at the time,[13] but was put off by the large number of required dependencies needed to get this up and running as well as the lack of cohesive documentation. So, for one of the first times in my web development career, I settled on a non-jQuery solution, and I was a bit lost at first.

---

[12]www.widen.com/digital-asset-management-software/
[13]https://github.com/blueimp/jQuery-File-Upload

The library I decided to replace our Java applet uploader with was, at the time, called valums/ file- uploader (due to its location on GitHub). It was unique in the respect that it was completely dependency free. I was a bit skeptical at first as I was trained to put a lot of faith in the jQuery ecosystem, but was pleasantly surprised at the ease at which I was able to integrate the plug-in.

However, the plug-in had fallen into disrepair. It was no longer actively maintained, and needed a few bugs addressed and features tweaked in order to make it production-ready for Widen Collective. Though the work required wasn't substantial, it took a significant amount of time me for to address these issues due to the large gaps in my knowledge of JavaScript, HTML, and CSS. I pushed some of my changes back up to a forked GitHub repository. My code was sloppy and flawed, but it was sufficient.[14]

My efforts were apparently noticed by the creator of the library, Andrew Valums, who asked if I was interested in maintaining the library. Even though I had very little practical experience outside of jQuery, I jumped at the opportunity and accepted. I was now the sole maintainer of a large and very popular non-jQuery plug-in, to be renamed Fine Uploader.

When I took over maintenance and development of Fine Uploader, a large cross-browser file upload library in mid-2012, my first instinct was to rewrite it all using jQuery, because that would make my life easier (I thought). The existing user community was very much against bringing any 3rd- party dependencies into the library, so I was forced to deal with the native web API and vanilla JavaScript instead.[15]

My inexperience certainly slowed the evolution of Fine Uploader initially. I was forced to gain an expert-level understanding of the core concepts. I wrote my own small shims to account for cross- browser differences in the web API and JavaScript. A good deal of my time was spent reading and experimenting. Over time, I was able to successfully shed my blind dependence on the oppressive magic of jQuery. I didn't need jQuery, and neither do you.

Focus on the Implementation, Not the Magic

The magic of jQuery and its promise of easy web application development is alluring. But we've discussed how and why you can become a stronger developer by understanding your environment first. Learn your trade by following the proper route: JavaScript, HTML, CSS, and the web API first. Worry about libraries later.

Let me be frank with you and admit that it is truly both interesting and surreal for a former clueless rookie web developer to now be playing the part of the wise "I've seen everything" developer. But I can say, with a high degree of confidence, that you are in a much better position to decide when you need to use jQuery, and when you don't, if you are more familiar with the fundamentals of web development. Knowledge and experience give you the freedom to make this choice and justify it with facts. You aren't permanently attached to any library. You have *options*.

Don't hide behind your tools—own your code. Become a web developer and a teacher, not a jQuery developer and a library user. There is something liberating about saying "I don't need jQuery anymore. I can do it myself!" and actually meaning it. Don't get into the habit of taking shortcuts. Start out on a trajectory that you can be proud of as a professional. Don't put off learning the fundamentals until later, because later never happens. Avoid helplessness when your library of choice fails to shield you from the browser. You cannot realistically expect to hide behind a layer of abstractions for your entire career. The fundamentals are building blocks that will propel you further and empower you to master your trade.

---

[14]https://github.com/FineUploader/fine-uploader/compare/82c8d5b0c383738ed84c771e90dbf202bd3 acd68…55b3ca6e9f7a18fd3adc5ba7537124ae12b63e71
[15]https://github.com/FineUploader/fine-uploader/issues/326

CHAPTER 2

■ ■ ■

You Don't Need jQuery (Anymore)

The primary goal of this chapter is to explain why a web developer like yourself should or should not use jQuery when developing a library or application. For example, file size is one common consideration when choosing browser-based dependencies. I cover the importance of this attribute and determine how it factors into your decision to utilize this library. Including exploration of the file size argument, the usefulness of jQuery will be further analyzed. As part of this particular exploration effort, I will contrast the common reasons why developers choose to use jQuery against the problems that the same developers may run into as a result of this choice. I may even briefly investigate and discuss other libraries that may be used in place of jQuery or even propel it into obsolescence, though this will mostly be limited. The focus of third-party code will be centered around adopting smaller and more focused libraries and shims. The future of the native functionality provided by the browser will also be a point of discussion.

Upon completion of this chapter, you will in a better position to decide whether jQuery should be part of your current or future projects. Your understanding of the importance of such a library will become clear, and many common meritless excuses will be refuted. You will also be empowered with choices. If you do desire a bit of help on a complex project with ambitious goals, jQuery is never your only option. The future of web development, in terms of the evolving native browser tools, will give you confidence if you *do* decide to leave jQuery behind. The term *anymore* in the title of this chapter has a double meaning. You don't need jQuery anymore because the web API and JavaScript are sufficiently evolved such that a wrapper library can be omitted in favor of a closer-to-the-metal approach. You don't need jQuery anymore because your confidence and knowledge as a web developer will also be sufficiently evolved after reading this book.

Need vs. Want

The struggle between *need* and *want* is not specific to software development, but it is a particularly prudent conflict to be aware of when planning a web project. Often when we make decisions regarding dependencies, IDEs, and build tools, our choices are more focused on want than need. Why do some of us choose WebStorm over vim? Certainly vim provides us with everything we need to develop a full-stack web application, but we may feel more comfortable with WebStorm due to its flashy UI and exceptional usability and intuitiveness. Why not use Make or shell scripts instead of grunt or gulp? We can define tasks to automate aspects of our project's build system with a Makefile, but grunt provides a more intuitive set of conventions and integrations that JavaScript developers can easily grasp.

What we *need* is often trumped by what we *want*. New developers are often more motivated to produce observable progress, above all else, in each and every project, each and every time. Emerging coders aim to prove themselves and use any help they can get from their tools in their pursuit of recognition and self-confidence. I know this to be true, as I was a new developer once myself, and observed the same qualities in many of my peers. As a more experienced developer, I now have a much more minimalistic approach to my toolset. I see this same state of mind in *some* others, but many seem to continue to center on churning out code and features above all else.

© Ray Nicholus 2016
R. Nicholus, *Beyond jQuery*, DOI 10.1007/978-1-4842-2235-5_2

Some get satisfaction from masterful understanding and application. But most seem to be more interested in adopting new bleeding-edge high-level tools that promise to take them further than the traditional set ever could. Closer-to-the-metal solutions are seen as primitive, weak, and unnecessarily complex. Their years of existence are glossed over in favor of an abstraction that vows to be more powerful than the old tool and easier to use. Maintaining a modest set of tools is admirable to some, but generally not a goal.

Pulling jQuery into a project is often the result of a *want* or an *unfounded need*. Its magical reputation is due more to lore than an objective analysis of need versus want. The truth is, it isn't magic. jQuery, while potentially elegant and helpful, is nothing more than a wrapper around the web API and an extension of JavaScript. It's an abstraction, a simplification, and a mechanism for convenience. But make no mistake about it, the real power comes from the underlying language and the tools native to the browser. While jQuery can indeed be helpful in some ways, we never literally *need* jQuery. Of course, the same is true of many other abstractions. And although the title of this chapter may suggest otherwise, the goal here is not to quibble about semantics.

Both Sides of the Acceptable Use Argument

The goal of this book is not to declare jQuery to be "persona non grata." My intention is not to pick on jQuery, but rather to teach about the browser's native tools and provide you with the confidence to develop your web projects without feeling helplessly dependent on a library. So, let's discuss frankly when it is acceptable to put the "magic" of jQuery to use in your project and when it is not. Let's put necessity aside for a bit and focus more on *want*. With a proper understanding of the instances in which jQuery is an acceptable choice, you will be able to make the correct decision when planning future projects.

When Is It Acceptable to Use It?

If you are quite comfortable with front-end web development and are just looking to write more elegant code, admittedly there aren't many good reasons to avoid jQuery as a project dependency. This doesn't mean that you absolutely *should* use it, but feel free to do so if you desire. If you also feel comfortable with jQuery, and you are familiar enough with how jQuery works its magic, then, by all means, keep using it.

There are certain aspects of "ancient" browsers that may make jQuery, or at least certain modules of the library, worthwhile. Let's define an *ancient* browser as one that is older than Internet Explorer 9. Anything that isn't an ancient browser can be considered a *modern* browser. I talk more about ancient, modern, and evergreen browsers in the next chapter.

Ancient browsers tend to have substantial API differences compared to modern browsers. Take event handling as an example. In Internet Explorer 8 and older, event handlers must be registered with the `attachEvent()` method, and event names passed to `attachEvent()` must be prefixed with "on". Also, some important properties and methods of the `Event` object are non-standard. Input element "change" events do not bubble, and event capturing is not supported at all.

These browsers also leave a lot to be desired in terms of API and feature support. Ancient browsers lack CSS3 selector support. The useful `indexOf` method is missing on the `Array` prototype. Very old browsers cannot natively parse or create JSON and lack a way to easily distinguish an element from an object. These are just a few of the struggles ancient browsers present. In *some* cases, jQuery was especially important when these browsers were commonly supported. If you are in the unusual and unfortunate position to require support for such an old browser, jQuery *may* not be a bad library to use.

There is usually little benefit to extracting jQuery from a large legacy project. In cases where an enterprise web application has shed support for ancient browsers, it may be tempting to try to eradicate unnecessary browser-based dependencies. I have found myself in this very situation more than once. From my experience, large multi-purpose all-encompassing libraries such as this tend to become firmly entrenched in a complex project over time. Perhaps a planned major rewrite of the application is a prudent excuse to remove these types of monolithic dependencies, but anything short of this would likely render such an undertaking fruitless. Unless your suite of front-end automated tests are exceptionally comprehensive, you may find that the risk of removal far outweighs any perceived drawbacks to leaving the library in place.

When writing unit tests for your front-end code—and you should always write tests—jQuery is an acceptable dependency. In a testing environment, performance and page load time are not notable factors, nor is file size. In fact, writing unit tests using some higher-level language or abstraction has some observable benefits. A common thought is that unit tests should not only serve to test your code, but to document it in terms of expected behaviors. An elegant and terse testing framework certainly makes tests more maintainable and, most importantly, readable.

Finally, there is no shame in using a little help on a one-off project. Someone without any career ambitions in the web development space working on a small and straightforward project is probably not giving up anything by leaning on jQuery to expedite the process. If you're simply not a developer and need to get, for example, a WordPress site up and running, jQuery can be a notable asset. This is a situation where the car and driver analogy holds up. In this case, you are a driver, not a mechanic. The browser is a merely convenience and not a central tool of your trade.

When Should You Refrain from Using It?

If your project only supports modern browsers, especially evergreen browsers, you may find it especially easy to do without the conveniences that a wrapper library provides. As browsers evolve, so does the web API and JavaScript. The higher-level amenities that a library like jQuery provides are quickly being represented natively in modern browsers as the associated specifications evolve. For example, the ability to add, remove, and check for CSS classes was previously a chore without jQuery's addClass(), removeClass(), and hasClass() methods. But the web specification caught up and now provides a native classList property on every element with add(), remove(), and contains() methods. This is perhaps an example of jQuery's powerful influence on the web specification. As the browser's native API continues to push forward, the necessity of jQuery also decreases. Instead of pulling a redundant dependency into new projects, consider relying on the power of the browser instead.

When writing a generic reusable library, especially open source, your instinct should be to keep third-party dependencies to a bare minimum. Your library's dependencies become your user's dependencies as well. Due to the current ubiquitousness of jQuery, you might think it safe to use in any exported code. Odds are, projects making use of your library are already using jQuery. But what if they aren't? Will a discerning web developer pull in a large transitive client-side dependency solely for the use your library? Perhaps not. This scenario will become much more common as the web evolves and developers elect to shed these types of abstractions. Personally, I would skip over a library with otherwise unnecessary dependencies, and I don't believe that this position is unique, based on input I have received from users of a large JavaScript library I maintain. As a library developer, your job is to solve complex problems and package them up in a box that is proportional to the size and scope of the problem you are solving.

Performance of your application is perhaps another reason to reject some dependencies, especially one as complex as jQuery. As the *user* of such a mature and popular library, you would naturally assume that the most basic and common areas of the codebase are all heavily optimized. In this context, efficiency is expected. Sure, perhaps some of the more complex and lesser-used functions have some performance implications. But all of the basic convenience methods should be quite performant. Unfortunately, in the case of jQuery, this is not always true.

Take the hide() method as an example of the potential performance issues that lay beneath the surface. This seems like a simple operation to implement efficiently. In fact, it *is* relatively simple to do this. One approach involves defining a proprietary CSS class name in the document tied to a style of display: none. Instead of using a CSS class, perhaps a hidden attribute can be tied to this style instead. On hide(), add the class or attribute to the element. On show(), remove it. This results in a simple and performant solution to a simple problem. However, jQuery's solution to a problem that *should* be simple is quite complex and inefficient.

One major performance bottleneck in jQuery's implementation of the hide() method is due to the use of getComputedStyle(), a web API method that computes the actual set of styles of an element, taking into account CSS files, <style> elements, and inline or JavaScript modifications to the element's style property. The use of getComputedStyle() is appropriate in some cases, but hiding an element may not be one of them. The use of this method in jQuery's hide() implementation has *serious* performance implications. Benchmark testing[1] indicates that this approach is about *90 times slower* than simply defining a style via an attribute and setting that attribute on the element to be hidden. This specific performance issue is likely to be an unexpected one, even to a seasoned developer. There are other similar issues in jQuery revolving around the use of its CSS support, which will be covered in more detail in Chapter 7.

The performance issues with jQuery's hide() method are so substantial, that the implementation was significantly simplified in version 3.0, which removed this particular performance bottleneck. Still, for any developers using jQuery 2.x or 1.x, the problem remains, and the changes to hide() in 3.0 are so drastic that it may be a bit of work for some to migrate to jQuery 3.0 in a large project that has depended heavily on this method. This is a good example of how blind faith in an all-encompassing library can lead you down the wrong path.

If you want to maintain ultimate control over the performance of your code, you should think twice before pulling in this type of library, lest you unexpectedly run across other efficiency bottlenecks. Of course some performance issues may be more related to your use of the library than anything else. But still, it is surprisingly simple to unknowingly write inefficient code with jQuery. Consider the following code listing that loops over a set of elements that contain a CSS class of "red" and removes any that include an attribute of "foo" with a value of "bar":

Listing 2-1. Removing Elements with jQuery: Naïve Approach

```
1  $('.red').each(function() {
2      if($(this).attr('foo') === 'bar') {
3          $(this).remove();
4      }
5  });
```

The preceding code certainly works, but it has some notable performance issues. A novice developer and jQuery user without a good understanding of CSS selectors and the implications of looping over a large set of elements may not know that there is a much simpler and more efficient way to solve the same problem. Here is a much more performant and elegant solution to the same problem:

```
1  $('.red[foo="bar"]').remove();
```

The execution time between the two approaches is not noticeably different given a small document. But if the document domains a large number of elements with a CSS class of "red", say, 200, the consequences of the first approach are notable. The former solution is about six times slower than the one-line solution with a complex CSS selector[2] — Chrome 42 using jQuery 1.11.2.).

You *can* still write highly performant code with jQuery, provided you know which methods in the API to avoid, and when. The same is true of the browser's API, but libraries often provide a false sense of security. Code that makes use of the web API directly is a bit more explicit and specific in its intentions. jQuery, on the other hand, provides a more high-level and seemingly magical API that obscures many details of the implementation and glosses over potential performance tradeoffs. We often don't want to look past the abstraction's conveniences, but you must. If you want to write solid and highly efficient code, you must not only understand jQuery itself (if you choose to use it) but how jQuery makes use of the web API. Blind faith here can present problems in many forms.

---

[1]http://jsperf.com/jquery-hide-vs-set-attr
[2]http://jsperf.com/jquery-loop-vs-complex-selector

Another consideration that may require avoidance of jQuery involves page load time. An over- reliance of jQuery's `ready()` method is one example. The `ready()` method executes a passed function only after all elements in the document have been loaded on the page. This doesn't really have a notable effect on *actual* page load time, but it does affect *perceived* page load time. Commonly, any code to be executed by jQuery's `ready()` method is imported at the top of the document (usually in the <head> element). And if all scripts are loaded at the top of the document, this may result in a noticeable delay in page rendering, since the scripts must be loaded and executed before the elements. The recommended approach, wherever possible, is to load all scripts at the *bottom* of the document instead. This results in a much faster perceived page load time as the document elements load before anything else. If you follow this convention, using `$.ready()` is no longer necessary. The use of jQuery's `ready()` method is widespread and even used regularly in the example code on jQuery's learning site. This is another instance where you would be better off understanding all the possible options (such as loading your scripts at the bottom of the page) instead of blindly relying on the convenience methods that jQuery provides, such as `ready()`.

Somewhat connected to page load time is file size. I'm referring to the size, in bytes, of any resources that your page must load in order to fully render on page load. One common argument against depending on libraries such as jQuery revolves around file size. The reality is that bandwidth is limited, and all client-side dependencies downloaded by the browser on page load consume some of this bandwidth. If your users all have a 60 Mbps downstream pipe available, the scripts pulled down by your application will probably not have any noticeable effect on page load times. But what if your users are not so lucky? What if they only have access to DSL, which maxes out at 6 Mbps downstream? What if you are targeting mobile devices? In that case, downstream bandwidth may not exceed 4 Mbps. In developing nations, your users may only have access to EDGE, which peaks at about 400 Kbps. Are you considering *all* of your users?

The size of jQuery may or may not be significant to you and your users. If you decide to load jQuery from a CDN, there is a greater chance that the round trip will be avoided altogether. Because this library is so popular, there is a chance that many of your users have already cached jQuery in their browser from another application. But this is certainly not guaranteed. The sheer number of versions of jQuery in active use makes it less likely that the specific version your project depends on will be cached by the majority of your users. There are also potential disadvantages to depending on a third-party server for your production runtime dependencies. If this server experiences technical issues, your application is likely to be crippled as a result, even if all servers under *your* control are functioning as expected.

If you host jQuery yourself or via a private CDN, you have much more control over how it is served, and where it is served from (taking the user's location into account). Or perhaps you are worried about the overhead of individual HTTP requests, and elect to serve jQuery combined with all other page resources as the response to a single request. Combined with GZIP compression, this is not a bad strategy. But when your user base relies on exceptionally low-bandwidth connections, keeping your resource list small is still of utmost importance. If the first page load takes a noticeable amount of time, you may just lose a potential customer.

To be fair, I should mention that jQuery 1.8 exposed a build task in the project source that allows jQuery to be "custom" built, excluding any modules that that may not be needed for a specific project. This perhaps negates the file size argument. But a question remains: Will new and inexperienced developers really know what parts of jQuery they need? Do most developers even know the ability to create a custom build of jQuery exists? The answer to both questions is, most likely, "no". Unfortunately, the ability to create a custom build is hidden inside of a build file in jQuery's source tree. In order to make use of it, you must pull down the entire repository, install the development dependencies required to build jQuery, search through the build file or page through the README.md in the project's GitHub repository for instructions, and run the task using their grunt build tool with any undesired modules excluded. With all these steps, it is unlikely that most jQuery-dependent developers will use anything other than the full build files available on the user-facing download page.

All those points bring to light the compromises made when developing popular monolithic libraries. There is no disputing that a great deal of care and detail has gone into development of jQuery since its inception. But it may not have *you* in mind or *your* edge cases, or even *your* goals. Do you want both convenience *and* speed? These two goals may be at odds with each other, depending on your workflow and intended use of the library. Do you desire seamless file uploading or a minimal footprint? Neither of these is a jQuery goal either. jQuery, like any other large library with a huge user base, has to take great care to focus mostly on the greatest common divisor in terms of features and workflow.

Should You Use Other Libraries Instead?

One goal of this book is to push you to remove your dependence on jQuery. But the only alternative I have offered to a monolithic wrapper is a direct attachment to the browser's native API. This is certainly an admirable goal, and in a sense, the browser is all we need to develop all of our front-end projects. But realistically, we may need a bit more help to reduce the inevitable hand-wringing that occurs when putting together something overly complex. The assumption is that we are targeting modern browsers, and this is reasonable given the current state of the web. But even "modern" browsers with an evolved API may have inconsistent support for some of the powerful features that we need for our projects. If only there was some way to make consistent use of modern web and JavaScript features across all modern browsers, without wrapping the entire stack. . . .

Small Shims Over Large Wrappers

There is a concept in web development that describes a very specific type of library, a *regressive library*. This is a new term, one you have probably never heard of before, because I just coined it myself. Regressive libraries are a reasonable alternative to large wrapper libraries. While they are *usually* small (though not always), their true appeal is evident in the name—they are *regressive*. Though most libraries evolve in size and feature sets over time, regressive libraries devolve. The ultimate goal of a regressive library is to disappear, to be replaced entirely by the browser's native API.

Regressive libraries are more popularly known as *shims* or *polyfills*. They don't provide any new APIs. Their job is to temporarily fill in missing implementations for standardized APIs in non-compliant browsers. These libraries keep us focused on native tools. There are no abstractions to cloud our understanding and hide the true nature of the web. Polyfill code is usually constructed such that it is only ever used if the browser *does not* contain a matching native implementation. If the browser *does* contain appropriate native code, the library delegates directly to the browser instead.

One example of a commonly used polyfill is the json2 library by Douglas Crockford.[3] It contributes an implementation for the JSON object in browsers that do not contain their own native implementation. As expected, the API of json2.js is a one-to-one match to the JSON API standardized in the ECMAScript 5 specification.[4] The specification describes a JavaScript object that contains methods for turning a JSON string into a JavaScript object, and a JavaScript object back into a JSON string again. These methods are quite useful and important when serializing and deserializing data as part of communication with a JSON aware endpoint. Json2.js ensures that this API is available in older browsers that do not implement this particular ECMAScript 5 specification (such as Internet Explorer 7).

There are quite a few other popular shims such as webcomponents.js, and fetch. Their names give a good indication as to the native APIs they are responsible for patching. Currently, both of these polyfills contribute implementations for bleeding edge specifications. Webcomponents.js contributes patches for browsers that do not completely implement the Web Components browser specification (meaning all browsers other than Chrome at the moment). Fetch allows developers to make use of the new WHATWG-created fetch specification,[5] an eventual replacement for XMLHttpRequest. Some of this will be explored later on in this book, such as in the next chapter.

---

[3]https://github.com/douglascrockford/JSON-js
[4]www.ecma-international.org/publications/files/ECMA-ST/Ecma-262.pdf
[5]https://fetch.spec.whatwg.org

Writing Your Own Shim

When we want to use some new and exciting cutting-edge features of the web API and JavaScript in our projects *and* maintain support for a wide range of browsers *and* ensure that the footprint of our dependencies is as small as possible and temporary, we turn to regressive libraries. But what exactly does a polyfill look like? How does one go about creating such a library? These questions are more pragmatic than academic when you find yourself needing to use a common and useful native API method in an older browser without an available pre-existing polyfill at your disposal. Creating your own polyfill *may* not be as complicated as you might expect. Don't believe me? Let's create one right now.

Take the find() method, available in JavaScript Arrays, which is part of the ECMAScript 2015 specification. Array.find returns an entry in an array that satisfies a provided condition. While this sounds fairly useful, browser support is missing in all versions of Internet Explorer. But we can make use of this method in all browsers by writing our own shim, as shown in Listing 2-2.

Listing 2-2. Conditionally Creating an Array.prototype.find Shim

```
1  if (!Array.prototype.find) {
2    Array.prototype.find =
3      function(callback, ctx) {
4        for (var i = 0; i < this.length; i++) {
5          var el = this[i];
6          if (callback.call(ctx, el, i, this)) {
7            return this[i];
8          }
9        }
10     };
11 }
```

If (and only if) the browser does not natively implement Array.prototype.find, the preceding code will register an implementation. So, with this shim, you may use Array.prototype.find just as it is presented in the ECMAScript 2015 specification[6] in any browser, even Internet Explorer 6! Essentially, the shim, just like a native implementation, will iterate over all items in the array until it finds one that satisfies the passed predicate function, or until it runs out of elements to examine. For each element in the array, the passed predicate function is called, passing the current array element, the current array index, and finally the entire array. Notice that the ctx argument, which is optional, allows the calling code to specify an alternate value of *this* (also known as the context) to be used by the predicate function. If this context argument is omitted, the actual context of the passed predicate function will be the "global object," which happens to be the window object if this code is executing in a browser. An array element satisfies the predicate function if the function returns a "truthy" value. The shim will return the element that satisfies the predicate, or undefined if *no* element is satisfactory.

Using our shim, the function in Listing 2-3 returns the element in the array with a name property of "foobar". This happens to be the third element in the array.

Listing 2-3. Using the Array.prototype.find Shim

```
1  function findFoo() {
2    return [
3      {name: 'one'},
4      {name: 'two'},
5      {name: 'foobar'},
```

---

[6]http://people.mozilla.org/~jorendorff/es6-draft.html#sec-array.prototype.find

```
 6        {name: 'four'}
 7     ].find(function(el) {
 8        return el.name === 'foobar';
 9     });
10   }
```

The Final Word

jQuery isn't part of the future of web development, but neither is any of the other large and currently popular libraries or JavaScript frameworks. Libraries come and go; the browser's API and JavaScript will outlive them all. The future of the web, and of your career as a web developer, is codified in the web and ECMAScript specifications. These specifications are rapidly evolving—they are quickly catching up to the libraries. Native solutions to common problems usually result in improved performance and increased convenience.

There is nothing necessarily wrong with using wrapper libraries like jQuery. However, it is imperative that you have a proper understanding not only of the code that jQuery itself depends on, but also of the reasons why you have chosen to use it. You do not really *need* jQuery, but if you still *want* to use it, be sure to take note of the situations where its use is acceptable *and* of those where you may want to consider forgoing this particular abstraction.

■ ■ ■

CHAPTER 3

Understanding the Web API and "Vanilla" JavaScript

Before we further explore the mysteries of the browser, JavaScript, and jQuery, there are a number of important concepts and terms to cover. If your plan is to better understand all the different native tools available to you in the browser, it is imperative that you are aware of the history of these tools *and* how they are interrelated.

Browsers can be lumped into a few different categories. You'll hear about many terms used to describe these categories, such as *modern* and *evergreen* browsers, both in this book and elsewhere—something that will be discussed in more detail in this very chapter. A discerning look at the necessity of these categorizations will reveal why some of the groupings are moving targets and potentially of dubious importance. And in addition to browser-based JavaScript, you'll even learn about how the language can be used *outside* of browsers, such as on the server, thanks to Node.js.

Both the web API and the language of JavaScript are main topics of discussion in this book. Before covering the intricacies of the syntax and use of these two items, you will need to be clear about their role and importance. I go into great detail defining the web API and JavaScript and how these two essential concepts are related. Another important goal of this chapter is to illustrate how these two technologies have been influenced by standardization. The organizations that curate these standards will be detailed. After completing this chapter, you will be quite comfortable with the various specifications that make up the native browser stack.

Everything You Need to Know About Browsers

In the beginning (1990), there was Nexus—the first web browser—developed by Tim Berners-Lee, one of the founders of the modern Internet. Mosaic, the first fully graphical browser, followed shortly after in 1993. In 1994 and 1995, Netscape Navigator and Microsoft Internet Explorer 1.0 were released, respectively. By the mid-1990s, Netscape and Explorer accounted for almost all of the browsers in common use. They both offered a rapidly growing set of proprietary features, setting themselves apart from each other but also favoring polarity over standardization. This, in part, lead to the later popularity of tools (such as jQuery) that allowed web developers to more effectively target multiple browsers. While Nexus, Mosaic, and other similar browsers of the time were relatively short-lived and fell out of favor with users and developers, Netscape and Explorer ushered in an era of intense browser competition.

The early web was, by today's standards, uninspired and primitive. On the browser side, the web was exclusively populated with static content. Information was loaded from the server one entire page at a time, even if only a small portion of the page needed to be updated. Upon clicking on an anchor link, an HTTP GET request was sent to the server, which responded with the contents of the next page—header, body, footer, and all. This did not facilitate an exceptional user experience or good use of the *very* limited bandwidth at the time. Then came Java Applets and Flash around the late 1990s, which allowed developers to create dynamic, in-browser applications. However, both of these technologies required installation of third-party software on top of the browser. Long before an official standard was codified by the World Wide Web Consortium, Microsoft allowed developers to create a page that could be partially updated by sending a request to the server that returned a fragment of a document. This fragment was then used to replace existing content *or* create additional content without changing the rest of the page. This has been commonly known as an AJAX request, and its invention brought dynamic content creation to the *native* browser. Microsoft's implementation of this concept was introduced in the late-1990s, soon after Flash and Java Applets came about. Although AJAX requests were first introduced around 1999, they did not appear elsewhere until their inclusion in the Mozilla Firefox browser in 2002, and they remained non-standard until 2006. This was a time when standardization of the web crept far behind the desire for more modern features.

Although Internet Explorer and its proprietary features dominated the browser market for quite some time, notable competition arrived in the early 2000s. Mozilla Firefox was the first such viable adversary to Microsoft's offering. The introduction of a free and open source browser caught Microsoft entirely off-guard and ushered in a new era of the web. Firefox's Gecko engine was the first such challenger to Microsoft's Trident. A few years after Gecko, Apple developed the WebKit rendering engine to power its Safari browser. WebKit was initially a fork of the KHTML rendering engine used by the Konqueror browser, which was a browser for the Linux desktop. Shortly after, Google developed its own browser, Chrome, also using Apple's WebKit engine. Later on, Google created its own rendering engine—Blink—which itself started as a fork of WebKit, similar to Apple's initial fork of KDE's KHTML engine. Interestingly: Opera, somewhat of a niche browser that relied on its homegrown "Presto" rendering engine for most of its life, switched to Chrome's "Blink" engine in 2013. While Firefox initially grabbed a substantial share of the market on Windows, and Safari did the same on OS X, Chrome began its ascent into cross-OS dominance shortly after its introduction. Chrome's success can be attributed to its rapid evolution and significant influence on web standardization. This was a time where formal specifications began to match and affect browser development. With a mature standards track and relatively solid browser quality assurance, the necessity of libraries like jQuery began to seem less important.

The history I just outlined describes a number of different mobile and desktop browsers, which, like most things, can be categorized in many different ways. In the context of this book, a reasonable set of categories will be used to speak to their modernity, portability, and updatability. In the following sections, you will become familiar with some of the more common browser categories. I'll also comment on the state of all currently available browsers and provide some words of caution to consider when thinking of browsers in terms of these categories.

Ancient Browsers

Ancient browsers, also known as legacy browsers, are usually considered to be older versions of Microsoft's Internet Explorer. At the writing of this book, in mid-2016, ancient browsers are those older than Internet Explorer 9. Explorer 7 is generally thought of as the oldest browser to realistically target for any purposes, though even Internet Explorer 10 and below are no longer supported by Microsoft and should only be supported in your new web applications if a significant chunk of your users cannot upgrade. IE6, Mosaic, Netscape, and other similar browsers are not only out-of-date but also mostly unused. They are not part of any set of currently in-use browsers, so we will not consider these in any future discussions throughout this book. As of June 2016, ancient browsers *thankfully* only account for about 1% of currently in-use browsers across the measured web.[1]

Ancient browsers are the most undesirable of all the browser categories. They suffer many drawbacks that make them difficult to develop against and support, and are generally considered to be quite slow compared to more modern choices. Their support of the DOM API and other related web APIs is primitive. They support limited JavaScript convenience methods due to lack of modern specifications at the time. Many of them, especially Internet Explorer 6, are infested with notable and serious layout bugs. For these reasons, ancient browsers have fallen out of favor, replaced with more stable, efficient, and convenient choices.

---

[1]https://www.w3counter.com/globalstats.php?year=2016&month=6

But we have to be careful when categorizing browsers using age as the key property. Ancient browsers represent a moving target. A new browser today will likely be considered an ancient browser several years from now. An ancient browser today will be considered dead in the near future when its market share effectively drops to 0. This type of categorization is not a particularly pragmatic one, but is arguably effective enough for the purposes of separating those browsers that can be reasonably addressed without jQuery in all cases from those that cannot. However, future chapters explore other more effective techniques to distinguish between capable and non-capable browsers through the practice of programmatic feature detection.

Modern Browsers

The *modern* adjective can be used to describe all browsers newer than those thought of as ancient. At the time of writing, modern browsers are all those newer than and including Internet Explorer 9. This list also includes Chrome, Firefox, and Safari version 6+. But this modern categorization does share a common trait with the ancient one. The trailing edge of this category is a moving target. What is modern now may be ancient in a few years. Similar to *ancient, modern* is simply to be used as context when reading this book. I will often use these terms when describing the browser support for a fragment of code.

Modern browsers are, compared to their ancient counterparts, much easier to work with due to their relatively evolved developer tools, web API and JavaScript support, and stability. They account for a set of browsers that can be eloquently addressed without the help of a wrapper library like jQuery. The urge to programmatically identify this class of browser is great. If we can easily determine if we are dealing with Internet Explorer 9 versus 8, or Safari 8 versus 5, then perhaps we can then define two discrete code paths—one for ancient browsers, and another for modern ones. But you should resist this urge.

This blanket classification of browsers, based mainly on age, is frivolous. Even worse is identifying browsers in this category and making all your code path decisions based on the browser's user agent identification string. The correct approach is to test a browser's API implementation for the presence of, or lack of, a specific feature and *then* take the appropriate code path for *that specific feature*. I want to make this clear to be sure that the classifications I have proposed thus far are seen in the proper context and not elevated to a higher level of importance than they deserve.

■ **Note** A user agent string is a series of characters that identifies a particular type and version of web browser. You can obtain the browser's UA string via JavaScript by checking the userAgent property of the navigator object.

Evergreen Browsers

There is a third class of browser, one that is ageless and ever evolving. *Evergreen* browsers are the future of the web. Browsers that fit into this category update themselves without any required user intervention. Although they are versioned, most who use an evergreen browser are likely unaware of their browser's current version number (with the exception of Internet Explorer 10+ and possibly Safari). Updates are completely transparent, even major version upgrades. This allows the browser to seamlessly evolve its web API and JavaScript support. There is generally no option for the user to (easily) remain on an older version. This allows these browsers to more quickly realize new web specifications, and ensure the entire user base is current. The whole ecosystem wins.

Currently, Chrome, Firefox, Safari, Opera, Internet Explorer 10+, and Microsoft Edge are considered to be evergreen browsers. This concept is quite popular and accounts for the majority of browsers available today. The model of tying a browser version to a specific set of operating system versions or "service packs" mostly died with Internet Explorer 9 and Windows Vista. Microsoft's newest redesigned browser, known as Microsoft Edge, is more like the other traditional evergreen browsers in the sense that the version number will be less prominent compared to earlier Microsoft-created offerings. As evergreen browsers take over the web, we can expect to take advantage of the rapidly evolving specifications, security improvements, and bug fixes faster than ever before. In this world, the need for a library to fill in the browser's gaps becomes much less important.

Mobile Browsers

Desktop browsers still account for the majority of web traffic, at least in the United States. However, current measurements show that mobile browser use is rising while desktop traffic is falling. As of June 2016, mobile/tablet devices account for about 42% of web traffic,[2] with the remainder mostly attributable to desktop browsers. The steady rise in mobile device use, along with a consistent (and important) mantra of "mobile first",[3] reveal that mobile browsers are just as big a part of the future of the web as evergreen browsers. The mobile web is still arguably in its infancy, but it cannot and should not be ignored.

In some respects, many mobile browsers are very much evergreen browsers as well, due to the fact that a portion of them are automatically updated without user intervention. Just as on the desktop, this behavior allows mobile browsing to evolve rapidly and ensures that users are always equipped with the most up-to-date version of their browser of choice. But the benefits of an automatically updating browser have historically been tied to the capabilities of the physical device. For example, old phones running Android 2.x are likely not able to handle a 4.x version, cutting them off from the latest versions of mobile Chrome. The same problem exists on other mobile platforms, such as on older Apple devices stuck on outdated builds of iOS.

The mobile landscape is largely dominated by Apple's iPhone and iPad running iOS and a multitude of other devices running Google's Android operating system. Though Microsoft is beginning to make a small impression with their Windows Phone operating system.[4] Research in Motion's Blackberry OS is, for the purposes of this book (and most other contexts), irrelevant due to its small and declining share of mobile web traffic. Regardless of the mobile device, keep in mind that the code and techniques used to replace jQuery in this book will apply equally to all modern/evergreen browsers, so the distinction between mobile and desktop is not particularly important in this context, other than for performance considerations.

Even with the rising ubiquitousness of the mobile web, the current situation is not all roses and sunshine. Mobile browsers present unique challenges. Profile and battery considerations make performance consequences of our code more noticeable, compared to desktop systems. Mobile browsers in particular are a bit less mature than their larger form-factor counterparts. Along with this immaturity comes more inconsistency in specification support between the various browsers. This is often more noticeable when comparing a mobile browser to its desktop counterpart. Chrome and Safari are two examples of browsers that have a presence both on mobile and desktop devices. While these browsers may share the same name across multiple platforms, their goals vary, leading to differing experiences.

In some cases, due to very mobile-unique concerns, such as data use, common portions of web specifications behave differently. Take the `autoplay` Boolean attribute on the HTML5 `<video>` element as an example, which will ensure the associated video begins playing immediately after loading.[5] Desktop browsers all support this standard feature, but support on the mobile side is a bit different. Safari running on iOS does not observe this attribute to ensure that auto-playing videos do not adversely affect a user's limited (and relatively expensive) mobile data consumption.[6] There are other similar examples where the unique environment of a mobile browser may result in unexpected implementation gaps. This reality must be considered when writing "mobile first" libraries and applications.

---

[2]http://gs.statcounter.com/#all-comparison-ww-monthly-201404-201606
[3]http://stratechery.com/2015/mobile-first/
[4]www.gartner.com/newsroom/id/2944819
[5]www.w3.org/TR/html5/embedded-content-0.html#attr-media-autoplay
[6]https://developer.apple.com/library/safari/documentation/AudioVideo/Conceptual/Using_HTML5_Audio_Video/Device-SpecificConsiderations/Device-SpecificConsiderations.html

Non-browsers

This section may seem a bit out of place, but to be complete I figured it is important to at least *touch* on another environment where JavaScript is thriving. Full stack software development with JavaScript on both ends is possible due to the existence of Node.js—a server-side runtime that uses Chrome's JavaScript engine.[7] Server-side JavaScript development does not include any type of web API, for obvious reasons. So, although the web-based discussions presented throughout this book (and there are many) do not apply to the Node.js world, many of the pure JavaScript areas *do* transcend the browser.

If you're not quite sure about the differences between browser-specific JavaScript and JavaScript that is codified in the language specification (and useable outside of the browser), this will be discussed a bit more later on when I compare, contrast, and define the web API and the language of JavaScript. The important takeaway here is simply to understand that *some* of this book's content will in fact apply to server-based JavaScript development. And for the most part, JavaScript on the server provides you with relatively up-to-date support for the language specification, which means that most non-browser-specific examples in this book will be usable on the server as well.

What Is This Web API and Why Is It Important?

I have been referring to the *web API* throughout the book and will continue to do so. But the term *web API* is not a standard or even a common term, so a bit of explanation is warranted to clear up any potential ambiguity. Simply put, the web API refers to all the JavaScript methods and objects that specifically allow developers to programmatically address and manipulate the browser. This generalized browser API is made up of two distinct parts: one is the Document Object Model (DOM) API, which is a set of methods and properties attached to HTML document nodes, and the second is a collection of other methods and functions available only in the browser environment but not directly related to HTML. If these terse definitions are still a bit murky, no need to worry. I promise to explain the DOM and the non-DOM APIs in *much* more detail later on in this section.

I hope by now you are a *bit* more comfortable with the term *web API* and how it relates to the browser. But one question still remains: why should you care? Aside from the fact that it is a key property of the majority of the chapters and concepts in this book, it is also *the* most important tool available to web developers. The web API provides everything necessary to create an exceptionally customized and dynamic experience for end users and even other developers. It is constantly and rapidly evolving, such that the web is destined to ultimately replace installed applications. As a professional developer, your understanding of the web API (or lack thereof) will have a substantial effect on your ability to efficiently design and develop rich complex web applications and libraries. This book's goal is to inculcate this reality and teach you how to not only make good use of the web API in lieu of jQuery, and also to gain a better understanding of the browser environment so that you can more effectively use libraries that wrap this native API if you so choose.

The DOM API

The DOM is a set of methods and objects used to represent an HTML document. These representations are often (but not exclusively) expressed using the most common language of the web: JavaScript. The DOM provides JavaScript objects that mirror elements in a document. It allows elements to be created, located, manipulated, and described. This language binding exposes a host of potential control points among all HTML elements. For example, the DOM API defines a `className` property on the the DOM's `Element` interface. This specific property allows for programmatic reading and changing of any element's CSS `class` attribute. All other HMTL elements, such as anchors (`HTMLAnchorElement`), `<div>` elements (`HTMLDivElement`), and `<span>` elements (`HTMLSpanElement`), inherit from the `Element` interface and therefore *also* include the `className` property in their JavaScript object representations.

---

[7]`https://code.google.com/p/v8/`

The element hierarchy exposed in the previous className example is an important one to understand. Common properties and methods available on specific elements are often inherited from a more common element type. The EventTarget type is at the top of the chain, with all other representations of HTML nodes inheriting from this. The EventTarget type defines methods to register event handlers, which all other HTML items inherit. A Node is a sub-type of EventTarget that all other elements inherit from as well. This Node interface provides methods to clone HTML items and locate sibling nodes, among other behaviors. Sub-types of Node include Element and CharacterData. Element objects are, as you might expect, all nodes that can be expressed with standardized HTML tags, such as <div> and <span>. CharacterData items are either text or comments in a document.

In addition to per-element control, the document as a whole may also be manipulated using JavaScript. In fact, there is a particular representation of a document, aptly named the Document interface. A Document object inherits from Node (which, if you remember, inherits from the base type—EventTarget). Documents contain properties that, for example, allow all style sheets associated with the markup to be examined. A number of important methods are available as well, such as one that facilitates creation of new HTML elements. Note that *nothing* inherits from Document. All properties and methods on the browser's document object can also be considered part of the DOM specification, for the purposes of discussion in this book. Figure 3-1 shows the DOM element hierarchy.

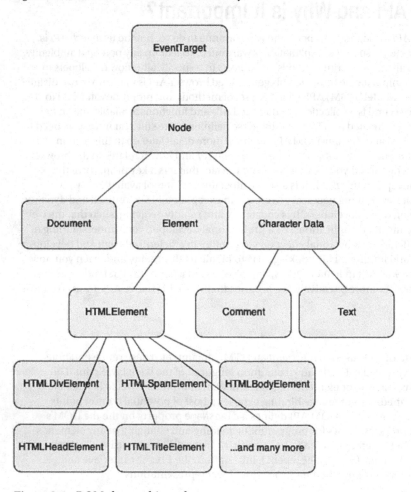

Figure 3-1. DOM element hierarchy

All of these types, behaviors, properties, methods, and relationships are part of a standard - the DOM specification.[8] This standard was first created in 1998 by the World Wide Web Consortium (W3C) as DOM Level 1.[9] There have traditionally been two specific standards paths that deal with the DOM: DOM Core and DOM HTML. DOM Core, as the spec summary points out, is "a platform- and language-neutral interface that allows programs and scripts to dynamically access and update the content, structure, and style of documents." At the time of writing, the latest such standard (which became a recommendation in late 2004) is DOM Level 3 Core,[10] which defines new properties on elements, such as the textContent property that can be used to read or set the text of a node.

The DOM HTML specification summary sounds similar to DOM Core but is actually a bit different. It claims that the spec is "a platform- and language-neutral interface that allows programs and scripts to dynamically access and update the content and structure *of HTML 4.01 and XHTML 1.0 documents*" (emphasis added by me). In other words, the DOM Core specification defines, as you might expect, core functionality that is common to all documents, and the DOM HTML specification extends this core specification a bit and provides a more HTML-specific API. The DOM HTML spec defines common properties of elements, such as id, className, and title. At the writing of this book, the latest DOM HTML standard is DOM Level 2 HTML, which became a recommendation in late 2003.[11]

There are other related standards, such as the Selectors API[12] which covers, as you might expect, selecting elements. For example, the querySelector and querySelectorAll methods are defined on both the Document and the Element interfaces to allow selection of elements in a document using CSS selector strings defined in the Selectors specification (currently at Level 4.[13] Another related specification is the UI Events specification,[14] which defines native DOM events such as mouse and keyboard events. The DOM4 specification attempts to aggregate all of these standards and more.[15]

Then there is the most widely known standard, HTML5, which became a recommendation in late 2014.[16] It is one of the latest DOM specifications and carries forward the goals of DOM4 along with a host of other non-DOM-related specifications (which I touch on in the next section). In the context of the DOM, HTML5 defines new elements (such as <section>, <footer>, and <header>), new attributes (such as placeholder and required), and new element methods and properties (such as naturalWidth and naturalHeight properties of image elements). This is, of course, a very small list of changes. The W3C maintains a document that describes, in quite a bit of detail, the changes brought on by HTML5.[17] Currently, the latest in-progress specification is HTML 5.2, also curated by the World Wide Web Consortium. HTML 5.1 and 5.2 bring some even newer elements to the DOM. The most notable of these new elements is <picture>,[18] which allows multiple image sources to be specified alongside cues to the browser that indicate which image to load. Picture sources can be tied to browser window size or pixel density, for example.

In short, the DOM APIs provide a way to read, update, traverse, and create document elements using JavaScript. The elements themselves and their properties are also defined by this family of specifications. The real power in the web is, in part, defined by the DOM APIs. Without it, dynamic web applications would simply not exist in their current form. The only option would be, perhaps, embedded Flash or Java applets—two technologies that are quickly becoming obsolete due to the power of the modern DOM API. And let's be clear about another thing: jQuery is built *on top of the DOM API*. Without the DOM API, jQuery would not exist either. jQuery is mostly a wrapper around the DOM API, providing a level of abstraction. A large portion of *Beyond jQuery* is dedicated to using the DOM APIs with and without the aid of jQuery.

---

[8]www.w3.org/DOM/DOMTR
[9]www.w3.org/TR/1998/REC-DOM-Level-1-19981001/
[10]www.w3.org/TR/DOM-Level-3-Core/
[11]www.w3.org/TR/DOM-Level-2-HTML/
[12]http://dev.w3.org/2006/webapi/selectors-api2/
[13]http://dev.w3.org/csswg/selectors-4/
[14]https://dvcs.w3.org/hg/dom3events/raw-file/tip/html/DOM3-Events.html
[15]www.w3.org/TR/domcore/
[16]www.w3.org/TR/html5/
[17]www.w3.org/TR/html5-diff/
[18]www.w3.org/html/wg/drafts/html/master/semantics.html#the-picture-element

Everything Else (non-DOM)

In addition to the DOM API(s), there is another set of APIs specific to the browser that makes up all properties attached to the browser's window object. A browser "window" contains an HTML document and the document object (which is defined by the DOM API). This window can be programmatically accessed through the JavaScript window object—a global variable. Although the DOM API defines everything attached to the document object, everything else attached to the window object is defined by a large number of other specifications. For example, the File API,[19] which defines a set of methods and properties use to read, write, and identify files in the browser, is represented by two interfaces: Blob and File. Both interface definitions are available on the window object.

Another well-known API specification with bindings to the Window interface is XMLHttpRequest,[20] which defines a set of methods and properties used to communicate with a server asynchronously over HTTP. And in addition to new DOM API features, the HTML5 standard defines a large swath of the properties attached to window. One example is the History interface,[21] which provides programmatic access to the browser's history. This is exposed as a history object on window. Yet another example is the Storage interface,[22] which includes representations on window as sessionStorage and localStorage for managing temporary storage of small amounts of data in the browser.

Though the HTML 5.1 specification, discussed in the previous section on the DOM, also plays a part in the evolution of the non-DOM APIs, it does so to a much lesser extent than the HTML5 standard. The most notable non-DOM reference in the current version of W3C's HTML 5.1 specification is the fetch API,[23] which was actually drafted by a different standards group: WHATWG. And this brings us to a *short* discussion regarding this relatively new phenomenon: competing web standards. On one side, we have the W3C, which has been crafting standards for the web since 1994.[24] It is lead by Tim Berners-Lee, the inventor of the Web. The origins of the web specifications we all use and love today were formally standardized by the W3C. Ten years after the W3C came along, the Web Hypertext Application Technology Working Group (WHATWG) was formed.

The WHATWG promotes a "Living Standard," one that is not tied to version numbers or "levels." For example, instead of an HTML5, or an HTML 5.1 spec, they simply have an HTML spec that is updated over time. The group has drafted some original new standards themselves, such as the previously referenced Fetch API, along with the Notifications API,[25] which enables web applications to display notifications to the user. According to the FAQ page, the group was created out of frustration with "the W3C's direction with XHTML, lack of interest in HTML and apparent disregard for the needs of real-world authors".[26] The WHATWG does appear to be a healthy counterbalance to the W3C, apparently promoting faster evolution of the web, which is of course a *good* thing.

JavaScript: A Less Elegant Version of jQuery?

A common reason to pull in jQuery is to make up for perceived shortcomings in the underlying language itself—JavaScript. This is one of the most frivolous excuses. It's a bit much to pull in a third-party dependency like jQuery simply for a marginally better way to loop over object properties and array elements. In fact, this is completely unnecessary with the existence of forEach and Object.keys(), both of which are available in modern browsers. Or perhaps you think $.inArray() is an important utility function to have at your disposal. The truth is, since Internet Explorer 9—where Array.prototype.indexOf was made available as part of the language—the most elegant solution is to make use of "vanilla" JavaScript instead. There are, of course, many more examples which will become apparent throughout this book.

---

[19]www.w3.org/TR/FileAPI/
[20]https://xhr.spec.whatwg.org/
[21]www.w3.org/TR/html5/browsers.html#the-history-interface
[22]www.w3.org/TR/html5/browsers.html#the-history-interface
[23]https://fetch.spec.whatwg.org
[24]www.w3.org/Consortium/facts#history
[25]https://notifications.spec.whatwg.org
[26]https://wiki.whatwg.org/wiki/FAQ#What_is_the_WHATWG.3F

Among front-end developers, especially those with limited knowledge of web development, there is often thought to be two possible options in terms of "languages" to utilize when coding your client-side application: jQuery or JavaScript. The flaw in this set of options is obvious to seasoned web developers. Only one of these two "languages" is *actually a language*. JavaScript is, in fact, a standardized language, whereas jQuery simply provides a collection of utility methods that aim to make solving common problems with JavaScript easier and more elegant across a wide range of browsers. jQuery is nothing more than a collection of web API wrapper methods.

JavaScript is both ubiquitous and unavoidable when developing web applications, and with the advent of Node.js, JavaScript is now a viable option on the server as well. In the following sections, I explain the significance of JavaScript, as a language, in the context of web development. *Beyond jQuery* does not have an explicit goal to dive deep into language syntax and core concepts such as inheritance and scope, though these forms of language details *may* appear at times throughout the book if there is a clear tie-in to the layer of abstraction offered by jQuery. Instead, you will gain an understanding of JavaScript's connection to the web API. The history and standardization of the language will be explored as well, similar to our previous discussion of the web API.

■ **Note**   Actually, JavaScript is technically avoidable, especially since the advent of WebAssembly, but that standard is in its infancy. If you are writing in a non-traditional front-end language that compiles to WebAssembly, assuming WebAssembly is solid (which is currently not the case), then you are probably safe from JavaScript. But short of that, it is still quite important and unavoidable.

The Language vs. the Web API

JavaScript is an integral component of the web API. Take the DOM, for example. While the browser DOM is usually *implemented* in C or C++ and packaged as a layout engine (such as Safari's WebKit and Chrome's Blink), the DOM is most commonly *manipulated* using JavaScript. For example, consider working with DOM element attributes for a moment. To do this, there are three attribute-related methods described in DOM Level 1: getAttribute,[27] setAttribute,[28] and removeAttribute.[29] Additionally, DOM Level 2 provides hasAttribute).[30] All four of these methods are defined in the Element interface, which has a corresponding (and commonly known) implementation in JavaScript. Given any HTML element, you can read and manipulate its attributes in JavaScript just as they are defined in these specifications. Chapter 5 will include *much* more detail on the topic of attributes.

In addition to the DOM, JavaScript is also used when interacting with portions of the web API that are not tied to the DOM, such as the Web Messaging API,[31] which is part of the W3C's HTML5 specification. The Web Messaging API provides a way for different browsing contexts to communicate with each other via message passing. This opens up an easy way for two iframes on differing domains to communicate, or even communication between the browser's main UI thread and a Web Worker threads.[32] This specification defines a MessageEvent interface,[33] which allows a client to listen for passed messages. In JavaScript, this event object is implemented in all modern browsers and allows developers to listen for messages using the addEventListener method available on the window, document, and element objects. These objects get this method from the EventTarget interface, which you may remember from earlier in this chapter, is the top-level interface from which many other native browser objects inherit from. I will go into much more detail regarding event handling in Chapter 9. The Web Messaging API will be covered in a bit more detail as part of Chapter 8.

---

[27]www.w3.org/TR/REC-DOM-Level-1/level-one-core.html#method-getAttribute
[28]www.w3.org/TR/REC-DOM-Level-1/level-one-core.html#method-setAttribute
[29]www.w3.org/TR/REC-DOM-Level-1/level-one-core.html#method-removeAttribute
[30]www.w3.org/TR/DOM-Level-2-Core/core.html#ID-ElHasAttr
[31]www.w3.org/TR/DOM-Level-2-Core/core.html#ID-ElHasAttr
[32]www.w3.org/TR/workers/
[33]www.w3.org/TR/webmessaging/#the-messageevent-interfaces

Although JavaScript is key to working with native browser-specific APIs, as a language it is *not* to be confused with the web specifications themselves. JavaScript is used to interface with implementations of these web specifications in the browser, but the language itself has its *own* specification: ECMAScript,[34] which I will discuss a bit more in the next section. Note that it is *not* tied to the Web, though it is implemented in all web browsers. The web API, in some ways, builds on the foundation provided by the JavaScript API. Arrays,[35] Objects,[36] Functions,[37] and primitives such as Booleans and strings[38] are all defined in the JavaScript spec and available in the browser (among other environments). And these core elements of the ECMAScript specification are further defined to have additional properties. For example, Arrays contain a method to retrieve the index of a specific item, implemented as indexOf.[39] And the Function interface contains apply[40] or call[41] methods that make it easy to invoke a function with an alternate context (value of this)[42] as well as pass arguments. Chapter 12 includes a great amount of detail relating to JavaScript-specific utility functions, comparing them to jQuery's higher-level wrapper methods.

History and Standardization

The story of JavaScript starts with Brendan Eich, who, as an employee of Netscape in 1995, developed the first working version of the language in ten days. A scripting language to run inside Netscape Navigator was to be created, and it was ordered to be "like Java." Eich was appointed to undertake this vision and make it a reality. The result was a mix of C, Self,[43] and Scheme,[44] with a hint of Java.[45] More details of the incarnation of JavaScript can be found in Brendan Eich's blog.[46]

Before a formal standardization process was created, JavaScript was, for all intents and purposes, a proprietary language only used by Netscape in its flagship browser. But shortly after implementing the language in Netscape Navigator, Microsoft created its own implementation, JScript, which was first introduced in Internet Explorer 3. Similar in name, JScript was mostly identical to Netscape's JavaScript. The name was chosen by Microsoft to avoid any potential trademark disputes by the owner of the Java trademark,[47] which was Sun Microsystems at the time.

Very shortly after the arrival of JScript, a formal language specification was drafted and later adopted. But the lack of standardization, even for a relatively short amount of time, had taken a noticeable toll on the web. In late 1996, Netscape approached the European Computer Manufacturer's Association (ECMA) to create a formal language specification. This was, in part, prompted by the divergence between implementations of the language between Netscape Navigator and Microsoft Internet Explorer 3. The first spec was completed in June 1997 under the name ECMA-262, also known as ECMAScript. The specification is currently curated by ECMA Technical Committee 39, also known as TC39, a group of individuals entrusted to evolve and maintain the language.[48] Members of TC39 include heavy-hitters such as Douglas Crockford, Brendan Eich, and Yehuda Katz (who is also a member of the jQuery Foundation).

---

[34]www.ecmascript.org
[35]www.ecma-international.org/ecma-262/5.1/#sec-15.4
[36]www.ecma-international.org/ecma-262/5.1/#sec-15.2
[37]www.ecma-international.org/ecma-262/5.1/#sec-15.3
[38]www.ecma-international.org/ecma-262/5.1/#sec-4.3.2
[39]www.ecma-international.org/ecma-262/5.1/#sec-15.4.4.14
[40]www.ecma-international.org/ecma-262/5.1/#sec-15.3.4.3
[41]www.ecma-international.org/ecma-262/5.1/#sec-15.3.4.4
[42]www.ecma-international.org/ecma-262/5.1/#sec-10.3
[43]http://handbook.selflanguage.org/4.5/intro.html
[44]www.scheme.com/tspl4/intro.html
[45]www.oracle.com/technetwork/topics/newtojava/downloads/index.html
[46]https://brendaneich.com/2008/04/popularity/
[47]http://yuiblog.com/blog/2007/01/24/video-crockford-tjpl/
[48]www.ecma-international.org/memento/TC39.htm

The first version of the ECMAScript language specification was released in 1997, titled "ECMAScript- 262, 1st Edition." At the time of writing, the 7th edition was just completed. Although releases of new specifications were inconsistent throughout the life of the language, as of the 6th edition, the concept of an annual release of updated specifications seems to be gaining momentum. Lending some credence to this goal, the 6th edition of the spec is also titled "ECMAScript 2015," the 7th is titled "ECMAScript 2016", with the assumption that the 8th edition will be "ECMAScript 2017," and so forth. A set of "harmony" specification(s) has also been a point of discussion, and the crux of this nomenclature seems to be related to the general order of the spec. Version 4 and earlier were *not* harmonious, while version 5 and on *are*, earning this period of the specification the name "harmony." It should be noted that version 4 of the specification was never actually completed. Instead, it was rolled into ECMAScript 5. Harmony,[49] in this context, may refer to the goals and requirements, such as "Be a better language for writing," and "Keep the language pleasant for casual developers." Another goal of the harmony movement of the language specification is to "build on ES5 strict mode to avoid too many modes." In other words, simplification and usability bring harmony to the language. At the time of writing, browser support of ECMAScript 3 includes all browsers in existence. ECMAScript 5 support is covered entirely by all "modern" browsers. ECMAScript 2015 has decent support across most current versions of all browsers at this time. ECMAScript 2016 support is spotty at the moment, but that of course will improve over time.

---

[49]http://wiki.ecmascript.org/doku.php?id=harmony%3Aharmony

CHAPTER 4

■ ■ ■

Finding HTML Elements

How many times have you come across a project that uses jQuery simply to perform seemingly trivial element selection? How many times have *you* written $('#myElement') or $('.myElement')? If you have depended on jQuery for most (or all) of your projects, you may not be aware of the fact that you don't *need* jQuery to select elements! This task is fairly straightforward with the help of the plain 'ole boring web API. Much like jQuery, there are abundant examples (such as this book) that demonstrate how to properly harness the power of the browser to swiftly select any and all elements in your document. None of this is a well-kept secret, but the pervasiveness of jQuery has lead many to believe that the *only* sane way to find elements is with the help of the almighty dollar sign. Nothing could be further from the truth, and all of this will become clear as you read on.

All the methods described here to select elements are supported in *all* modern browsers. In fact, many are supported in ancient browsers as well. In other words, unless you are supporting an aging legacy web application, even the most complex native solutions for selecting elements are available to you without the help of *any* library. And for those old applications still tied to browsers of the past? You can easily replicate any of the missing native methods with a few lines of code. In fact, I'll provide some simple and intuitive solutions to help you fill in important gaps in ancient browsers.

Although jQuery does admittedly save you some keystrokes, you *will* sacrifice performance. That type of higher-level abstraction is understandably slower than relying directly on native APIs. So what if you want the convenience of jQuery without the sheer size of the dependency and the potential for hidden performance issues? Simple, create your own *very* thin wrapper around the web API to save you some keystrokes. I'll explore this possibility with some example code before we close out this chapter.

Core Element Selectors

In this first section on the topic of finding HTML elements in a document, I discuss selecting elements by using some of the more traditional element properties, such as ID, class, and tag name. Here, I compare element selection in jQuery with "vanilla" JavaScript through examples that interface directly with the DOM by making use of the functionality codified in various web API specifications. After completing this section, you will have the necessary confidence and understanding to select elements in the DOM using the most common methods—without relying on jQuery at all.

© Ray Nicholus 2016
R. Nicholus, *Beyond jQuery*, DOI 10.1007/978-1-4842-2235-5_4

IDs

The W3C HTML4 specification[1] defines the id attribute as one that *must* be unique among all IDs defined inside of a document. This part of the specification goes on to describe its primary uses,[2] such as element selection and navigation to other sections of a page using anchor links. The DOM Level 1 specification defines the HTMLElement interface,[3] from which all other elements inherit from. The id property is defined in this interface, which is directly connected to the id attribute defined on the corresponding element in the markup.

For example, consider the following markup:

```
1  <div id="my-element-id"></div>
```

The <div> element's id attribute is also accessible via the JavaScript representation of the element. This is exposed by the element object's id property:

```
1  // `theDiv` is the <div> from our sample HMTL above
2  theDiv.id === 'my-element-id'; // returns true
```

jQuery

In jQuery-land, obtaining a handle on the <div> element object looks something like Listing 4-1.

Listing 4-1. Select by ID: jQuery

```
1  // returns a jQuery object with 1 element -
2  // the <div> from our sample HMTL above
3  var result = $('#my-element-id');
4
5  // assuming our element has been found in the document
6  result.is('#my-element-id'); // returns true
```

In the jQuery example, we are using the ID selector string, which was first defined in the W3C CSS1 specification.[4] The jQuery object returned by this selection attempt is a pseudo-array (which Chapter 12 discusses in more detail). This pseudo-array contains the HTMLElement object representation of this element in the document.

Web API

Selecting the same exact element without the help of jQuery is surprisingly easy, and in fact the code to achieve this looks surprisingly similar. There are two different ways to select an element by ID using the web API. The first such method involves using the getElementById method defined on the Document interface, first formalized in the DOM Level 2 Core specification.[5] This method is supported in *all* browsers in existence (first implemented in Internet Explorer 5.5):

```
1  // returns the matching HTMLElement - the <div> from our sample
2  var result = document.getElementById('my-element-id');
3
```

---

[1]www.w3.org/TR/REC-html40/cover.html
[2]www.w3.org/TR/REC-html40/struct/global.html#adef-id
[3]www.w3.org/TR/REC-DOM-Level-1/level-one-html.html#ID-58190037
[4]www.w3.org/TR/REC-CSS1/#id-as-selector
[5]www.w3.org/TR/DOM-Level-2-Core/core.html#ID-getElBId

```
4  // assuming our element has been found in the document
5  result.id === 'my-element-id'; // returns true
```

A second approach makes use of the querySelector method, which was first defined on both the Document and Element interfaces in the W3C Selectors API Level 1 specification.[6] Remember that the HTMLElement interface, on which the id attribute is defined, inherits from the Element interface, so Elements have an id property as well. The querySelector method is available in all modern browsers, as well as Internet Explorer 8. In Listing 4-2, you will start to notice some stark similarities between the native approach and the jQuery shortcut.

Listing 4-2. Select by ID: Web API, Modern Browsers and Internet Explorer 8

```
1  // returns the matching HTMLElement - the <div> from our sample
2  var result = document.querySelector('#my-element-id');
3
4  // assuming our element has been found in the document
5  result.id === 'my-element-id'; // returns true
```

■ **Performance Note**   querySelector is a bit slower than getElementById,[7] but this performance gap is closing as browser JavaScript engines evolve.

Classes

Contrary to the focus of IDs, class attributes do *not* uniquely identify an element in a document. Instead, classes are traditionally used to semantically group elements in the context of an application as a whole. While IDs can certainly be used to style elements via CSS, this role is most often tied to class attributes. Elements may also be assigned multiple class names, while they are limited to one ID (for obvious reasons). The HTML 4.01 specification goes into more detail regarding the role of class attributes.[8] Chapter 5 discusses working with element attributes in much more detail.

Generally speaking, a valid CSS class is case-insensitive, can only contain alphanumeric characters or hyphen or underscore, and may not start with a digit or two hyphens or a hyphen and a digit. These rules also apply to IDs, along with other element properties used to target elements via CSS. You can read about all of the allowed values in CSS selectors in the CSS 2.1 specification.[9]

For example, consider the following markup:

```
1  <span class="some-class"></span>
```

The span element's class attribute is also accessible via the JavaScript representation of the element on the object's className property. Notice the inconsistency here—the attribute name is class, whereas the corresponding Element property is className. This is due to the fact that class is a reserved word in many languages, such as JavaScript (even as late as the ECMAScript 5.1 edition specification),[10] which is why an alternate name exists in the JavaScript representation of an element. For example:

```
1  // `elementObject` is the <span> in our sample markup above
2  elementObject.className === 'some-class'; // returns true
```

---

[6]www.w3.org/TR/selectors-api/#queryselector
[7]http://jsperf.com/getelementbyid-vs-queryselector/11
[8]www.w3.org/TR/html401/struct/global.html#adef-class
[9]www.w3.org/TR/CSS21/syndata.html#characters
[10]www.ecma-international.org/ecma-262/5.1/#sec-7.6.1.2

jQuery

Selecting an element by class in jQuery looks very similar to the approach used to select an ID. In fact, all element selection in jQuery follows the same pattern:

```
1  // Returns a jQuery object with 0 elements (element not found)
2  // or all elements with the 'some-class' class attribute.
3  var result = $('.some-class');
4
5  // assuming our element has been found in the document
6  result.is('.some-class'); // returns true
```

If there happen to be three different elements in the document with a class name of some-class, the result jQuery object will have three entries, one for each match.

Web API

As with IDs, there are several different way to select elements by class name using the web API. I will demonstrate two of them—both available in modern browsers as well as Internet Explorer 8 (the last example). Listing 4-3 is the most performant, but Listing 4-4 is clearly the most elegant.

Listing 4-3. Select by Class: Web API, Modern Browsers

```
1  // Returns an HTMLCollection containing all matching elements,
2  // which is empty if there are no matches.
3  var result = anyElement.getElementsByClassName('some-class');
4
5  // assuming our element has been found in the document
6  result[0].className === 'some-class'; // returns true
```

The first noticeable difference between getElementById and getElementsByClassName is the fact that the latter returns an array-like object containing *all* matching elements, instead of a *single* element. Remember, a document can contain many elements that share the same class name. You may also notice another difference, one which may not be particularly obvious in the simple example provided. The getElementsByClassName method is available on the Document interface, just like getElementById. However, it is also defined to be a method on the Element interface in the W3C DOM4 specification.[11] This means that you may restrict your query to a specific subset of elements when looking for class name matches by specifying an element in the document. When executed on a specific element, only descendant elements are examined for matches. This allows for more focused and efficient DOM traversal.

The getElementsByClassName method's return value is an HTMLCollection, which is a pseudo-array, and it provides sequentially ordered numeric properties (0, 1, 2, . . .), one for each matching element, along with a length property and some other methods (of limited usefulness). The most notable attribute of an HTMLCollection is the fact that it is a *live* collection. That is, it is updated automatically to match the underlying elements in the DOM that it represents. For example, if an element contained in the returned HTMLCollection is removed from the DOM, it will *also* be removed from any HTMLCollection in scope. Note that getElementsByClassName is defined in the W3C DOM4 specification.

A second approach, shown in Listing 4-4, to selecting elements by class name involves a cousin to the previously demonstrated querySelector.

---

[11]www.w3.org/TR/2015/WD-dom-20150428/#dom-document-getelementsbyclassname

Listing 4-4. Select by Class: Web API, Modern Browsers and Internet Explorer 8

```
1  // Returns a NodeList containing all matching elements,
2  // which is empty if there are no matches.
3  var result = anyElement.querySelectorAll('.some-class');
4
5  // assuming our element has been found in the document
6  result[0].className === 'some-class'; // returns true
```

Like getElementsByClassName, querySelectorAll returns all matches in an array-like object. The differences end there, though. For one, querySelectorAll returns a NodeList object, an interface which was first formally defined in the W3C DOM Level 3 Core specification.[12] NodeList differs in one important way from an HTMLCollection: it is *not* a "live" collection. So, if a matching element contained in a NodeList is removed from the DOM, it will *not* be removed from any NodeList.

querySelectorAll is available both on the Document interface *and* the Element interface, according to the W3C Selectors API (just like getElementsByClassName).[13] The querySelector method, which can *also* be used when looking for an element with a specific class name, will *only* return the *first* matching element, which may actually be desirable in some instances. In either case, a CSS selector string must be passed. When looking for a class name, we must include a "." prefix, which was first described in the CSS 1 specification,[14] although more detail was included in the later CSS 2.1 specification.[15] Although getElementsByClassName is not available in IE8, you can alternatively locate elements by class name in this browser simply by passing a CSS class selector string into the querySelectorAll method.

If you *must* support Internet Explorer 7, or older, the approach for selecting elements by class name can be a bit cumbersome. Since this type of support is rapidly falling out of favor, I have elected to omit the ugly and inefficient legacy solution (which jQuery must rely on anyway). You can have a look at how a library I maintain solved the issue[16] back when it supported ancient browsers.

Element Tags

The most basic property of any element is its name. In the IETF HTML specification drafted in part by Tim Berners-Lee way back in 1993,[17] a valid element/tag name may "consist of a letter followed by up to 33 letters, digits, periods, or hyphens." This specification goes on to say "names are not case sensitive." There were also a small number of elements defined in this document, such as the anchor tag (<a>), the paragraph tag (<p>), and the <address> element for supplying contact information. Since this first specification, many more elements have been added, such as <video>[18] and <audio>,[19] added in the relatively recent HTML5 specification.

Although custom elements have not been explicitly banned by browsers, there was little motivation to create them, until the Web Components specification came along.[20] Web Components is a collection of specifications, one being the custom elements specification,[21] which details a way to create new HTMLElements with their own API and properties, or even extensions of existing elements—such as the ajax-form custom element,[22] which extends and adds features to a native <form>.

[12]www.w3.org/TR/DOM-Level-3-Core/core.html#ID-536297177
[13]www.w3.org/TR/2007/WD-selectors-api-20071221/#documentselector
[14]www.w3.org/TR/REC-CSS1/#class-as-selector
[15]www.w3.org/TR/CSS21/selector.html#class-html
[16]https://github.com/FineUploader/fine-uploader/blob/5.2.1/client/js/util.js#L107
[17]www.w3.org/MarkUp/draft-ietf-iiir-html-01.txt
[18]www.w3.org/TR/html5/embedded-content-0.html#the-video-element
[19]www.w3.org/TR/html5/embedded-content-0.html#the-audio-element
[20]www.w3.org/wiki/WebComponents/
[21]www.w3.org/TR/custom-elements/
[22]https://github.com/rnicholus/ajax-form

To set up our examples, consider the following very simple HTML block:

```
1   <code>System.out.println("Hello world!");</code>
```

If you are given an element reference, you can easily determine the element's name via the `tagName` property, which is defined on the Element interface as part of DOM Level 1 Core:[23]

```
1   // `elementObject` is the <code> element from our above HTML
2   elementObject.tagName === 'CODE'; // returns true
```

jQuery

Selecting elements by jQuery is, predictably, facilitated by passing a CSS element selector into the $ or jQuery function:

```
1   // Returns a jQuery object with 0 elements (element not found)
2   // or all elements with a matching tag name.
3   var result = $('CODE');
4
5   // assuming our element has been found in the document
6   result.is('CODE'); // returns true
```

Nothing magical here. In fact, the syntax for an element name selector string is defined in the first CSS specification.[24] jQuery has simply provided a simple alias for the native methods available to select elements by tag name, explored next.

Web API

Let's start with a quick look at the traditional method for selecting elements by tag name by interfacing directly with the native web API:

```
1   // Returns a HTMLCollection containing all matching elements,
2   // which is empty if there are no matches.
3   var result = anyElement.getElementsByTagName('CODE');
4
5   // assuming our element has been found in the document
6   result[0].tagName === 'CODE'; // returns true
```

The preceding method has been available as early as DOM Level 1 Core, and, like getElementsByClass-Name, is available on both the Document interface[25] *and* the Element interface.[26] So, this approach is available on all browsers in existence.

A more "modern" approach involves, as you might expect, querySelector or querySelectorAll:

```
1   // Returns a NodeList containing all matching elements,
2   // which is empty if there are no matches.
3   var result = anyElement.querySelectorAll('CODE');
4
```

---

[23]www.w3.org/TR/REC-DOM-Level-1/level-one-core.html#ID-1950641247
[24]www.w3.org/TR/REC-CSS1/#basic-concepts
[25]www.w3.org/TR/REC-DOM-Level-1/level-one-core.html#i-Document
[26]www.w3.org/TR/REC-DOM-Level-1/level-one-core.html#ID-745549614

```
5   // assuming our element has been found in the document
6   result[0].tagName === 'CODE'; // returns true
7
8   // -OR-
9
10  // ...you can use this if you know there is only one <code>
11  // element to find, or if you only care about the first.
12  // Returns true.
13  anyElement.querySelector('CODE').tagName === 'CODE';
```

There is currently a potentially noticeable performance difference between getElementsByTagName and querySelectorAll(tagName).[27] The performance consequences of using querySelectorAll are apparently attributable to the fact that getElementsByTagName returns a live collection of matching elements in the DOM (an HTMLCollection), while querySelectorAll returns a static collection (a NodeList). The latter requires iterating over all elements in the DOM, while the former returns cached matching elements and then queries the document for updates when the list is accessed.[28] This performance difference is similar to that of getElementsByClassName versus query- SelectorAll(classSelector) for the same reason.

Pseudo-classes

While the prevalence and number of pseudo-classes has grown substantially in recent versions of the CSS specification, pseudo-classes have existed since the earliest versions of the CSS specification.[29] Pseudo-classes are keywords that add state to a selector string or group of elements. For example, the :visited pseudo-class on an anchor selector string will target any links that the user has already visited. Another example, the :focus pseudo-class will target the element that is determined to have focus, such as a text input field that the user is currently interacting with. We will use the latter in our following examples, as browsers prevent programatic selector access in JavaScript to visited links due to privacy concerns.[30]

To set up our examples, let's create a simple form with a couple text inputs, and imagine that the user has clicked on (or tabbed to) the last text input (named "company"). This last input will be the one that is "focused":

```
1   <form>
2       <label>Full Name
3           <input name="full-name">
4       </label>
5       <label>Company
6           <input name="company">
7       </label>
8   </form>
```

jQuery

Say we want to select the input that is currently focused, using jQuery:

```
1   // Return value will be a jQuery object containing the
2   // "company" input element
3   var focusedInputs = $('INPUT:focus');
```

---

[27]https://jsperf.com/queryselectorall-vs-getelementsbytagname
[28]www.nczonline.net/blog/2010/09/28/why-is-getelementsbytagname-faster-that-queryselectorall/
[29]www.w3.org/TR/CSS1/#anchor-pseudo-classes
[30]www.w3.org/TR/selectors-api/#privacy

The preceding is, once again, a standardized CSS selector string. We are making use of a tag name selector with a pseudo-class modifier. jQuery isn't doing anything special for us at all. In fact, it's simply delegating directly to the web API.

Web API

Consider the following:

```
1  // Return value will be the "company" text input field element
2  var companyInput = document.querySelector('INPUT:focus');
```

That code avoids all of the overhead associated with filtering the call through jQuery. If we were to use jQuery instead (as we have done in the previous example) querySelectorAll would have been invoked internally by jQuery's selector code with the exact same selector string. Since only one element can have focus at once, querySelector is more appropriate than querySelectorAll. And it's also a bit faster, for the same reason why any of the getElementsBy methods are faster than querySelectorAll.

Selecting Elements Based on Their Relations

With some rudimentary approaches to selecting elements fresh in our heads, we're ready to move on to the next step in our trip through element selectors. The following sections cover selecting elements based on their relation to other elements. We will examine locating children and descendants, parents of children, and elements that are siblings of other elements. The DOM is organized as a tree-like structure. With this in mind, it is often advantageous to be able to navigate this hierarchy of nodes with relations in mind. Just as we already witnessed in the core selectors section, finding elements based on their relations is fairly straightforward *and* more performant *without* jQuery.

Parents and Children

Remember from our discussion on the DOM API that an Element is a specific type of Node. A Node or Element may have zero *children* if it is a "leaf" node. Otherwise, it will have one or more immediate children. But every Node or Element in a document has exactly *one* immediate parent. Well, almost. There are two exceptions to this rule: one occurs with the <html> tag (HTMLHtmlElement)[31] which is the root Element in a document, and therefore has no parent Element (though it does have a parent Node: document). This brings us to the second exception, the document object (Document),[32] which has neither a parent Node *nor* a parent Element. It is *the* root Node.

Listing 4-5 shows a simple HMTL fragment.

Listing 4-5. Example Markup for Parent/Children Traversal Examples

```
1  <div>
2      <a href="http://fineuploader.com">
3          <span>Go to Fine Uploader</span>
4      </a>
5      <p>Some text</p>
6      Some other text
7  </div>
```

---

[31] www.w3.org/TR/html5/semantics.html#the-html-element
[32] www.w3.org/TR/html5/dom.html#the-document-object

In the following code examples, a distinction will be made between targeting child/parent Nodes and Elements. If this distinction is not already clear, first understand that Listing 4-5 is made up of Element type object, such as the <div>, the <a>, the <span>, and the <p>. These Elements are *also* Nodes, since the Element interface is a subtype of the Node interface. But the "Go to Fine Uploader", "Some text", and "Some other text" portions of the fragment are *not* Elements. But they *are* Nodes. More specifically, they are Text items. The Text interface[33] is a subtype of the CharacterData interface,[34] which itself implements the Node interface.

jQuery

jQuery's API includes a parent method. To keep things simple, we'll assume that the "current jQuery object" only represents *one* element. When calling the parent method on this object, the resulting jQuery object will contain either the parent Element, or, in rare instances, a parent Node that is not an Element. See Listing 4-6.

Listing 4-6. Get Parent Element/Node: jQuery

```
1  // Assuming $a is a reference to the anchor in our example HTML,
2  // $result will contain the <div> above it.
3  var $result = $a.parent();
4
5  // Assuming $span is a reference to the <span> in our example HTML,
6  // the first parent() call references the <a> element, and the
7  // $result will contain the <div> root element.
8  var $result = $span.parent().parent();
9
10  // Assuming someText is a reference to the "Some text" Text node,
11  // the result will contain the <p> element in our example HTML.
12  // Note: selecting a text node requires locating the node in the result of
13  // using the `contents()` method, as illustrated in the next code block.
14  var $result = $someText.parent();
```

To locate children, jQuery provides a children() method that will return all immediate child Elements of a given element. You may also select child elements given a reference element using the child selector standardized in the CSS 2.1 W3C specification.[35] But since children() will *only* return Elements, we must use jQuery's contents() API method to obtain any Nodes that are not also Elements, such as Text nodes. Again, to keep this simple, Listing 4-7 assumes that the reference jQuery object in our example only refers to *one* specific element in the DOM.

Listing 4-7. Get Child Elements and/or Child Nodes: jQuery

```
1  // Assuming $div is a jQuery object containing the <div> in our example HTML,
2  // $result will contain 2 elements: <a> and <p>.
3  var $result = $div.children();
4
5  // $result contains the <p> element in the sample markup
6  var $result = $('DIV > P');
7
8  // Again, assuming $div refers to the <div> in our example markup,
9  // $result will contain 3 nodes: <a>, <p>, and "Some other text".
```

---

[33]www.w3.org/TR/DOM-Level-3-Core/core.html#ID-1312295772
[34]www.w3.org/TR/DOM-Level-3-Core/core.html#ID-FF21A306
[35]http://www.w3.org/TR/CSS21/selector.html#child-selectors

```
10  var $result = $div.contents();
11
12  // Assuming $a refers to the <a> element in our example markup,
13  // $result will contains 1 element: <span>.
14  var $result = $a.children();
15
16  // This returns the exact same elements as the previous example.
17  var $result = $('A > *')
```

Web API

For the most part, locating the parent of an element/node without jQuery is simple. DOM Level 2 Core was the first specification to define a parentNode property on the Node interface,[36] which, as you might expect, is set to the parent Node of the reference element. Of course, this value may be an Element or any other type of Node. Later on, in the subsequent W3C DOM4 specification, a parentElement property was added to the Node interface.[37] This property will *always* be an Element. If the parent of a reference Node is some type of Node other than an Element, the parentElement will be null. But in most cases, parentElement and parentNode will be identical, unless the reference node is <html>, in which case parentNode will be document, and parentElement will be of course null. In a general sense, and especially due to wide browser support, the parentNode property is the best choice, but parentElement is nearly just as safe. See Listing 4-8.

Listing 4-8. Get Parent Element/Node: Web API

```
1   // Assuming "a" is the <a> element in our HTML example,
2   // "result" will be the the <div> above it.
3   var result = a.parentNode;
4
5   // Assuming "span" is the <span> element in our HTML example,
6   // the first parentNode is the <a>, while "result" is the <div>
7   // at the root of our example markup.
8   var result = span.parentNode.parentNode;
9
10  // Assuming "someText" is the "Some text" Text node in our HTML example,
11  // "result" will be the the <p> that contains it.
12  var result = someText.parentNode;
```

There are a number of different ways to locate immediate children of an element using the web API. I will demonstrate two such ways next, and briefly discuss a third approach. The simplest and most common method of locating an element's children in all modern browsers involves using the children property on the ParentNode interface.[38] ParentNode is defined to be implemented by both the Element *and* Document interfaces, though it is only commonly implemented on the Element interface. It applies to a Node that may potentially have children. It was first defined in the W3C DOM4 specification[39] and is only available in modern browsers. ParentNode.children returns all children of the reference Node in an HTMLCollection, which you may remember from earlier in this chapter represents a "live" collection of Elements:

```
1   // Assuming "div" is an Element object containing the <div> in our example HTML,
2   // result will contain an HTMLCollection holding 2 elements: <a> and <p>.
3   var result = div.children;
```

[36]www.w3.org/TR/DOM-Level-2-Core/core.html#ID-1060184317
[37]www.w3.org/TR/2015/WD-dom-20150428/#node
[38]www.w3.org/TR/2015/WD-dom-20150428/#parentnode
[39]www.w3.org/TR/2015/WD-dom-20150428/

A second method used to locate child Elements involves using querySelectorAll along with the CSS 2 child selector.[40] This approach allows us to support Internet Explorer 8, in addition to all modern browsers. Remember that querySelectorAll returns a NodeList, which differs from an HTMLCollection in that it is a "static" collection of elements. The collection in this case contains all Element children of the parent Node:

```
1  // The result will contain a NodeList holding 2 elements: <a> and <p>
2  // from our HTML fragment above.
3  var result = document.querySelectorAll('DIV > *');
4
5  // The result will be all <p> children of the <div>, which, in this case
6  // is only one element: <p>Some text</p>.
7  var result = document.querySelectorAll('DIV > P');
```

A third option used to select children with the web API involves the childNodes property on the Node interface.[41] This property was declared on the original W3C DOM Level 1 Core specification.[42] As a result, it is supported by all browsers, even ancient ones. The childNodes property will reveal *all* child Nodes, even Text and Comment nodes. You *can* filter out the non-Element objects in the collection simply by iterating over the results and ignoring any that have a nodeType property[43] that is *not* equal to 1. This nodeType property was *also* defined on the original Node interface specification:

```
1  // Assuming "div" is an Element object containing the <div> in
2  // our example HTML, result will contain a NodeList
3  // holding 3 Nodes: <a>, <p>, and "Some other text".
4  var result = div.childNodes;
```

Given a parent Node, you may also locate either the first and last child, via the aptly named firstChild and lastChild properties, respectively. Both properties have existed since the original Node interface specification, and they refer to child Nodes, so the first or last child may be a Text Node *or* an HTMLDivElement, for example. The firstChild property can be used as part of a *fourth* method of obtaining the children of a parent Node. This approach is discussed as part of the sibling element selection section below.

Siblings

DOM Nodes are siblings if they share the same immediate parent. They may be adjacent siblings (next to each other) or "general" siblings (not necessarily next to each other). There are a number of ways to find and navigate among sibling Nodes. While I will go over how this is done using jQuery for the purpose of reference, you will see just how easy it is to do this *without* jQuery as well. Listing 4-9 will be used as a reference point for all demonstration code.

Listing 4-9. Working with Siblings: Markup for Following Demos

```
1  <div id="parent">
2      <a href="https://github.com/rnicholus">GitHub</a>
3      <span>Span text</span>
4      <p>Paragraph text</p>
5      <div>Div text</div>
6      Text node
7  </div>
```

---

[40]http://www.w3.org/TR/CSS21/selector.html#child-selectors
[41]www.w3.org/TR/REC-DOM-Level-1/level-one-core.html#ID-1950641247
[42]www.w3.org/TR/REC-DOM-Level-1/level-one-core.html
[43]www.w3.org/TR/REC-DOM-Level-1/level-one-core.html#ID-1950641247

jQuery

To find all sibling Elements of a given Element, jQuery provides a siblings method as part of its API. For traversing through the siblings of a given Element, there are next() and prev() methods as well. To keep things simple, I'll simply review how we have all used jQuery to find and traverse through the siblings of a given element, starting with Listing 4-10.

Listing 4-10. Find and Traverse Through Siblings: jQuery

```
1  // $result will be a jQuery object that contains <a>, <span>, <p>,
2  // and <div> elements inside of the #parent <div>.
3  var $result = $('SPAN').siblings();
4
5  // $result will be a jQuery object that contains the <a> element
6  // that precedes the <span>.
7  var $result = $('SPAN').prev();
8
9  // The first next() refers to the <p>, and the 2nd next()
10 // refers to the <div>Div text</div> element, which is also
11 // the element contained in the jQuery $result object.
12 var $result = $('SPAN').next().next();
13
14 // The first next() refers to the <p>, and the 2nd next()
15 // refers to the <div>Div text</div> element. The final next()
16 // does not reference any element, since the final Node in the
17 // fragment is a Text Node, and not an element. So, the $result
18 // is an empty jQuery object.
19 var $result = $('SPAN').next().next().next();
```

You can also use CSS sibling selectors in jQuery, which we explore a bit in the next section. jQuery actually permits standardized W3C CSS selectors strings for this and other operations.

Web API

To mirror the behaviors provided by jQuery's API, I'll cover the following topics associated with sibling traversal and discovery:

1. Locating all siblings of a specific Element or Node.

2. Navigating through preceding and subsequent siblings of a specific Element or Node.

3. Locating general and adjacent siblings of an Element using CSS selectors.

4. Locating *children* using the sibling properties on the Node interface.

The simplest way to locate all sibling Elements of another Element is to make use of the CSS3 general sibling selector.[44] This approach will work as far back as Internet Explorer 8, and provides you with a NodeList of all sibling Elements. The W3C CSS2 specification defined an "adjacent" sibling selector,[45] which only selects the first Element matching the selector that occurs after the reference element. Both of the sibling selectors described here are demonstrated in Listing 4-11.

---

[44]www.w3.org/TR/css3-selectors/#general-sibling-combinators
[45]www.w3.org/TR/CSS21/selector.html#adjacent-selectors

Listing 4-11. Find Siblings Using CSS Selectors: Web API, Modern Browsers, and Internet Explorer 8

```
1  // "result" contains a NodeList of all siblings that occur after the <span>
2  // in our example HMTL at the start of this section. These siblings are
3  // the <p> and the <div> elements.
4  var result = document.querySelectorAll('#parent > SPAN ~ *');
5
6  // Another general sibling selector that specifically targets any
7  // subsequent siblings of the <span> that are <div>s. In our case,
8  // there is only one such element - <div>Div text</div>. The
9  // "result" variable is a NodeList containing this one element.
10 var result = document.querySelectorAll('#parent > SPAN ~ DIV');
11
12 // This is an adjacent sibling selector in action. It will target
13 // the first sibling after the <span>. So, "result", is the same
14 // as in the previous general sibling selector example.
15 var result = document.querySelector('#parent > SPAN + *');
```

You'll notice that the general sibling selector (~) does *not* select any elements that precede the reference element—only the ones that follow it. If you *do* need to account for any siblings that come before the reference element, you'll need to make use of either the Node.previousSibling property first defined in W3C DOM Level 1 Core[46] or the previousElementSibling property, which is part of the ElementTraversal interface[47] first defined in the W3C Element Traversal specification.[48]

ElementTraversal is an interface that is implemented by any object that also implements the Element interface. Simply put, all DOM elements have a previousElementSibling property. This is demonstrated in Listing 4-12.

Listing 4-12. Find Both Preceding and Subsequent Siblings of a Reference Element: Web API, Modern Browsers

```
1  // Find all siblings that follow the <span> in our example HTML
2  var allSiblings = document.querySelectorAll('#parent > SPAN ~ *');
3
4  // Converts the allSiblings NodeList into an Array.
5  allSiblings = [].slice.call(allSiblings);
6
7  var currentElement = document.querySelector('#parent > SPAN');
8
9  // This loop executes until we run out of previous siblings,
10 // starting with the sibling before the <span>. Each sibling
11 // is added to the allSiblings array. After this loop is complete,
12 // the allSiblings array will contain all siblings of the <span>
13 // (before and after).
14 do {
15   currentElement = currentElement.previousElementSibling;
16   currentElement && allSiblings.unshift(currentElement);
17 } while (currentElement);
```

---

[46]www.w3.org/TR/REC-DOM-Level-1/level-one-core.html#ID-1950641247
[47]www.w3.org/TR/ElementTraversal/#attribute-previousElementSibling
[48]www.w3.org/TR/ElementTraversal/

■ **Note**   Another approach may be to select the parent of the reference element, then collect its children, omitting the reference element. The code in this section was created specifically to demonstrate some standard CSS selectors and element properties.

For Internet Explorer 8 support, you will have to use `Node.previousSibling` instead of `Element.previousElementSibling`. This is due to lack of support for the Element Traversal spec in any version of Explorer older than 9. This property returns any `Node`, so you will want to be sure you add a `nodeType` property check if you only want to accept `Elements`. See Listing 4-13.

Listing 4-13. Find Both Preceding and Subsequent Siblings of a Reference Element: Web API, Modern Browsers, and Internet Explorer 8

```
1  var allSiblings = document.querySelectorAll('#parent > SPAN ~ *');
2
3  // Converts the allSiblings NodeList into an Array.
4  var allSiblings = [].slice.call(allSiblings);
5
6  var currentElement = document.querySelector('#parent > SPAN');
7
8  do {
9    currentElement = currentElement.previousSibling;
10   // This differs from the previous example in that we must
11   // exclude non-Element Nodes by examining the nodeType property.
12   if (currentElement && currentElement.nodeType === 1) {
13     allSiblings.unshift(currentElement);
14   }
15 } while (currentElement);
```

The web API also exposes a `nextSibling` property on the `Node` interface and a `nextElementSibling` property on the `ElementTraversal` interface.[49] As Listing 4-14 shows, browser support of these properties is identical to their "previous" cousins.

Listing 4-14. Traverse Through All Subsequent Siblings: Web API, Modern Browsers, and Internet Explorer 8

```
1  // The first nextSibling refers to the <p>, and the 2nd nextSibling
2  // refers to the <div>Div text</div> element. The final nextSibling
3  // refers to the "Text node" Text Node, since nextSibling targets
4  // any type of Node. So, the result is this Text Node.
5  var result = document.querySelector('SPAN')
6                      .nextSibling.nextSibling.nextSibling;
7
8  // Same as the above example, but the final nextElementSibling returns null,
9  // since the last Node in the example markup is not an Element. There are only
10 // 2 Element siblings following the <span>. Note that nextElementSibling
11 // is not available in ancient browsers.
12 var result = document.querySelector('SPAN')
13                      .nextElementSibling.nextElementSibling.nextElementSibling;
```

---

[49]www.w3.org/TR/ElementTraversal/#attribute-nextElementSibling

In addition to the methods used to select children outlined in the previous section using the web API, another such option exists to select *only* Element children of a parent Node in *any* browser. This involves obtaining the firstChild of the parent Node, locating for the sibling Node of this first child, and then continuing to traverse through all sibling elements using the nextSibling property on each Node until there are no remaining siblings. And finally, to exclude all non-Element siblings (such as Text Nodes), simply check the nodeType property of each Node, which will have a value of 1 if the Node is more specifically an Element. This is how jQuery implements its children method, at least in the late 1.x versions of the library. This implementation choice is likely due to the fact that all of these properties on the Node interface have wide browser support, even among ancient browsers. However, there are much simpler approaches that are supported in modern browsers, so the path just described is really only relevant from an academic or historic perspective.

Ancestors and Descendants

To illustrate the ancestor/descendant Node relationship, let's start out with a brief HTML fragment:

```
1  <body>
2    <div>
3      <span>random text</span>
4        <ul>
5          <li>
6            <span>item 1</span>
7          </li>
8          <li>
9            <a href="#some-content">item 2</a>
10         </li>
11       </ul>
12   </div>
13 </body>
```

An element's ancestors are any elements that appear before it in the DOM. That is, its parent, its parent's parent (or grandparent), its parent's parent's parent (great-grandparent), and so on. In the preceding HTML fragment, the anchor element's ancestors include its immediate parent (the <li>), along with the <ul>, <div>, and finally the <body> element. Conversely, an element's descendants include its children, its children's children, and so on. In the preceding markup, the <ul> element has four descendants: the two <li> elements, the <span>, and the <a>.

jQuery

jQuery's API provides a single method used to retrieve all of an element's ancestors - parents():

```
1  // Using our HTML example, $result is a jQuery object that
2  // contains the following elements: <li>, <ul>,
3  // <div>, and <body>
4  var $result = $('A').parents();
```

But what if you only want to retrieve the first ancestor that matches a specific condition? In our case, say we are only looking for the first ancestor of the <a> that is also a <div>. For that, we would use jQuery's closest() method. jQuery implements closest() by brute-force—through examination of each parent of the reference Node:

```
1  // Using our HTML example, $result is a jQuery object that
2  // contains the <div> element.
3  var $result = $('A').closest('DIV');
```

45

For locating descendants, you may use jQuery's find() method:

```
1  // Using our HTML example, $result is a jQuery object that
2  // contains the following elements: both <li>s, the <span>,
3  // and the <a>.
4  var $result = $('UL').find('*');
5
6  // $result is a jQuery object that contains the <span>
7  // under the first <li>.
8  var $result = $('UL').find('SPAN');
```

Web API

The native web does not provide a single API method that returns all ancestors of an element. If this is required in your project, you can accumulate these Nodes with a simple loop, making use of the Node. parentNode property[50] or Node.parentElement. Remember that the latter targets only a specific type of Node: an Element. This is usually what we want anyway, so we will make use of parentElement in our examples. See Listing 4-15.

Listing 4-15. Retrieve All Element Ancestors: Web API, Any Browser

```
1  // When this code is complete, "ancestors" will contain all
2  // ancestors of the anchor element: <li>, <ul>,
3  // <div>, and <body>
4  var currentNode = document.getElementsByTagName('A')[0],
5      ancestors = [];
6
7  while (currentNode.parentElement) {
8     ancestors.push(currentNode.parentElement);
9     currentNode = currentNode.parentElement;
10 }
```

We already know that jQuery provides a method that allows us to easily find the first matching ancestor of an element, closest. The web API has a similar method on the Element interface, also called closest. Element. closest()[51] is part of the WHATWG DOM "living standard".[52] This method behaves exactly like jQuery's closest(). Browser support for this method is missing from any version of Internet Explorer and Microsoft Edge as of mid-2016, but is supported in Chrome, Firefox, and Safari 9. In the next example, I demonstrate how the web API's closest() method can be used, and I even include a simple fallback for browsers *without* native support. Let's again use our example markup and try to locate the closest ancestor of the <a> that is a <div>. See Listings 4-16 and 4-17.

■ **Note**   You may remember from Chapter 3 that the WHATWG develops a set of web specifications that differ a bit from the traditional W3C specs.

Listing 4-16. Retrieve Closest Element Ancestor: Web API, All Modern Browsers Except IE and Edge

```
1  function closest(referenceEl, closestSelector) {
2     // use Element.closest if it is supported
```

---

[50]www.w3.org/TR/DOM-Level-2-Core/core.html#ID-1060184317
[51]https://dom.spec.whatwg.org/#dom-element-closestselectors
[52]https://dom.spec.whatwg.org

```
 3      if (referenceEl.closest) {
 4          return referenceEl.closest(closestSelector);
 5      }
 6
 7      // ...otherwise use brute force (like jQuery)
 8      // To find a match for our closestSelector, we must use the
 9      // Element.matches method, which is still vendor-prefixed
10      // in some browsers.
11      var matches = Element.prototype.matches ||
12          Element.prototype.msMatchesSelector ||
13          Element.prototype.webkitMatchesSelector,
14
15          currentEl = referenceEl;
16
17      while (currentEl) {
18        if (matches.call(currentEl, closestSelector)) {
19          return currentEl;
20        }
21        currentEl = currentEl.parentElement;
22      }
23
24      return null;
25  }
26
27  // "result" is the <div> that exists before the <a>
28  var result = document.querySelector('A').closest('DIV');
```

Listing 4-17. Retrieve Closest Element Ancestor: Web API, All Modern Browsers

```
 1  function closest(referenceEl, closestSelector) {
 2    // use Element.closest if it is supported
 3    if (referenceEl.closest) {
 4        return referenceEl.closest(closestSelector);
 5    }
 6
 7    // ...otherwise use brute force (like jQuery)
 8
 9    // To find a match for our closestSelector, we must use the
10    // Element.matches method, which is still vendor-prefixed
11    // in some browsers.
12    var matches = Element.prototype.matches ||
13        Element.prototype.msMatchesSelector ||
14        Element.prototype.webkitMatchesSelector,
15
16        currentEl = referenceEl;
17
18    while (currentEl) {
19      if (matches.call(currentEl, closestSelector)) {
20        return currentEl;
21      }
22      currentEl = currentEl.parentElement;
23    }
```

```
24
25    return null;
26  }
27
28  // "result" is the <div> that exists before the <a>
29  var result = closest(document.querySelector('A'), 'DIV');
```

Note that the cross-browser solution makes use of Element.matches,[53] which is also defined by WHATWG in their DOM living spec. This method will return true if the element it is called on matches the passed CSS selector. Some browsers, namely IE and Safari, still implement a naming convention consistent with an older version of the specification along with vendor-specific prefixes. I've accounted for these in my example.

The preceding solution may be less elegant, but it makes better use of the browser's native power. jQuery's closest() function *always* uses the most primitive brute-force approach, even if the browser supports Element.closest natively.

Finding descendants using the web API is just as easy as with jQuery (Listing 4-18).

Listing 4-18. Retrieve Element Descendants: Web API, Modern Browsers, and Internet Explorer 8

```
1  // Using our HTML example, result is a NodeList that
2  // contains the following elements: the two <li>s, <span>,
3  // and <a>.
4  var result = document.querySelectorAll('UL *');
5
6  // "result" is a NodeList that contains the <span>
7  // under the first <li>.
8  var result = document.querySelectorAll('UL SPAN');
```

Mastering Advanced Element Selection

What follows are some more advanced methods used to select even more specific elements or groups of elements. While jQuery provides API methods to deal with each scenario, you'll see that modern web specifications *also* provide the same support, which means that jQuery is not needed in modern browsers for *any* of these examples. Web API Solutions here will mostly involve the use of various CSS3 selectors,[54] which are also usable from jQuery.

All the native examples in this section are supported in all modern browsers. In some cases, I also touch on how to achieve the same goals using the web API in ancient browsers as well. Should you find yourself needing some of the following selectors in support of an ancient browser, perhaps you'll forgo pulling in jQuery after understanding how to approach the problem using the browser's native tools instead. Or not, but at least the solution will shed some light on jQuery's inner-workings, which is still beneficial if you insist on making it part of your core toolset.

Excluding Elements

Although the ability to exclude specific matches in a set is part of the jQuery API, we'll also see how we can achieve the same results natively with another appropriately named pseudo-class. Before we dive into code, let's consider the following HTML fragment:

```
1  <ul role="menu">
2      <li>choice 1</li>
```

---

[53]https://dom.spec.whatwg.org/#dom-element-matchesselectors
[54]www.w3.org/TR/css3-selectors/

```
3      <li class="active">choice 2</li>
4      <li>choice 3</li>
5  </ul>
```

Imagine this is some sort of menu, with three items to choose from. The second item, "choice 2", is currently selected. What if you want to easily gather all of the menu items that are *not* selected?

jQuery

jQuery's API provides a not() method that will remove any elements that match a selector from the original set of elements:

```
1  // $result is a jQuery object that contains all
2  // `<li>`s that are not "active" (the first and last).
3  var $result = $('UL LI').not('.active');
```

Although the preceding example is idiomatic jQuery, you don't *have* to use the not() function. Instead, you can make use of a CSS3 selector, discussed next.

Web API

The native solution for modern browsers is arguably just as elegant as jQuery's, and certainly just as easy. Below, we are using the W3C CSS3 negation pseudo-class[55] to locate the non-active list items. There is no library overhead, so this is of course more performant than jQuery's implementation:

```
1  // "result" is a NodeList that contains all
2  // `<li>`s that are not "active" (the first and last).
3  var result = document.querySelectorAll('UL LI:not(.active)');
```

But what if we still need to support Internet Explorer 8, which unfortunately does not support the negation pseudo-class selector? Well, the solution isn't as elegant, but still not particularly difficult if we need a quick fix and don't want to pull in a large library:

```
1  var allItems = document.querySelectorAll('UL LI'),
2      result = [];
3
4  // "result" will be an Array that contains all
5  // `<li>`s that are not "active" (the first and last).
6  for (var i = 0; i < allItems.length; i++) {
7    if (allItems[i].className !== 'active') {
8        result.push(allItems[i]);
9    }
10 }
```

The preceding solution is *still* more performant than jQuery's implementation of the not() method.[56]

---

[55]www.w3.org/TR/css3-selectors/#negation
[56]http://jsperf.com/jquery-not-vs-looping-through-results1

Multiple Selectors

Suppose you want to select several groups of disparate elements. Consider the following HTML fragment:

```
1  <div id="link-container">
2      <a href="https://github.com/rnicholus">GitHub</a>
3  </div>
4  <ol>
5      <li>one</li>
6      <li>two</li>
7  </ol>
8  <span class="my-name">Ray Nicholus</span>
```

What if you want to select the "link-container" *and* the "my-name" element, along with the ordered list? Let's also assume you want to accomplish this without loops—in one simple line of code.

jQuery

jQuery allows you to select multiple unrelated elements simply by providing one long comma-separated string of CSS selectors:

```
1  // $result is a jQuery object that contains 3 elements -
2  // the <div>, <ol> and the <span> from this section's
3  // HTML fragment.
4  var $result = $('#link-container, .my-name, OL');
```

Web API

The exact same result can be obtained without jQuery, using the web API. And the solution looks eerily similar to the jQuery solution. jQuery is, in this case and many others, simply a very thin wrapper around the web API. jQuery fully supports and uses the CSS specification to its advantage. The ability to select multiple unrelated groups of elements has always been part of the CSS specification.[57] Since jQuery supports standard CSS selector strings, the jQuery approach looks nearly identical to the native path:

```
1  // "result" is a NodeList that contains 3 elements -
2  // the <div>, <ol> and the <span> from this section's
3  // HTML fragment.
4  var result = document.querySelectorAll('#link-container, .my-name, OL');
```

Element Categories and Modifiers

jQuery's API provides quite a few of its own *proprietary* CSS pseudo-class selectors, such as :button, :submit, and :password. In fact, jQuery's documentation for these non-standard selectors *advises against using them*, due to the fact that there are much more performant alternatives—*standardized* CSS selectors. For example, the jQuery API docs for the :button pseudo-class contain the following warning:

> Because :button is a jQuery extension and not part of the CSS specification, queries using :button cannot take advantage of the performance boost provided by the native DOM querySelectorAll() method.

---

[57]www.w3.org/TR/REC-CSS1/#grouping

I'll demonstrate how to mimic the behavior of a few of jQuery's own pseudo-classes using querySelectorAll. These solutions (shown in Listings 4-19 and 4-20) will be far more performant than using the non-standard jQuery selectors. We'll start with :button, :submit, :password, and :file.

Listing 4-19. Implementing jQuery's :button Pseudo-class: Web API, Modern Browsers, and Internet Explorer 8

```
1  // "result" will contain a NodeList of all <button> and
2  // <input type="button"> elements in the document, just like
3  // jQuery's :button pseudo-class.
4  var result = document.querySelectorAll('BUTTON, INPUT[type="button"]');
```

Listing 4-20. Implementing jQuery's :submit Pseudo-class: Web API, Modern Browsers, and Internet Explorer 8

```
1  // "result" will contain a NodeList of all <button type="submit"> and
2  // <input type="submit"> elements in the document, just like
3  // jQuery's :submit pseudo-class.
4  var result = document.querySelectorAll(
5        'BUTTON[type="submit"], INPUT[type="submit"]'
6  );
```

The native solutions in Listings 4-21 and 4-22 are a bit wordier, but not particularly complex, and certainly more performant that jQuery's :submit. You can see the same performance differences between jQuery's :button selector and the native solution for more:[58]

Listing 4-21. Implementing jQuery's :password Pseudo-class: Web API, Modern Browsers, and Internet Explorer 8

```
1  // "result" will contain a NodeList of all <input type="password">
2  // elements in the document, just like jQuery's :password pseudo-class.
3  var result = document.querySelectorAll('INPUT[type="password"]');
```

Listing 4-22. Implementing jQuery's :file Pseudo-class: Web API, Modern Browsers, and Internet Explorer 8

```
1  // "result" will contain a NodeList of all <input type="file">
2  // elements in the document, just as jQuery's :file pseudo-class.
3  var result = document.querySelectorAll('INPUT[type="file"]');
```

Even this fairly straightforward native CSS selector is much faster than jQuery's non-standard :file pseudo-class.[59] Is the performance loss really worth saving a few characters in your code?

jQuery also offers a non-standard :first pseudo-class selector. As you might expect, it filters all but the first match in a query's result set. Consider the following markup:

```
1  <div>one</div>
2  <div>two</div>
3  <div>three</div>
```

Suppose we want to select the first <div> in this fragment. With jQuery, our code would look something like this:

```
1  // $result is a jQuery object containing
2  // the first <div> in our example markup.
```

_____

[58]http://jsperf.com/jquery-submit-vs-queryselectorall
[59]http://jsperf.com/jquery-file-vs-queryselectorall

```
3  var $result = $('DIV:first');
4
5  // same as above, but perhaps more idiomatic jQuery.
6  var $result = $('DIV').first();
```

The native solution is surprisingly simple and exceptionally performant[60] compared to jQuery's primitive implementation:

```
1  // result is the first <div> in our example markup.
2  var result = document.querySelector('DIV');
```

Since querySelector returns the first match for a selector string, this is actually a very elegant alternative to jQuery's :first pseudo-class or first() API method. You'll find many other proprietary CSS selectors in jQuery's arsenal that have straightforward alternatives in the web API.

A Simple Replacement for $(selector)

Throughout this chapter, you've seen a number of element selection approaches that involve passing a CSS selector string into the jQuery function (aliased as $). The native solution often involves the same selector string passed into either querySelector or querySelectorAll. All things being equal, and assuming we are only using valid CSS selector strings, we can replace the jQuery function with a native solution that is both simple to wire up *and* more performant than jQuery.

If we focus exclusively on selector support, and only need support for modern browsers, we can get pretty far by forgoing jQuery entirely and replacing it with a surprisingly concise native alternative, as shown in Listing 4-23.

Listing 4-23. Native Replacement for jQuery Function: All Modern Browsers, Internet Explorer 8 for CSS2 Selectors

```
1  window.$ = function(selector) {
2    return document.querySelectorAll(selector);
3  };
4
5  // examples that use our replacement
6  $('.some-class');
7  $('#some-id');
8  $('.some-parent > .some-child');
9  $('UL LI:not(.active)');
```

The performance benefits seen in some of the more complex selectors exist for the same reason as described earlier when contrasting selecting these same elements using jQuery with the web API. Let's take a look at the child selector in our above code. Our native solution is definitively faster than jQuery,[61] and the syntax is exactly the same between the two. Here, we give up nothing by abandoning jQuery, and gain performance along with a leaner page—a noteworthy theme of this chapter.

---

[60]http://jsperf.com/jquery-first-vs-queryselector
[61]http://jsperf.com/jquery-select-children-vs-native-replacement

CHAPTER 5

■ ■ ■

Using and Understanding HTML Element Attributes

Here in chapter five, prepare yourself for a full-scale, in-depth, no-holds-barred discussion on everything related to element attributes. Everything you learned in Chapter 4 will prove to be useful as you apply this knowledge during your journey through attributes. I'll make sure you have a proper understanding of attributes, how they came about and became part of HTML, and how they fit into the web API. Additionally, you'll learn how to use attributes to locate DOM elements. Although this is covered a bit in Chapter 4, you'll find that the coverage here is much more comprehensive. And finally, I'll dive deeper into attributes and demonstrate how you can read, add, and update them on any DOM element. Special sections on data- and class attributes will be included as well.

Other than a couple exceptions, most of the web API code in this chapter has full support across *all* modern browsers *and* even Internet Explorer 8 in many instances. After you complete this chapter, you will not only have a complete understanding of attributes, you will also have the confidence to read them, modify them, *and* use them to select elements in all browsers, even those as old as Internet Explorer 8. Read on to continue your quest to move Beyond jQuery!

What Is an Attribute?

HTML elements, declaratively speaking, are made up of three parts: name, content, and attributes, with the last two being optional. Take a look at the following simple fragment, which I'll reference as I explain these three parts a bit more.

```
1  <form action="/rest/login.php" method="POST">
2    <input name="username" required>
3    <input type="password" name="password" required>
4  </form>
```

In that markup, you see three elements tags: one <form> and two <input>s. The <form> element has a tag name of "FORM". In fact, tagName is a property available on every object in the DOM that implements the Element interface. This property was standardized as part of W3C's DOM Level 2 Core specification.[1] In the preceding HTML, the <form> element, represented as a HTMLFormElement object,[2] has a tagName property with a value of "FORM". The two <input> elements are represented as HTMLInputElement objects,[3] and unsurprisingly they each have tagName values of "INPUT".

---

[1]www.w3.org/TR/2000/REC-DOM-Level-2-Core-20001113/core.html#ID-104682815
[2]www.w3.org/TR/html5/forms.html#the-form-element
[3]www.w3.org/TR/html5/forms.html#the-input-element

Content, the second part of an element, describes any other nodes that are descendants of an element. My example `<form>` has two `<input>` elements as content, while the two `<input>` elements have *no* content. In fact, `<input>` elements are not allowed to have any content. This restriction was likely in place since `<input>` elements were first introduced in the HTML 2 specification,[4] but was only first explicitly mentioned in the HTML 3 official standard document.[5]

■ **A note about my example form markup** Normally you would want to associate each form field with a `<label>` that contains a text node with the field's display name. Also, a submit button is usually prudent, but I left all of these out of my preceding markup to keep it simple and focused on the discussion of attributes.

Attributes, the third and final part of an element, also optional, provide a way to annotate elements directly in your markup. You may use them to provide data or state. For example, the `<form>` element above contains two such attributes: `action` and `method`, which together tell the form to send a POST request (`method`) to the "/rest/login.php" server endpoint (`action`) when the form is submitted. The first input has a `name` attribute of "username" and the second has a `name` of "password". This information is used to construct the request and tie these elements to their values when the server parses the form submit. Although not evident in the preceding HTML, you can even create your own proprietary attributes and reference them in your code for the purposes of associating state or data with elements in your markup. Though not strictly required, the more standard way to do this is with `data-` attributes, which will be mentioned later on in this chapter.

In addition to providing data or state, some attributes are used to define specific behaviors for multipurpose elements. Take a look at the `type` attribute on the second input in the preceding fragment for an example of this. This `type` attribute defines the second input to be a password input, which signals the browser to mask any characters entered into this field by the user. The first input *could* include a `type` attribute with a value of "text," but this is not necessary as all `<input>` elements are, by default, text inputs. This default has been in place since the inception of HTML, and is visible in one of the earliest drafts of the specification.[6] Another example of a behavior imposed by an attribute can be seen on both of the preceding inputs. Notice the `required` attributes on each of the inputs—this is a signal to any browser that supports the `constraints API` to prevent form submission if either of these fields are left empty by the user.[7]

History and Standardization

Attributes have always been a part of HTML and were described in the first document that details HTML tags, written by Tim Berners-Lee in 1992.[8] In this article, Berners-Lee describes the same two general types of attributes that are used in HTML today—Boolean and variable—both of which I will elaborate on further shortly. The passage that calls out attributes is near the start of the document:

> Some tags take parameters, called attributes. The attributes are given after the tag, separated by spaces. Certain attributes have an effect simply by their presence, others are followed by an equals sign and a value.

Berners-Lee went on to mention a few such attributes, using the `href`, `type`, and `name` attributes of anchor tags as an example. Note though that the `name` attribute on `<a>` elements is no longer available as it was removed in the HTML5 specification.[9] Since this first description of HTML, the number and importance of element attributes has increased greatly.

---

[4]www.w3.org/MarkUp/html-spec/html-spec_toc.html
[5]www.w3.org/MarkUp/html3/input.html
[6]www.w3.org/MarkUp/HTMLPlus/htmlplus_41.html
[7]www.w3.org/TR/html5/forms.html#constraints
[8]www.w3.org/History/19921103-hypertext/hypertext/WWW/MarkUp/Tags.html
[9]www.w3.org/TR/html5/text-level-semantics.html#the-a-element

Unbounded custom attributes are not and have never been *officially* supported in any HTML specification. But you may prefix an attribute name of your choice with "data-" as of the HTML5 spec (more on that later). However, if you would like to introduce a purely custom attribute into your markup, such as "myproject-uuid", you are certainly free to do so. The page will render without issue, and there will be no errors in your browser's developer tools console. Everything will work just fine. The only drawback is that your document will fail validation, as it will contain *non-standard* attributes—attributes that are not mentioned in any accepted HTML standard. Non-standard custom attributes are actually quite common and are even prevalent in popular JavaScript frameworks, such as AngularJS, which relies on non-standard custom attributes heavily to facilitate communication with element directives.

The latest *recommended* HTML spec—HTML5—defines four different types of attributes.[10] One type commonly known as a "Boolean attribute"[11] is expressed as an element attribute without any explicit value. Take the `required` attribute commonly found on `<input>` elements as one example (seen in the previous section's HTML fragment). As the specification states, "The presence of a boolean attribute on an element represents the true value, and the absence of the attribute represents the false value." The HTML 5.1 standardized `hidden` attribute,[12] which instructs the browser to *not* render any element bearing the attribute, is another example of this first type.

A second type of attribute is described as "unquoted." A little known fact is that you may omit quotes around your attribute values, provided the attribute value does not contain spaces, equal signs, or angle brackets (`<` and `>`), or an empty string (among other less notable character restrictions). So, the HTML fragment in the previous section can be re-written as follows:

```
1  <form action=/rest/login.php method=POST>
2    <input name=username required>
3    <input type=password name=password required>
4  </form>
```

The final two types of HTML element attributes are very similar: single-quoted and double-quoted. Both are similar in that they largely have the same restrictions and are much more common than unquoted attributes, although double-quoted attributes are arguably the *most* common of all types. In contrast to unquoted attribute values, those that are surrounded by either single or double quotation marks *may* contain spaces, equal signs, angle brackets, or an empty string. The portion of the latest W3C specification that describes attribute values mentions only that they may never contain any ambiguous ampersand characters. An "ampersand character" is an & sign followed by a standardized ASCII character code and terminated with a semicolon (`;`). An "ambiguous ampersand character" is one where this ASCII character code does *not* match any of the character codes defined in the named character references[13] portion of the spec.

How Do Attributes Differ from Properties?

Now that you have a solid understanding of what element attributes are, you may *still* be confused regarding their relation to element "properties," *especially* if you have been using jQuery for a while.[14] At a very basic level, properties and attributes are entirely different from each other. While attributes are declared at the HTML level in the element's markup, properties are declared and updated on the element's object representation. For example, consider the following element:

```
1  <div class="bold">I'm a bold element</div>
```

---

[10]www.w3.org/TR/html5/syntax.html#attributes-0
[11]www.w3.org/TR/html5/single-page.html#boolean-attributes
[12]www.w3.org/TR/html51/editing.html#the-hidden-attribute
[13]www.w3.org/TR/html5/syntax.html#named-character-references
[14]http://blog.jquery.com/2011/05/03/jquery-16-released/

The `<div>` has a `class` attribute with a value of "bold". But we can set properties on this element too. Suppose we want to set a property of `index` with a value of 0:

```
1  <div class="bold">I'm a bold element</div>
2
3  <script>
4      document.querySelector('.bold').index = 0;
5  </script>
```

After executing the preceding fragment, our `<div>` now has a `class` attribute with a value of "bold" *and* a property of `index` with a value of 0. The property is set on the underlying JavaScript object, which in this case is an implementation of the `HTMLDivElement`[15] interface. Element object properties such as our `index` are also known as "expando" properties, which is just a terse way to classify non-standard element object properties. Understand that not *all* element properties are expando properties. Don't worry if this is still not entirely clear. I'll talk more about standardized element properties before this section is complete.

Although properties and attributes are conceptually and syntactically different, they are very closely linked together in some cases. In fact, all standardized element attributes have corresponding properties defined in the element's object representation. For the most part, each standard attribute and property pair share the same value. And in all but one case, the attribute and property share the same name as well. These standardized attributes are special in that you can update them without touching the markup. Updating the corresponding element object's property value will cause the browser to update the attribute's value in the document, and updating the attribute value will in turn up the element's property value. Let's take a look at a simple example, where we define an anchor link with an initial `href`, and then update the anchor to point to a different location using JavaScript:

```
1  <a href="http://www.widen.com/blog/">Read the Widen blog</a>
2
3  <script>
4  document.querySelector('A').href = 'http://www.widen.com/blog/ray-nicholus';
5  </script>
```

After executing the script in the above code block, the anchor now appears in the document as follows:

```
1  <a href="http://www.widen.com/blog/ray-nicholus">Read the Widen blog</a>
```

In this case, the `HTMLAnchorElement`,[16] which is the object representation of an `<a>`, has an `href` property defined on its prototype that is directly connected to the `href` attribute on the element tag. This `href` property is actually inherited from the `URLUtils` interface,[17] which the `HTMLAnchorElement` object also implements. `URLUtils` is an interface formally defined in the WHATWG URL Living Standard[18] specification.

There are many other element attributes with connected properties, such as `id` (all elements), `action` (form elements), and `src` (script elements), to name a few. Remember that all attributes that appear in the HTML specifications fall into this category. But there are a few special cases and points to consider. First, `class` attributes are a bit different in that the corresponding property name is not `class`, but `className`. This is due to the fact that "class" is a reserved word in many languages, such as JavaScript.[19] More on the

---

[15]www.w3.org/TR/html5/grouping-content.html#the-div-element
[16]www.w3.org/TR/html51/semantics.html#the-a-element
[17]https://url.spec.whatwg.org/#urlutils
[18]https://url.spec.whatwg.org
[19]www.ecma-international.org/ecma-262/6.0/#sec-keywords

class attribute later on. Also keep in mind that the checked attribute, common to radio and checkbox input elements, is only *initially* connected to the corresponding element property value. Consider the following code to demonstrate this limitation a bit more clearly:

```
1  <input type="checkbox" checked>
2
3  <script>
4      // this does not remove the checked attribute
5      document.querySelector('INPUT').checked = false;
6  </script>
```

After executing the preceding script, you may expect the checked attribute to be removed from the input element, since this would happen for other Boolean attributes, such as required and disabled. However, the checked attribute remains on the element, even though the property value has been changed to false and the checkbox is indeed unchecked.

"Custom" attributes, that is, attributes that are *not* defined in any accepted specification, are not linked in any way to a similarly named property on the element object. Any properties you create to match non-standard attributes are also considered expando properties.

Finding Elements Using Attributes

Building upon the class and ID selector examples from Chapter 4, this section is going to provide a much more comprehensive guide to selecting any and *all* attributes using the web API. Although ID and class attribute selection is commonly accomplished using a selector syntax specific to these two types of attributes, you can use the more general attribute selection approaches found in this chapter as well. In some cases, some of the generic but powerful attribute selectors demonstrated here are most appropriate when looking for multiple elements that follow a known ID or class pattern.

For the sake of consistency and reference, jQuery examples will be provided throughout this section. But attributes can be selected in a number of ways without jQuery, simply by using either querySelector or querySelectorAll. Since attribute selectors were first introduced as part of the W3C CSS 2 specification,[20] *all of the simple web API examples here (but not all of the more complex ones) are supported all the way back to Internet Explorer 8!* You truly don't need jQuery to write simple but powerful attribute selectors.

Finding Elements Using Attribute Names

I cover values in quite a bit of detail shortly, but let's first focus on attribute names. Why might you want to only focus on an attribute name? Perhaps for many reasons:

1. Locating disabled elements or required form fields.

2. Finding one or more elements that include a custom attribute that groups these elements in some way.

3. Locating invalid markup in a document, such as <img> elements without a src attribute.

---

[20]www.w3.org/TR/CSS2/selector.html#attribute-selectors

The following jQuery and web API examples will revolve around #1 above. For this, a small HTML fragment will be used for reference:

```
1  <form action="/submitHandler.php" method="POST">
2      <input name="first-name">
3      <input name="last-name" required>
4      <input type="email" name="email" required>
5      <button disabled>submit</button>
6  </form>
```

jQuery

There is one way to select elements given their attributes in jQuery, and that is by passing a valid CSS 2+ attribute selector string into the jQuery function:

```
1  var $result = $('[required], [disabled]');
```

The preceding code will result in a $result jQuery object that contains the "last-name" and "email" <input> elements, along with the disabled submit <button>. In case the comma in the selector string is causing you some confusion, I covered this in the previous chapter's multiple element selector section. This jQuery code relies entirely on the web API behind the scenes.

Web API

As with many of the native solutions in the Chapter 4, the code required to locate elements using attribute names is eerily similar to the jQuery solution you have just seen (shown in Listing 5-1).

Listing 5-1. Selecting by Attribute Name: Web API, All Modern Browsers, and Internet Explorer 8

```
1  var result = document.querySelectorAll('[required], [disabled]');
```

Similar to the jQuery example, the preceding code will populate the result variable with a NodeList containing the "last-name" and "email" inputs, along with the disabled submit button.

While disabled and required are Boolean attributes, the preceding code will yield the same results even if we assigned them values. The attribute selector simply matches on the attribute name—the value (or lack of one) is irrelevant. This means you can easily locate all elements in a document that have *any* CSS classes assigned to them. For example, Listing 5-2 shows a simple attribute selector.

Listing 5-2. Selecting All Elements with a Class Attribute: Modern Browsers and Internet Explorer 8

```
1  var result = document.querySelectorAll('[class]');
```

Given the following HTML:

```
1  <div class="bold">I'm bold</div>
2  <span>I'm not</span>
```

... the result variable in the previous selector will yield one element: the <div>. But beware, simply adding an *empty* class attribute to the <span> may result in an unexpected result set:

```
1  <div class="bold">I'm bold</div>
2  <span class>I'm not</span>
```

Even though the <span> does not have any CSS classes assigned to it, the mere presence of the class attribute means that our selector includes it in the result set alongside the <div>. This is probably not what we wanted. This is not a deficiency of the selector API, but it *is* important to understand exactly how attribute name selectors function. Note that you will run into the same "problem" using jQuery if you don't have a firm grasp of this CSS selector.

Finding Elements Using Attribute Names and Values

Sometimes locating an element or group of elements by attribute name alone is not sufficient. You may want to, for example, locate all password input fields, in which case you would need to find all <input> elements with a type attribute of "password". Or perhaps you need to locate all anchor elements that link to a specific endpoint, in which case you'd need to key on the desired value of the href attribute of all <a> elements.

To set up our jQuery and web API examples, let's use the following HTML and state that our goal is to locate all anchors that link to the ajax-form web component documentation page:

```
1  <section>
2    <h2>web components</h2>
3    <ul>
4      <li>
5        <a href="http://file-input.raynicholus.com/">file-input</a>
6      </li>
7      <li>
8        <a href="http://ajax-form.raynicholus.com/">ajax-form</a>
9      </li>
10   </ul>
11 </section>
12 <section>
13   <h2>no-dependency libraries</h2>
14   <ul>
15     <li>
16       <a href="http://ajax-form.raynicholus.com/">ajax-form</a>
17     </li>
18     <li>
19       <a href="http://fineuploader.com/">Fine Uploader</a>
20     </li>
21   </ul>
22 </section>
```

jQuery

In order to find all anchor elements that point to the ajax-form library page, we'll use a standardized CSS selector string passed into the jQuery function, as we've seen so many times before:

```
1  var $result = $('A[href="http://ajax-form.raynicholus.com/"]');
```

The preceding selector returns a jQuery object containing the two ajax-form HTMLAnchorElement objects from our example markup.

Web API

You've already seen how a standard CSS selector is required to select by attribute name and value when using jQuery, so of course the same selector is most appropriate when attempting to find specific anchor elements without jQuery. The solution here is, as you have seen in most other element selection examples, almost identical to the jQuery approach, but more efficient:

```
1  var result =
2      document.querySelectorAll('A[href="http://ajax-form.raynicholus.com/"]');
```

The result variable is a NodeList containing both ajax-form anchors from our example HTML at the start of this section. Notice that I'm combining the attribute name/value selector with a tag name selector. This ensures that any other elements that may include a non-standard href attribute are ignored (along with any <link> elements), since we are only concerned with anchor links.

Remember the empty class attribute example from the selecting by attribute name section? During our search for all elements with CSS classes, we were unable to ignore empty class attributes with a simple attribute name selector. But if we pair an attribute name/value selector with the exclusion selector from Chapter 4, as shown in Listing 5-3, we can effectively filter out empty class attributes.

Listing 5-3. Find Anchors with Specific href Attributes: Web API, Modern Browsers

```
1  var result = document.querySelectorAll('[class]:not([class=""])');
```

Using the sample HTML from the initial empty class attribute example section, the preceding code block, result contains a NodeList containing *only* the <div> with a class attribute of "bold". The <span> with an empty class attribute has been successfully skipped over.

The Power of Wildcard and Fuzzy Attribute Selectors

This last part of the attribute selectors section focuses on more advanced use cases. In this section, I demonstrate four very powerful attribute selector tricks that are also easy to understand *and* supported in all modern browsers as well as Internet Explorer 8. The pattern you have already seen (many times) between the jQuery and the web API selector code continues in this last set of examples. So, let's just forgo the jQuery versus web API code snippets, as they are mostly redundant when discussing element selectors. If you really want to run the following examples "the jQuery way," just replace document.querySelectorAll() with $() and be prepared for your code to run a bit slower.

Looking for Specific Characters

Remember the example from the section on attribute names and values? We wanted to locate any anchor links in a document that pointed to a very specific endpoint. But what if we don't care about the entire URL? What if we are only concerned with the domain? Consider the following HTML fragment:

```
1  <a href="http://fineuploader.com/">home page</a>
2  <a href="http://fineuploader.com/demos">demos</a>
3  <a href="http://docs.fineuploader.com/">docs</a>
4  <a href="http://fineuploader.com/purchase">purchase</a>
```

If we want to locate all anchor links at `http://fineuploader.com`, the instance substring attribute selector, first standardized in the W3C CSS 3 specification,[21] allows us to do this:

```
1  var result =
2      document.querySelectorAll('A[href*="http://fineuploader.com"]');
```

The `result` variable above is a NodeList containing all anchor links *except* for the third one. Why is this? Well, we are looking for an href attribute that contains the string `"http://fineuploader.com"`. The third anchor link does *not* contain this string. Perhaps this is not our intent, and we simply want to find all anchor links that point in some way to fineuploader.com. Simple!

```
1  var result =
2      document.querySelectorAll('A[href*="fineuploader.com"]');
```

Looking for Specific Words

Instead of looking for groups of characters, perhaps we need to locate a specific "word" inside of an attribute value. For example, we can write an alternate CSS class selector using this attribute word selector. Consider the following HTML fragment:

```
1  <div class="one two three">1 2 3</div>
2  <div class="onetwothree">123</div>
```

Let's say we want to find only the element with a CSS class of "two". In addition to the CSS class selector I demonstrated in Chapter 4, we can make use of a special attribute selector to accomplish this as well:

```
1  var result = document.querySelectorAll('[class~=two]');
```

The `result` variable is a NodeList containing one entry—the first `<div>` in our sample element collection—exactly what we were looking for. But why do we need to create another class selector? We don't, and the preceding example is not exactly practical, though it does illustrate the behavior of this selector very well. A more realistic example may be to locate a specific word in an element `title` attribute. Consider this set of elements:

```
1  <a href="https://github.com/rnicholus/frame-grab.js"
2      title="frame-grab repo">frame-grab GitHub repo</a>
3
4  <a href="https://github.com/rnicholus/frame-grab.js/blob/master/docs/api.md"
5      title="frame-grab docs">frame-grab documentation</a>
6
7  <a href="https://www.youtube.com/watch?v=hHBhPO3JHIQ"
8      title="frame-grab + fine-uploader">Video frame uploader</a>
9
10 <img src="https://travis-ci.org/rnicholus/frame-grab.js.svg?branch=master"
11     title="frame-grab build status">
12
13 <a href="https://foo.bar/subframe-grabber"
14     title="window-subframe-grabber">
15     Locates all iframes inside of a given iframe</a>
```

---

[21]www.w3.org/TR/css3-selectors/#attribute-substrings

Imagine the two links and one image, all obviously related to the frame-grab library, exist among a number of other unrelated links and images in a large document. But we want to find only those resources that directly relate to the frame-grab library. We can't key on "frame-grab.js" using the substring attribute selector since not all of the elements contain an href or src attribute with "frame-grab.js". We also don't want to key on the phrase "frame-grab", as this would include the last link, which does *not* relate to the frame-grab library. Instead we need to select all elements with a title attribute that contains the specific phrase "frame-grab".

```
1  var result = document.querySelectorAll('[title~=frame-grab]');
```

result is a NodeList that contains all elements in our HTML sample *except* for the last anchor link, which is the exact result we are looking for.

Attribute Values That Start or End With . . .

The final set of useful advanced attribute selectors to be aware of allow you to locate elements in a document with attribute values that either start with or end with one or more specific characters. Perhaps you are wondering at this point why such a selector would be useful, pragmatically speaking. As we have done so many times before, let's start with a bit of HTML, and then discuss how these two attribute selectors may be important to us:

```
1  <img id="dancing-cat" src="/images/dancing-cat.gif">
2  <img id="still-cat" src="/images/still-cat.png">
3  <img id="dancing-zebra" src="dancing-zebra.gif">
4  <a href="#dancing-zebra">watch the zebra dance</a>
5  <a href="/logout">logout</a>
```

That fragment is likely to appear inside a large document, among many other anchor links and images, but can be considered representative of a number of such elements. Say we want to locate two things in this document:

1. All GIF images.

2. All anchors that reference elements on the current page.

The refreshing reality is that we can meet both goals in one line *without* any third-party dependencies:

```
1  var result = document.querySelectorAll('A[href^="#"], [src$=".gif"]');
```

The preceding selector combines a "starts with" and an "ends with" attribute value selector (respectively) using the multiple selectors syntax covered in Chapter 4. Our "starts with" selector targets any anchor element with an href attribute that starts with a hash mark, which would only include anchors that reference the current page. And the second selector focuses on elements with a src attribute value that ends with ".gif". This would include references to GIF images, assuming the image URL ends with the expected extension.

Reading and Modifying Element Attributes

So now you know exactly what attributes are (and what they are *not*), and you are well-versed in selecting elements by their attribute names and values. The final aspect of attributes for me to discuss involves reading and updating an element's attributes, as well as creating new attributes. You'll discover that the appropriate approach for parsing, adding, removing, and changing attributes may depend on the type of attribute. In this final section, I go over three distinct types of attributes: class attributes, data attributes, and all other generic native and custom attributes.

Class Attributes

Element class attributes seem to be a popular topic in "Beyond jQuery" so far. Chapter 4 discusses them at length, I mentioned how the `class` attribute differs from its element property name in the attributes vs. properties section earlier in this chapter, and I even showed you how to select elements using class attributes given various types of values recently in the finding elements with attributes section. Well, here we are again discussing classes. But this time, I'm going to show you how to read a specific element's classes, as well as add, toggle, and remove an element's classes.

Reading Classes

All of the situations in the reading and modifying attributes section assume you already have a handle on a specific element or elements. So, since we already have an element, perhaps we would like to know what specific CSS classes it is associated with. Or maybe we just want to find out if it is connected to one specific class. This section examines both of these needs.

Let's start with an actual element, for reference:

```
1  <p class="product-name out-of-stock manual-tool">saw</p>
```

Imagine this element is the name of a specific tool among many other such tools in a larger document. Let's say we want to know two things about the particular tool element we've landed on:

1. Is this tool in stock?

2. Is this a manual or a power tool?

The solution provided by jQuery makes use of its `hasClass` API method:

```
1  var inStock = !$toolEl.hasClass('out-of-stock');
2  var type = $toolEl.hasClass('manual-tool') ? 'manual' : 'power';
```

The `inStock` Boolean variable will be set to a value of `false` since the element contains an "out- of-stock" class. While `type` is "manual" due to the presence of a "manual-tool" class. No surprises here.

But we don't want to use jQuery! So, how do we do all of this without it? Luckily, the modern web API offers an equally elegant solution, thanks to the `classList` property on the `Element` interface.[22] The WHATWG web standards organization initially drafted the specification for `classList`, and the W3C has included it in its DOM4 document[23] as well.

Note that the `classList` property is a `DomTokenList`.[24] The `DomTokenList` interface contains four notable methods, each of which I will demonstrate throughout this section. You'll see how `classList` can be used to perform all sorts of operations on an element's `class` attribute soon, but first I'm going to focus one such method: `contains`.[25] To determine if a specific element contains a specific CSS class, the DOM API provides an intuitive property on the `classList` object: `contains`.

```
1  var inStock = !toolEl.classList.contains('out-of-stock');
2  var type = toolEl.classList.contains('manual-tool') ? 'manual' : 'power';
```

---

[22]https://dom.spec.whatwg.org/#dom-element-classlist
[23]www.w3.org/TR/dom/#dom-element-classlist
[24]https://dom.spec.whatwg.org/#domtokenlist
[25]https://dom.spec.whatwg.org/#dom-domtokenlist-contains

The preceding code is *identical* to the jQuery example—just replace hasClass with classList. contains and reap the performance benefits![26]

If you need to support older browsers, you will need to resort to a regular expression in order to determine if your target element contains a certain class. Luckily, this too is fairly simple (and works for any browser):

```
1  var hasClass = function(el, className) {
2    return new RegExp('(^|\\s)' + className + '(\\s|$)').test(el.className);
3  };
4  var inStock = !hasClass(toolEl, 'out-of-stock');
5  var type = hasClass(toolEl, 'manual-tool') ? 'manual' : 'power';
```

Whether you are using jQuery or not, if you want to get a list of *all* CSS classes associated with an element, you must either directly access the class attribute or the className property on the Element object. In both cases, the value will be a space-delimited string of all CSS classes attached to the element.

Adding and Removing Classes

Next, we have an element, and we need to remove the "red" class, and add a "blue" one instead:

```
1  <p class="red">I'm red. Make me blue!</p>
```

We all know that the addClass and removeClass jQuery functions are used to add and remove CSS classes from elements, respectively:

```
1  $pEl.removeClass('red').addClass('blue');
```

The jQuery solution is pretty, and we can do it all in one line without sacrificing readability. Can we do the same thing without jQuery? Well, the web API approach is a tad wordier, and chaining isn't built it, but it's just as easy. The non-jQuery solution is faster as well,[27] and works for all modern browsers except IE9:

```
1  pEl.classList.remove('red');
2  pEl.classList.add('blue');
```

Once again, classList to the rescue. Perhaps you are saying to yourself, "The native solution makes me type a few more character. This will greatly affect my productivity." Really? If you are adding and removing classes via JavaScript so often that a few more characters will have a profoundly negative impact on agility, then perhaps it is time to instead re-evaluate your application design.

Stuck supporting IE9 and older? A solution that covers every browser under the sun is similar to the fallback for contains from the previous section:

```
1  var removeClass = function(el, className) {
2    el.className =
3      el.className.replace(new RegExp('(^|\\s)' + className + '(\\s|$)'), ' ');
4  };
5  removeClass(pEl, 'red');
6  pEl.className += ' blue';
```

---

[26]http://jsperf.com/classlist-contains-vs-hasclass
[27]http://jsperf.com/jquery-addclass-removeclass-vs-dom-classlist

That *is* quite a bit harder than addClass(...) and removeClass(...). Luckily, classList is standardized and a suitable replacement for jQuery's class manipulation going forward.

Toggling Classes

Say we have an element and we'd like to toggle its visibility, perhaps in response to a button click. I cover events a bit later, so let's just focus on the logic required to toggle the visibility of this element:

```
1  <section class="hide">
2    <h1>User Info</h1>
3  </section>
```

jQuery provides the familiar toggleClass() method, used as follows:

```
1  // removes "hide" class
2  $sectionEl.toggleClass('hide');
3
4  // re-adds "hide" class
5  $sectionEl.toggleClass('hide');
```

This is *just as easy* without jQuery, provided you are using a modern browser (except for IE9):

```
1  // removes "hide" class
2  sectionEl.classList.toggle('hide');
3
4  // re-adds "hide" class
5  sectionEl.classList.toggle('hide');
```

The solution for IE9 and older is a bit hairier, but still possible. It involves checking whether the class exists and then either adding or removing it, depending on the current state:

```
1  var toggleClass = function(el, className) {
2    var pattern = new RegExp('(^|\\s)' + className + '(\\s|$)');
3    if (pattern.test(el.className)) {
4      el.className = el.className.replace(pattern, ' ');
5    }
6    else {
7      el.className += ' ' + className;
8    }
9  };
10
11  // removes "hide" class
12  toggleClass(sectionEl, 'hide');
13
14  // re-adds "hide" class
15  toggleClass(sectionEl, 'hide');
```

Note that you can refactor the preceding code example a bit to instead directly reference the hasClass() and removeClass() methods from the earlier code examples.

Data Attributes

Although CSS class attributes are typically used for styling elements, data attributes are, as you might expect, used to attach data to elements. Data attributes must be prefixed with "data-" and can contain stringified data associated with a particular element. Any valid attribute value is acceptable. Although it is possible to construct and use non-standard element attributes, the W3C HTML5 specification declares that custom attributes should in fact be data attributes.[28]

There are other ways to attach more complex data to elements. Chapter 6 covers data attributes, the HTML5 dataset object, the history of element data along with jQuery's role in solving this problem, and much, much more related to element data.

Working with Other Standard and Custom Attributes

As you have already seen, class attributes are special attributes that require a more specific approach to properly manipulate and read them. In fact, class attributes are among two types of "special" attributes, with data- being the other. But what about all of the other element attributes? How can we best work with them? This section covers reading, writing, removing, and creating both standard and custom attributes. You are probably already familiar and comfortable with jQuery's support for these tasks, but you'll see just how easy it is to work with attributes using the power of the browser.

Reading Attributes

Let's start with a simple input element that includes both a Boolean attribute and a standard string value attribute:

```
1   <input type="password" name="user-password" required>
```

Suppose we are given this element and we want answers to two questions:

1. What type of <input> is this element?

2. Is this <input> a required field?

This is one area (of many) where jQuery fails miserably to ease the burden on the developer. While reading an attribute value is simple, there is no API method dedicated to detecting the presence of an attribute on a specific element. Though it is still possible to do this with jQuery, the solution is not very intuitive and will likely require those new to the library to do a bit of web searching:

```
1   // returns "password"
2   $inputEl.attr('type');
3
4   // returns "true"
5   $inputEl.is('[required]');
```

jQuery does not define a hasAttr method. Instead, you must check the element using a CSS attribute name selector. The web API *does* provide these conveniences, and has done so since Internet Explorer 8:

```
1   // returns "password"
2   inputEl.getAttribute('type');
3
4   // returns "true"
5   inputEl.hasAttribute('required');
```

---

[28]www.w3.org/TR/html5/dom.html#embedding-custom-non-visible-data-with-the-data-%2A-attributes

The getAttribute method was first defined on the Element interface all the way back in 1997 as part of the W3C DOM Level 1 Core specification.[29] And hasAttribute was added to the same interface 3 years later, in 2000, in the DOM Level 2 Core spec.[30]

We can make the second half of the jQuery example a bit more intuitive simply by breaking out of the jQuery object and operating directly on the underlying Element:

```
1  // returns "true"
2  $inputEl[0].hasAttribute('required');
```

So if you're stuck with jQuery for whatever reason, consider the preceding example as a more straightforward way to determine whether an element contains a particular attribute. As an added bonus, you'll find that bypassing jQuery as much as possible here is, as always, more performant[31] than relying on the library wholesale.

Modifying Attributes

We have a handle on a specific <input> element in our document, and the element looks like this:

```
1  <input name="temp" required>
```

We want to modify this HTMLInputElement in three ways:

1. Make it an "email" input field.

2. Ensure it is *not* required.

3. Rename it to "userEmail".

jQuery requires we solve this problem using attr() to add and change attributes and removeAttr() to remove them:

```
1  $inputEl
2    .attr('type', 'email') // #1
3    .removeAttr('required') // #2
4    .attr('name', 'userEmail'); // #3
```

Without jQuery, our solution looks almost identical, and has the same wide browser support. The Element interface was defined to have a setAttribute method since W3C's DOM Level 1 Core specification.[32] With this method, we can change and add element attribute, just like jQuery's attr() method. To remove attributes, we have removeAttribute(), another method also defined on the Element interface in DOM Level 1 Core.[33] With these two methods, we can modify our input element as described earlier quite easily:

```
1  inputEl.setAttribute('type', 'email'); // #1
2  inputEl.removeAttribute('required'); // #2
3  inputEl.setAttribute('name', 'userEmail'); // #3
```

Apart from the lack of chaining support, the native approach is just as intuitive as the route that relies on jQuery. This is one area in which web standards have *always* been adequate, and jQuery has never provided more than a minor convenience advantage. As you have seen throughout this section, working with attributes in general is surprisingly easy without any assistance from a library.

---

[29]www.w3.org/TR/REC-DOM-Level-1/level-one-core.html#ID-666EE0F9
[30]www.w3.org/TR/DOM-Level-2-Core/core.html#ID-666EE0F9
[31]http://jsperf.com/hasattribute-vs-jquery-is
[32]www.w3.org/TR/REC-DOM-Level-1/level-one-core.html#method-setAttribute
[33]www.w3.org/TR/REC-DOM-Level-1/level-one-core.html#method-removeAttribute

CHAPTER 6

■ ■ ■

HTML Element Data Storage and Retrieval

In Chapter 5, I mentioned data attributes when going over the three types of HTML element attributes. Look no further for complete coverage of anything and everything related to connecting data of any kind to your document elements. All the details are in *this* chapter, which will also build on the general attribute and element properties from Chapter 5. JavaScript objects will be introduced briefly as well, during a demonstration on connecting non-trivial data structures to tags.

As you continue through this chapter, expect to understand why connecting data to your document elements is both important *and* potentially tricky. As always, I'll show you how data is attached to elements and then read back using jQuery initially. But most importantly, you'll see how to do all this *without* jQuery. I'll also explain exactly how jQuery makes use of the web API and JavaScript to provide its own support for element data.

The future of managing element data is exciting. I'll show you how the web API and JavaScript are prepared to eclipse jQuery's support for element data across *all* browsers in the very near future. And this "futuristic" native support is already available for many browsers. I'll be sure to include copious code examples detailing how you can make use of this built-in support *right now* in your project.

Why Would You Want to Attach Data to Elements?

Especially in modern web applications, there is a real need to tie data to the elements on a page. In this section, we will explore common reasons for attaching custom data to your markup, and how this is commonly accomplished, at a high level. You will see that there are many reasons why you may find it useful to track data alongside your elements.

Tracking State

Perhaps you are maintaining a page for a realtor that contains a table of properties that are currently on the market. Presumably, you'd want to order them from most popular to least, and maybe you'd like to be able to adjust this order via drag-and-drop directly on the page:

```
1   <table>
2     <thead>
3       <tr>
4         <th>Address</th>
5         <th>Price</th>
6       </tr>
7     </thead>
```

© Ray Nicholus 2016
R. Nicholus, *Beyond jQuery*, DOI 10.1007/978-1-4842-2235-5_6

```
 8    <tbody>
 9      <tr>
10        <td>6911 Mangrove Ln Madison, WI</td>
11        <td>$10,000,000</td>
12      </tr>
13      <tr>
14        <td>1313 Mockingbird Ln Mockingbird Heights, CA</td>
15        <td>$100,000</td>
16      </tr>
17    </tbody>
18  </table>
```

After a row is moved, or perhaps even as part of the initial markup, you may want to annotate each row with its original index in the table. This could potentially be used to revert any changes without calling the server. A data- or custom attribute (data-original-idx or original-idx respectively) is most appropriate here.

You may also want to track initial style information for an element, such as dimensions. If you allow the user to dynamically adjust the width and height of an element, you will likely want a simple way to reset these dimensions should your user have a change of heart. You can store the initial dimension alongside the element, possibly using data- attributes.

Connecting Elements

Seemingly disparate elements may very well need to be aware of each other. For example, two elements in which the visibility of each is determined by the visibility of the other. In other words, if one element is visible, the other is not. How can these elements coexist in this way? Answer: by maintaining references to each other.

This scenario has a number of possible solutions. One would be to embed CSS selector strings for each element's partner element inside of a data- or custom attribute. Assuming this is reasonable, and a unique selector is available, this is probably the best choice. If this is *not* possible, then you will need to resort to maintaining a map of the Node objects. This can be done a couple of different ways with the help of JavaScript objects. More on that later.

Storing Models Directly in Your Elements

You have a list of users on a page:

```
1  <ul>
2    <li>jack</li>
3    <li>jill</li>
4    <li>jim</li>
5  </ul>
```

Now, you may want to associate some common properties with each of these user elements for use by other JavaScript components on the page. For example: the user's age, ID, and email address. This may be best specified as JSON and *can* be attached directly to the user element via either a data- or custom attribute. You may find that such a solution is not appropriate for non-trivial data, such as JavaScript objects/JSON. In that case, pairing a unique key that identifies the element alongside its data in a "plain" JavaScript object is more appropriate. You can read more about this approach later in this chapter.

Common Pitfalls of Pairing Data with Elements

It's becoming easier to pair data with your elements, thanks to rapidly evolving web and JavaScript specifications. Don't worry, I'll cover specifics very soon. But life is not simple even with these advancements. There is still potential for trouble, provided this new power is not used responsibly. Of course, life *before* the modern web and JavaScript was much more difficult. Attaching trivial data to elements was done using primitive means. Storing complex data, such as other Nodes, could result in memory leaks. This section covers all of that.

Memory Leaks

When connecting two (or more) elements together, the natural instinct is to simply store a reference to the other elements in some common JavaScript object. For example, consider the following markup:

```
1  <ul>
2    <li>Ford</li>
3    <li>Chevy</li>
4    <li>Mercedes</li>
5  </ul>
```

Each of these car types responds to click events, and when one of the cars is clicked, the clicked car must be prominently styled, while all other cars must become less prominent. One way to accomplish that is to store references to all elements in a JavaScript array and iterate over all elements in the array when one of the list items is clicked. The clicked item must be colored red, while the others should be set to their default color. Our JavaScript might look something like this:

```
1  var standOutOnClick = function(el) {
2      el.onclick = function() {
3        for (var i = 0; i < el.typeEls.length; i++) {
4          var currentEl = el.typeEls[i];
5          if (el === currentEl) {
6            currentEl.style.color = 'red';
7          }
8          else {
9            currentEl.style.color = '';
10         }
11       }
12     };
13   },
14   setupCarTypeEls = function() {
15     var carTypes = [],
16       carTypeEls = document.getElementsByTagName('LI');
17
18       for (var i = 0; i < carTypeEls.length; i++) {
19         var thisCarType = carTypeEls[i];
20         thisCarType.typeEls = carTypes;
21         carTypes.push(thisCarType);
22         standOutOnClick(thisCarType);
23       }
24   };
25
26   setupCarTypeEls();
```

71

■ **Don't use inline event handlers** In the preceding example, I am assigning a click handler to an element via the element's `onclick` property. This is known as an *inline event handler*, and you should avoid doing it. Because I haven't covered events yet, I took this shortcut to keep the code example as simple as possible, but you should *never* use inline event handler assignments in your code. To learn more about how to properly deal with events without jQuery, take a look at Chapter 10.

Avoid inline style assignment In the preceding example, I change the color of a `<li>` by altering the `color` value of the element's `style` property. I took this shortcut to keep the example as simple as possible, but you should almost always avoid this type of style assignment in *your* code. The proper approach involves removing or adding CSS classes for each element, with the proper styles/colors defined in a style sheet for these specific classes. For more information on how to properly manipulate element CSS classes without jQuery, see Chapter 5.

The preceding code works in every browser available, including Internet Explorer 6, though a large hidden issue exists. It demonstrates a circular reference involving a DOM object (the JavaScript representation of the `<li>` element) and a "plain" JavaScript object (the `carTypeEls` array). Each `<li>` references the `carTypeEls` array, which in turn references the `<li>` element. This is a good example of a well-documented memory leak present in Internet Explorer 6 and 7. The leak is so severe that the memory may be unclaimed even after a page refresh. Luckily, Microsoft fixed this issue in Internet Explorer 8,[1] but this demonstrates some early challenges with storing data alongside HTML elements.

Managing Data

For trivial amounts of data, you can make use of `data-` attributes or other custom attributes. But what if you need to store a *lot* of data? You could perhaps attach the data to a custom property on the element. This is known as an *expando* property. This is was illustrated in the previous example. To avoid potential memory leaks, you may instead elect to store the data in a JavaScript object along with a selector string for the associated element(s). This ensures the reference to the element is a "weak" one. Unfortunately, neither of these approaches is particularly intuitive, and you get the feeling that you are either reinventing the wheel or writing kludgey, brittle code along the way. Surely there must be an easier route.

Then again, what *is* a "trivial" amount of data? When do attributes become a less-feasible storage and retrieval mechanism? To developers who have not come across this problem before, the large array of approaches may be a bit overwhelming. Can you simply make use of expando properties for all instances? What are the drawbacks and advantages to one approach over the others? Don't worry, you'll not only understand how and when to use a specific approach when storing element data, but you'll also learn how to do it easily and effectively in the final two sections of this chapter.

Using a Solution for All Browsers

Although there exist some pretty nifty ways to read and track element data in new specifications, such as ECMAScript 2015 and HTML5, I realize that the browser support for some of these APIs is not *yet* comprehensive. In a relatively short amount of time, these new tools will be implemented in the vast majority of all browsers in use. Until then, you should understand how to accomplish these same tasks with the most commonly available APIs. In some cases, the approaches described in this section are likely to withstand the test of time and remain most appropriate and simplest even as web standards continue to evolve.

---

[1]https://msdn.microsoft.com/en-us/library/dd361842(VS.85).aspx

Storing Small Bits of Data Using data- Attributes

Data attributes, which first appeared in the W3C HTML5 specification,[2] is one example of an existing standard that is simple enough to be usable in all current browsers. Its simplicity and flexibility is such that it may be leveraged in future incarnations of web specifications. In fact, data attributes already are a lot more powerful due to a relatively new Element interface property defined in the HTML5 spec (more on that soon).

The HTML5 specification declares data- attributes to be custom attributes. The two are one and the same. The only valid custom attribute is a data- attribute. The specification describes data- attributes as follows:

> A custom data attribute is an attribute in no namespace whose name starts with
> the string "data-" has at least one character after the hyphen. . . .

The spec also gives data- attributes a specific purpose. They are "intended to store custom data private to the page or application, for which there are no more appropriate attributes or elements." So, if you need to describe a title for an anchor link, use the title attribute.[3] If you must define a language for a paragraph that differs from the language defined on the <html> element for the rest of the document, you should use the lang attribute.[4]

But what if you need to store an alternate URL for an <img>, one that is used when the image either receives focus via the keyboard or when the user hovers over it with a pointing device, such as a mouse. In this instance, there is no standard attribute to store this information. So, we must make use of a custom data-attribute:

```
1  <img src="default.png"
2    data-zoom-url="default-zoomed.png"
3    alt="default image">
```

The image to display on focus/hover is stored in the data-zoom-url attribute. We may follow the same approach if we want to annotate a <video> with the offsets at which the scenes change:

```
1  <video src="my-video.mp4" data-scene-offsets="9,22,38">
```

The preceding video changes scenes at the 9-, 22-, and 38-second marks, according to the data-scene-offsets custom attribute we've tied to the element.

There are no drastic consequences for defining a custom element that does not confirm to the data-convention defined in the HTML5 spec. The browser will not complain or fail to render your document. But you *will* lose the ability to utilize any future portions of the API that build on this convention, including the dataset property. More on that specific property shortly.

Reading and Updating data- Attributes with jQuery

Now that we have a way to annotate our elements with a bit of data via our markup, how can we actually *read* this data in our code? If you are familiar with jQuery, you probably already know about the data() API method. Just in case the details are a little fuzzy, take a look at the following example:

```
1  <video src="my-video.mp4" data-scene-offsets="9,22,38">
2
3  <script>
```

---

[2]www.w3.org/TR/html5/dom.html#embedding-custom-non-visible-data-with-the-data-%2A-attributes
[3]www.w3.org/TR/html4/struct/global.html#edef-TITLE
[4]www.w3.org/TR/html4/struct/dirlang.html#adef-lang

```
4  // offsets value will be "9,22,38"
5  var offsets = $('VIDEO').data('sceneOffsets');
6  </script>
```

Notice that we must access the value of the data- attribute by referencing the unique portion of the attribute name as a camel-case string. Changing the value of the data attribute is very similar:

```
1  <video src="my-video.mp4" data-scene-offsets="9,22,38">
2
3  <script>
4  // Does NOT update the attribute. Updates jQuery
5  // internal data store instead.
6  $('VIDEO').data('sceneOffsets', '1,2,3');
7  </script>
```

Notice that there is something peculiar and unexpected about jQuery's data() method. When attempting to update the data- attribute via this method, nothing appears to happen. That is, the data-scene-offsets attribute value remains unchanged in the document. Instead, jQuery stores this value, and all subsequent values, in a JavaScript data store. There are a couple downsides to this implementation:

1.   Our markup is now out-of-sync with the element's data.

2.   Any changes we make to the element's data are *only* accessible to jQuery.

Though there are some good reasons for this implementation, it seems unfortunate in this situation.

Using the Web API to Read and Update data- Attributes

Later, I describe a more modern way to read and update data- attributes using JavaScript with the same elegance as jQuery's data() method but *without* the drawbacks. In the meantime, let's explore a solution that will work with *any* browser:

```
1  <video src="my-video.mp4" data-scene-offsets="9,22,38">
2
3  <script>
4  // offsets value will be "9,22,38"
5  var offsets = document.getElementsByTagName('VIDEO')[0]
6    .getAttribute('data-scene-offsets');
7  </script>
```

We've already seen this before back in the "reading attributes" section of the previous chapter. The data- attribute is, of course, just an element attribute, so we can easily read it in any browser using getAttribute().

As you might expect, updating data- attributes without jQuery makes use of the setAttribute() method, courtesy of the web API's Element interface:

```
1  <video src="my-video.mp4" data-scene-offsets="9,22,38">
2
3  <script>
4  // updates the element's data attribute value to "1,2,3"
5  document.getElementsByTagName('VIDEO')[0]
6    .setAttribute('data-scene-offsets', '1,2,3');
7  </script>
```

This primitive yet effective approach yields two benefits over jQuery's data() method in this situation:

1. Our markup is always in-sync with the element's data.

2. Any changes we make to the element's data are accessible to *any* JavaScript.

So, in this instance, the native solution may be a better route route.

Complex Element Data Storage and Retrieval

Simple element data consists of a short string, such as a phrase, word, or short sequence of characters or numbers. Perhaps even a small JSON object or array can be considered simple. But what about complex data? And what exactly *is* complex data?

Remember the list of cars from the memory leaks section earlier in this chapter? I demonstrated a way to link the individual list item elements such that we could easily highlight the clicked item while making the other items in the list less prominent. We were associating JavaScript representations of HTML elements with other elements. This can certainly be considered "complex" data.

If we expand upon the previous example with the <video> tag, another example of complex element data can be demonstrated. In addition to scene offsets, we also need to record a short description of each scene, along with a title and a location. What we are describing here is something that demands a proper JavaScript object instead of a single string of text stored as an attribute value.

The solution I proposed in the memory leaks section involved use of expando properties, which was, in part, responsible for a memory leak in older browsers. Even though this leak has been patched in all modern browsers, expando properties are discouraged, as is modifying JavaScript representations of elements in any non-standard way. The video data scenario I detailed earlier is far too much data to store in a data- attribute. And of course, we shouldn't resort to expando properties here either. So the proper way to associate these types of complex data with elements is to maintain a JavaScript object that is linked to one or more elements via a data- attribute. This is the approach jQuery takes, and we can do the same without jQuery fairly easily.

The Familiar jQuery Approach

The jQuery solution to our problem involves, as you might have already surmised, the data() method:

```
1  $('VIDEO').data('scenes', [
2    {
3      offset: 9,
4      title: 'intro',
5      description: 'introducing the characters',
6      location: 'living room'
7    },
8    {
9      offset: 22,
10     title: 'the problem',
11     description: 'characters have some issues',
12     location: 'the park'
13   },
14   {
15     offset: 38,
16     title: 'the resolution',
17     description: 'characters resolve their issues',
18     location: 'the cemetery'
19   }
20 ]);
```

Now, if we want to look up the title of the second scene:

```
1  // variable will have a value of 'the problem'
2  var sceneTwoTitle = $('VIDEO').data('scenes')[1].title;
```

jQuery maintains the array we supplied inside an internal cache object. Each cache object is given an "index," and this index is stored as the value of an expando property that jQuery adds to the HTMLVideoElement object, which is the JavaScript representation of a <video> tag.

Using a More Natural Approach

When deciding how to tie complex data to an element in this section, we must be aware of our three goals:

1. No jQuery.

2. Must work in all browsers.

3. No expando properties.

And we can respect the first two goals by mimicking jQuery's approach to storing element data. To respect the third, we must make some adjustments to jQuery's approach. In other words, we will have to tie our elements to the underlying JavaScript object via a simple data- attribute *instead of* an expando property:

```
1  var cache = [],
2    setData = function(el, key, data) {
3      var cacheIdx = el.getAttribute('data-cache-idx'),
4        cacheEntry = cache[cacheIdx] || {};
5
6      cacheEntry[key] = data;
7      if (cacheIdx == null) {
8        cacheIdx = cache.push(cacheEntry) - 1;
9        el.setAttribute('data-cache-idx', cacheIdx);
10     }
11   };
12
13 setData(document.getElementsByTagName('VIDEO')[0],
14   'scenes', [
15   {
16     offset: 9,
17     title: 'intro',
18     description: 'introducing the characters',
19     location: 'living room'
20   },
21   {
22     offset: 22,
23     title: 'the problem',
24     description: 'characters have some issues',
25     location: 'the park'
26   },
27   {
28     offset: 38,
29     title: 'the resolution',
30     description: 'characters resolve their issues',
```

```
31    location: 'the cemetery'
32  }
33 ]);
```

What's going on here? First, I've created a convenience method (the `setData` function) to handle association of data with a specific element, along with an array (`cache`) used to hold data for *all* my elements. The `setData` function has been set up to accept an element, data key, and data object, while the `cache` array holds one JavaScript object per element with data attached to (potentially) multiple key properties.

When handling a call, we first check to see whether the element is already tied to data in our `cache`. If it is, we look up the existing data object in `cache` using the array index stored in the `data-cache-idx` attribute on the element and then add a new property to this object that contains the passed data. Otherwise, we create a new object initialized to contain the passed data with the passed key. If this element does not yet have an entry in `cache`, a `data-cache-idx` attribute with the index of the new object in `cache` must be created as well.

As with the jQuery solution, we want to look up the title of second scene, and we can do that with just a bit more code:

```
1 var cacheIdx = document.getElementsByTagName('VIDEO')[0]
2   .getAttribute('data-cache-idx');
3
4 // variable will have a value of 'the problem'
5 var sceneTwoTitle = cache[cacheIdx].scenes[1].title;
```

We could easily create a `getData()` function to accompany our `setData()` that makes storing and looking up our element data a bit more intuitive. But this all-browser non-jQuery solution is surprisingly simple. For an even more elegant non-jQuery approach that targets more modern browsers, check out the next section, where I demonstrate the `dataset` element property and the `WeakMap` API.

Removing Data from Our Cache When Elements Are Removed from the DOM

One potential issue with the approach I just demonstrated is the fact that the cache will grow unbounded. It would be useful to remove items from the cache when corresponding elements are removed from the DOM. Ideally, we could simply "listen" to DOM element removal "events" and revoke elements from our cache accordingly. Luckily, this is possible in most modern browsers natively, thanks to `MutationObserver`, a web standard maintained by WHATWG as part of its DOM specification.[5] Internet Explorer 9 and 10 are holdouts, but a polyfill fills in[6] those two gaps. Before `MutationObserver`, there was still native ability to observe changes to the DOM via "Mutation Events," but these proved to be highly inefficient and are no longer part of any active specification. The polyfill I just referred to falls back to Mutation Events in IE10 and 9.

Mutation Observers allow for a callback function to be executed whenever any change to any DOM element (or its child or descendants) is detected. This is exactly what we are looking for. More specifically, when a DOM element attached to a cache item is removed, we'd like to be notified so the cache can be cleaned up. Take the `<video>` element from the cache example. Remember that we stored some data about various scenes present in the video in a cache object. When the `<video>` is removed, the cache entry should be removed as well to prevent our cache from growing needlessly. Using Mutation Observers, our code to accomplish that may look something like this:

```
1 var videoEl = document.querySelector('video'),
2     observer = new MutationObserver(function(mutations) {
3       var wasVideoRemoved = mutations.some(function(mutation) {
```

---

[5] https://dom.spec.whatwg.org/#mutation-observers
[6] https://github.com/webcomponents/webcomponentsjs/blob/v0.7.20/MutationObserver.js

```
4          return mutation.removedNodes.some(function(removedNode) {
5            return removedNode === videoEl;
6          });
7        });
8
9        if (wasVideoRemoved) {
10         var cacheIdx = videoEl.getAttribute('data-cache-idx');
11         cache.splice(cacheIdx, 1);
12         observer.disconnect();
13       }
14     });
15
16   observer.observe(videoEl.parentNode, {childList: true});
```

There, all changes to children of our video's parent element are being observed. If we observe the video element directly, we won't be notified when it is removed. The `childList` configuration option passed to our observer ensures that we are notified whenever our video or any of its siblings are changed. When our callback function is hit, if our video element *was* removed, we remove the corresponding entry in the cache and then disconnect our Mutation Observer, since we no longer need it. For more on `MutationObserver`,[7] have a look at Mozilla Developer Network.

The Future of Element Data

Storing trivial or complex data without jQuery in *all* browsers is not particularly difficult, but it's also not very elegant. Luckily for us, the web is evolving quickly, and two new APIs exist that should make our code more beautiful and maybe even a bit more performant. I'll show you how to manage trivial element data with the HTML5 dataset property, and complex data using the ECMAScript 2015 collection. Keep in mind that everything in this section is meant for the latest browsers only. In each case, nothing older than Internet Explorer 11 is an option. In a short amount of time all common browsers will be supported as the definition of "modern browsers" evolves and the world leaves Internet Explorer 9 and 10 behind.

The HTML5 Dataset Property

The HTML5 specification, which became a recommendation in October of 2014, defined a new property on the `HTMLElement` interface: `dataset`.[8] Think of this new property as a JavaScript object available on any element object. In fact, it *is* an object, more specifically a `DOMStringMap` object,[9] which is also defined in the HTML5 spec. Any property you add to the `dataset` object is reflected as data- attribute on the element's tag in your document. You can also *read* any data- attribute defined on the element's tag by checking the corresponding property on the element's `dataset` object. In this respect, `HTMLElement.dataset` provides all the behaviors you have come to love about jQuery's `data()` method. It's an intuitive way to read and write data to an element, without the drawbacks. Because changes to the properties on the `dataset` object are always synced to the element's markup, and vice-versa, this new standard property is a perfect way to deal with trivial element data.

`Element.dataset` is currently available on a subset of "modern" browsers—Internet Explorer 9 and 10 are *not* supported, though polyfills are available, such as `https://www.npmjs.com/package/dataset`.

---

[7]`https://developer.mozilla.org/en/docs/Web/API/MutationObserver`
[8]`www.w3.org/TR/html5/dom.html#dom-dataset`
[9]`www.w3.org/TR/html5/infrastructure.html#domstringmap-0`

Keep this in mind when viewing the following code examples. And for our first demonstration, let's re-write the first code block displayed in the earlier section on reading and updating data- attributes using the web API:

```
1  <video src="my-video.mp4" data-scene-offsets="9,22,38">
2
3  <script>
4  // offsets value will be "9,22,38"
5  var offsets = document.querySelector('VIDEO').dataset.sceneOffsets;
6  </script>
```

Here we've simplified the earlier example quite a bit. Notice how we must use the camel-case form of the data- attribute. Arguably, the dataset model is more intuitive to use than jQuery's data() method. We treat all of our data as properties on an object, which is exactly how jQuery represents this data internally. But when using jQuery's API, we are expected to call the function passing the key as a string argument.

Take a look at a more modern version of the second code example, which illustrates how to change or add data to an element:

```
1  <video src="my-video.mp4" data-scene-offsets="9,22,38">
2
3  <script>
4  // updates the element's data attribute value to "1,2,3"
5  document.querySelector('VIDEO').dataset.sceneOffsets = '1,2,3';
6  </script>
```

The element data has been updated along with the associated data- attribute, all with one simple and elegant line of code. But we can do more! Because dataset is a JavaScript object, we can easily remove data from our element, just as we would remove a property from any other JavaScript object:

```
1  <video src="my-video.mp4" data-scene-offsets="9,22,38">
2
3  <script>
4  // removes the element's data-scene-offsets attribute
5  delete document.querySelector('VIDEO').dataset.sceneOffsets;
6  </script>
```

You can now see how dataset actually exceeds the convenience of jQuery's data() method.

Leveraging ECMAScript 2015 WeakMap Collections

You already know how to leverage the latest web technology to connect trivial data to elements. But what about complex data? We *could* make use of our previous example, but maybe the latest and greatest web specifications bring us a more elegant solution, maybe something more intuitive that is a perfect fit for this type of problem.

ECMAScript 2015 brings a new collection called a WeakMap.[10] A WeakMap can contain keys that are objects and values that are *anything*—elements, objects, primitives, and so on. In this new collection, keys are "weakly" held. This means that they are eligible for garbage collection by the browser if nothing else references them. This allows us to safely use the reference elements as keys!

---

[10]www.ecma-international.org/ecma-262/6.0/#sec-weakmap-objects

Although WeakMap is only supported in the latest and greatest browsers (Internet Explorer 11+, Chrome 36+, Safari 7.1+) along with Firefox 6+, it provides an exceptionally simple way to associate HTML elements with data. Remember the all-browser code examples demonstrated earlier? Let's start rewriting them using WeakMap:

```
1  var cache = new WeakMap();
2  cache.set(document.querySelector('VIDEO'), {scenes: [
3    {
4      offset: 9,
5      title: 'intro',
6      description: 'introducing the characters',
7      location: 'living room'
8    },
9    {
10     offset: 22,
11     title: 'the problem',
12     description: 'characters have some issues',
13     location: 'the park'
14   },
15   {
16     offset: 38,
17     title: 'the resolution',
18     description: 'characters resolve their issues',
19     location: 'the cemetery'
20   }
21 ]});
```

Thanks to WeakMap, we've managed to eliminate *all* the boilerplate from our earlier non-jQuery example. The elegancy of this approach equals that of jQuery's data() method, which I also demonstrated earlier. Looking up data is just as easy:

```
1  // variable will have a value of 'the problem'
2  var sceneTwoTitle = cache.get(document.querySelector('VIDEO')).scenes[1].title;
```

And finally, we can clean up after ourselves by removing elements we no longer want to track with a simple API call:

```
1  cache.delete(document.querySelector('VIDEO'));
```

Once the element is removed from the DOM, the video element should be eligible for garbage collection by the browser, assuming there are no other references to this element. Since the video element reference is weakly held by WeakMap, this by itself does not prevent garbage collection. Since the video element should then be removed from the WeakMap automatically once the element is no longer in the DOM, we probably don't even need to explicitly delete this entry.

The web without jQuery is looking pretty powerful.

CHAPTER 7

■ ■ ■

Styling Elements

If you are used to using jQuery's css() method to work with styles in your document, this chapter is for you. I can certainly relate to blind dependence on this magical aspect of the API. Adjusting the dimensions, color, opacity, and any other style imaginable is *really* easy to do with the help of jQuery. Unfortunately, this simplicity sometimes comes at a substantial cost.

jQuery's internal code that backs its easy-to-use CSS API has some notable performance issues. If you value efficiency, and if you want to provide your users with an optimal experience, you should learn how to properly manipulate and read element styles using the web API. Instead of relying on a "one-size-fits-all" approach, you should choose the leanest route possible by bypassing jQuery's abstraction.

You may *continue* to rely on jQuery, *or* get rid of it entirely in favor of a more "natural" programmatic approach. But there are concepts to be aware of other than which JavaScript methods and properties to use. Consider the possibility that JavaScript is not always the best way to define styles in your document. In addition to HTML and JavaScript, the browser provides a third valuable tool: style sheets.

This book aims to provide you with a better understanding of the options provided natively by your browser, with each chapter building on your newfound knowledge. In this chapter, you'll learn some new things about working with element styles, both with and without JavaScript. You'll learn enough from this chapter to understand when to target elements using CSS rules in style sheets instead of resorting to JavaScript every time. Your strong knowledge of selectors and attributes, courtesy of the last few chapters, will make this much easier.

There Are Three Ways to Style Elements

Before I dive into examples and details related to actually adjusting and reading back style information from elements in your document, it's important to get a few key concepts out of the way first. In this chapter, I show you three distinct routes you may take when working with element styles. The first covers managing styles directly in your markup—something that is *not* recommended, but possible. Another method involves making changes to standardized properties on Element objects—one approach you may elect to take if you intend to read or update styles on demand. Finally, I go over writing CSS rules inside of style sheets as a third option.

Inline Styles

A couple chapters back, I introduced you to the class attribute. Although this attribute is *often* used for styling elements, it is also used for selecting and classifying them. This section introduces the style attribute, which is used *exclusively* for adjusting the appearance of an element. This attribute is not new; it was first introduced in 1996 as part of the first formal W3C CSS specification.[1]

---

[1] www.w3.org/TR/REC-CSS1/#containment-in-html

© Ray Nicholus 2016
R. Nicholus, *Beyond jQuery*, DOI 10.1007/978-1-4842-2235-5_7

Let's suppose you have a very simple document with a few heading elements and associated content. You've decided that each <h2> should be blue, and each <h3> should be green. As a novice web developer, or perhaps a developer without much knowledge of your styling options, you *may* choose to set the color of these headings using the style attribute, which is available on all elements, as shown in Listing 7-1.

Listing 7-1. Setting Styles Using the Style Attribute

```
1  <h1>Fake News</h1>
2  <div>Welcome to fakenews.com. All of the news that's unfit to print.</div>
3
4  <h2 style="color: blue">World</h2>
5
6  <h3 style="color: green">Valdimir Putin takes up knitting</h3>
7  <div>The infamous leader of Russia appears to be mellowing with age as he reportedly
   joined a local knitting group in Moscow.</div>
8
9  <h2 style="color: blue">Science</h2>
10
11 <h3 style="color: green">Sun goes on vacation, moon fills in</h3>
12 <div>Fed up after over 4 billion years without a day off, the sun headed off to the
   Andromeda galaxy for a few weeks of rest and relaxation.</div>
```

Looking at this example, you can see how the headings have been colored as desired. You can fit multiple styles on a single element, simply by separating the styles with a semicolon. For example, suppose we want to not only color each <h2> blue, but also ensure they stand out a bit more by making them bold:

```
1  <h2 style="color: blue; font-weight: bold">World</h2>
2
3  ...
4
5  <h2 style="color: blue; font-weight: bold">Science</h2>
```

Any standardized style[2] can be applied to any element, simply by using the style attribute as illustrated in the preceding code fragments. But there are other ways to style your elements, as you will learn shortly, so why would anyone choose this particular method? First, specifying your styles alongside your elements directly in the markup seems like an intuitive and reasonable approach. But using the style attribute is most likely done out of laziness or naivete more often than not. It's painfully obvious how easy it is to specify styles for your elements this way.

Styling your document using the style attribute, also known as *inline styling*, is something you should *almost always* avoid. Despite its simplicity and intuitiveness, there are a number of reasons why this practice will cause you grief. First, inline styles add quite a bit of noise to your markup. In addition to content, tags, and other attributes, now you have style attributes—perhaps for *many* of your elements. And these attributes could very well contain a number of semicolon-separated styles. As your document begins to grow and become more complex, this noise becomes more apparent.

In addition to cluttering up the document, defining styles directly on each element in your markup precludes you from easily re-skinning your page. Suppose a designer took a look at the preceding code and informed you that the "green" and "blue" color values are a bit too "generic-looking," and should be substituted for slightly different colors. The designer then supplies you with hex codes for the new colors, and this adjustment requires changing style attribute for *all* <h2> and <h3> elements in your document. This is a common consequence of not following the "Don't Repeat Yourself" principle[3] of software development. Overuse of the style attribute can result in a maintenance nightmare.

---

[2]www.w3.org/TR/CSS2/
[3]www.artima.com/intv/dry.html

Defining styles in your document via the `style` attribute is also a potential security risk. If you intend to implement a Content Security Policy,[4] styling elements using attributes is strictly prohibited in the most basic (and safest) policy definition. A strong Content Security Policy, also known as a CSP, is becoming more commonplace now that all modern browsers (with the exception of IE9) include support for at least the initial version of the specification.[5]

Finally, peppering your page with `style` attributes—or `<style>` elements, which can contain various sets of CSS rules—can result in more overhead. If a single style needs to be changed, now the entire document has to be re-fetched by the browser the next time a user loads the page. If your styles were defined in a more specific location, outside of your markup, style changes could be introduced while still allowing a portion of your page to be fetched from the browser's cache, avoiding an unnecessary round-trip to the server.

I strongly suggest avoiding the use of `style` attributes. There are other much more appropriate options. The initially visible benefits are shadowed by the hardships that will become a harsh reality further down the road.

Working with Styles Directly on the Element Object

The `style` property on the object representation of an element was first introduced in the year 2000 as part of DOM Level 2.[6] It was defined as the lone property of a new `ElementCSSInlineStyle` interface. The `Element` interface implements `ElementCSSInlineStyle`, which allows elements to be styled programmatically using JavaScript. And all CSS properties, such as `opacity` and `color`, are accessible as properties on the associated `CSSStyleDeclaration`[7] instance, where they can be read or updated.

If all this talk of style properties isn't clear, take another look at the code example from the previous section. Listing 7-2 rewrites it by taking advantage of the `style` property that is available on all `Element` objects.

Listing 7-2. Setting Styles Using the **style** Property: All Modern Browsers and Internet Explorer 8

```
1  <h1>Fake News</h1>
2  <div>Welcome to fakenews.com. All of the news that's unfit to print.</div>
3
4  <h2>World</h2>
5
6  <h3>Valdimir Putin takes up knitting</h3>
7  <div>The infamous leader of Russia appears to be mellowing with age as he report
   edly joined a local knitting group in Moscow.</div>
8
9  <h2>Science</h2>
10
11 <h3>Sun goes on vacation, moon fills in</h3>
12 <div>Fed up after over 4 billion years without a day off, the sun headed off to the
   Andromeda galaxy for a few weeks of rest and relaxation.</div>
13
14 <script>
15 var headings = document.querySelectorAll('h2, h3');
16
17 for (var i = 0; i < headings.length; i++) {
18   if (headings[i].tagName === 'H2') {
19     headings[i].style.color = 'blue';
20   }
```

---

[4]https://developer.mozilla.org/en-US/docs/Web/Security/CSP/Introducing_Content_Security_Policy
[5]www.w3.org/TR/2012/CR-CSP-20121115/
[6]www.w3.org/TR/DOM-Level-2-Style/css.html#CSS-ElementCSSInlineStyle
[7]www.w3.org/TR/DOM-Level-2-Style/css.html#CSS-CSSStyleDeclaration

```
21    else {
22       headings[i].style.color = 'green';
23    }
24 }
25 </script>
```

That seems a bit clumsy, but it illustrates how you can programmatically update styles using the web API.

In the last section, I extended the initial code fragment to illustrate how to define multiple styles on a single element. Let's see how we can do this with the `style` property:

```
1 <h2>World</h2>
2
3 ...
4
5 <h2>Science</h2>
6
7 <script>
8 var headings = document.querySelectorAll('h2');
9
10 for (var i = 0; i < headings.length; i++) {
11    headings[i].style.color = 'blue';
12    headings[i].style.fontWeight = 'bold';
13 }
14 </script>
```

Notice that the `font-weight` CSS style name has been converted to camel case, which is perfectly legal, but we can *still* change this style using the dashed name, if we really want to, like this: `headings[i].style['font-weight'] = 'bold'`.

We're not done just yet; there is *another* way to set multiple styles on a single HTML element using the `style` property. The `CSSStyleDeclaration` interface defines a special property: `cssText`. This allows you to read *and* write multiple styles to the associated element. The value string looks exactly like a collection of semicolon-separated CSS rules, as you can see in Listing 7-3.

Listing 7-3. Setting Multiple Styles Using the **style.cssText** Property: All Modern Browsers and Internet Explorer 8

```
1 <h2>World</h2>
2
3 ...
4
5 <h2>Science</h2>
6
7 <script>
8 var headings = document.querySelectorAll('h2');
9
10 for (var i = 0; i < headings.length; i++) {
11    headings[i].style.cssText = 'color: blue; font-weight: bold';
12 }
13 </script>
```

Why might you want to make use of the `style` property on an element (or elements)? Maybe you are writing a JavaScript library that needs to make a few quick adjustments to some elements based on environmental or user input. It may be inconvenient to create and depend on a library-specific style sheet for these styles. Also, styles set using this method will usually override any other styles previously set on the element, which may be your intent.

But be careful about overusing this power. Styles set in this manner are difficult to override via style sheet rules. This may be your intent, but it also may not. If it is not, and you want to allow style sheets to easily make adjustments to styles, you will likely want to avoid changing styles using the style property (or inline styles). Finally, using the style property can make it very difficult to track down style changes, and can clutter up your JavaScript. It seems unnatural for your code to be focused on setting specific element styles. This should be a rare practice. As you'll see in the next section, this job is better suited for style sheets.

Style Sheets

JavaScript isn't the only way to attack styling challenges in the browser. It probably isn't even the *best* way to change the appearance of your elements. The browser provides a dedicated mechanism for styling your document: style sheets. Through this medium you may define all CSS styles for your web document in dedicated files, encapsulated in a specific HTML element, or even add them to the document via JavaScript on demand. I'll demonstrate each of these three methods for working with styles in this section.

The <style> element, first defined in the W3C CSS 1 specification,[8] lets us group all of our styles for an entire document in one convenient location. Listing 7-4 is a rewrite of the previous code fragment, this time with style added courtesy of HTMLStyleElement.

Listing 7-4. Setting Styles Using the **<style>** Element: All Browsers

```
1  <style>
2  h2 { color: blue; }
3  h3 { color: green; }
4  </style>
5
6  <h1>Fake News</h1>
7  <div>Welcome to fakenews.com. All of the news that's unfit to print.</div>
8
9  <h2>World</h2>
10
11 <h3>Valdimir Putin takes up knitting</h3>
12 <div>The infamous leader of Russia appears to be mellowing with age as he report edly
   joined a local knitting group in Moscow.<div>
13
14 <h2>Science</h2>
15
16 <h3>Sun goes on vacation, moon fills in</h3>
17 <div>Fed up after over 4 billion years without a day off, the sun headed off to the
   Andromeda galaxy for a few weeks of rest and relaxation.<div>
```

As you can see, all the JavaScript code used to style these elements in the previous section is completely replaced by two lines of CSS. Not only is this a more efficient solution, it's also much more elegant and straightforward. And if we want to add additional styles, we can easily do so by including them among the existing styles, semicolon-separated:

```
1  <style>
2  h2 {
```

---

[8]www.w3.org/TR/REC-CSS1/

```
3    color: blue;
4    font-weight: bold;
5  }
6  h3 {
7    color: green;
8    font-weight: bold;
9  }
10 </style>
11 ...
```

The preceding styles could even be improved a bit using the power of the multiple selector, which you learned about earlier:

```
1  <style>
2  h2, h3 { font-weight: bold; }
3  h2 { color: blue; }
4  h3 { color: green; }
5  </style>
6  ...
```

Jamming your styles into a <style> element may be fine for a small set of rules, but this is probably not ideal for a complex document. Perhaps you even want styles to be shared across documents/pages. Duplicating these styles in each HTML document doesn't seem like a scalable approach. Luckily, there is a better way—style sheets—as shown in Listings 7-5 and 7-6.

Listing 7-5. styles.css External Style Sheet: All Browsers

```
1  h2 { color: blue; }
2  h3 { color: green; }
```

Listing 7-6. index.html Setting Styles Using an External CSS Style Sheet File: All Browsers

```
1  <link href="styles.css" rel="style sheet">
2
3  <h1>Fake News</h1>
4  <div>Welcome to fakenews.com. All of the news that's unfit to print.</div>
5
6  <h2>World</h2>
7  ...
```

We've defined two files here: styles.css and index.html. The first houses our style sheet, the second contains our markup. In our index file, we can pull in all of these styles simply by referencing the styles.css file via the <link> element, which can be seen as early as the HTML 2.0 specification.[9] This may not be new knowledge for many of you, but it's easy to lose sight of the entire picture when you are accustomed to using a tool like jQuery, which sometimes seems to be a solution to all browser problems.

It is rarely appropriate to rely exclusively on JavaScript in any form (including through jQuery's API) to style your markup. Cascading Style Sheets exist for this purpose. But that does not mean that there is *never* an occasion where it is appropriate to dynamically change styles directly through JavaScript. Perhaps you

---

[9]www.w3.org/MarkUp/html-spec/html-spec_toc.html#SEC5.2.4

have constructed a web application that allows your users to create their own custom landing page. Your user needs to display all secondary headings in italics. To easily do this, you can programmatically add a CSS rule to the document using the `insertRule` method on the `CSSStyleSheet` interface:

```
1  // This grabs the first loaded style sheet on the current page.
2  // This also assumes the first style sheet is appropriate here.
3  var sheet = document.style Sheets[0]
4
5  sheet.insertRule(
6    'h2 { font-style: italic; }', sheet.cssRules.length - 1
7  )
```

The preceding example will create a new style that will display all `<h2>` elements in italics. The rule will be appended to the end of a style sheet. The `style sheet` variable can refer to a `<style>` element we've created on demand for these sorts of dynamic styles, or even an existing style sheet imported using a `<link>` tag. If you need to support Internet Explorer 8, you'll have to use `addRule` instead, if it is defined in the browser's implementation of the DOM API.

Using style sheets is almost always the preferred approach over a JavaScript- only solution. Even so, it is often acceptable to take a holistic approach, incorporating JavaScript, HTML, and style sheets into your solution as the situation dictates.

Now that you have a more complete understanding of the possibilities, you are in a better position to make these kinds of decisions correctly in your own projects. The rest of this chapter is dedicated to more specific styling situations. As is customary in *Beyond jQuery*, I use the familiar jQuery approach as a reference, followed by copious web API examples as part of a discussion of alternatives.

Getting and Setting Generalized Styles

After describing and demonstrating several distinct ways to add style to your HTML elements, it's now time to examine working with CSS a bit closer. If you are familiar with jQuery (and if you are reading this book, you probably are), then you already know that there is typically one narrow path to adjusting document look and feel when using jQuery. I'll provide a demonstration, for the purposes of reference. But the native route provided by the browser stack is much richer. In this section, you'll see how to *properly* get styles and set them dynamically without any assistance from jQuery.

To set up the jQuery and non-jQuery demonstrations below, let's start with a simple HTML fragment:

```
1  <button>cookies</button>
2  <button>ice cream</button>
3  <button>candy</button>
```

Suppose you would like to style a button a bit differently after it is clicked (or selected via the keyboard). The clicked button should be styled in some way to indicate that it has been selected. I haven't covered event handlers yet (though I will in a later chapter), so just assume that a function already exists with the associated button element passed in as a parameter whenever the button is selected. Your job is to fill in the implementation of this function by changing the background and border color of the selected button to blue, and the button text to white.

And to demonstrate reading styles (and further demonstrate setting them), consider an element that has already been styled as a box. Whenever this box is clicked, it becomes slightly more opaque, until it disappears entirely. Again, assume you are passed a function whenever the box is clicked. Your job is to make the box 10% more opaque whenever this function is called. I walk you through both solutions in this section, starting with the (likely) familiar jQuery approach.

Using jQuery

jQuery, being a very popular JavaScript library relied upon by far too many developers, has a duty (in my humble opinion) to teach these developers the proper way to adjust element styles. Unfortunately, it fails to do so. Even the jQuery Learning Center article on styling[10] only briefly touches on how to properly style elements, without any real demonstration of this technique at all. The reason for this is simple: idiomatic jQuery is often at odds with best practices. That fact was one of several inspirations for this book. Let's see how most jQuery-minded developers would solve the problem:

```
1  function onSelected($selectedButton) {
2    $selectedButton.css({
3      color: 'white',
4      backgroundColor: 'blue',
5      borderColor: 'blue'
6    });
7  }
```

When writing styles to elements, the `css` method acts as a wrapper around the `style` property on the `HTMLElement` interface. This is elegant, no doubt, but is it really the proper approach? The answer, of course, is "no." I covered this earlier. Granted, the previously described way is not the *only* solution to this problem using jQuery, but it is the most common one among jQuery developers.

Now, let's examine how one would typically solve the second problem using jQuery:

```
1  function onClicked($clickedBox) {
2    var currentOpacity = $clickedBox.css('opacity');
3
4    if (currentOpacity > 0) {
5      $clickedBox.css('opacity', currentOpacity - 0.1);
6    }
7  }
```

Unfortunately, jQuery's `css` API method is quite inefficient. Each call to this method to look up a style requires jQuery to utilize the `getComputedStyle()` method on the `window` object, which is completely unnecessary after the first call and adds a notable amount of processing overhead to this solution.

Without jQuery

The proper way to solve the first problem is to include the CSS rules in an external style sheet and trigger these rules using minimal JavaScript. Remember, we are looking to style a button, when it is selected/pressed, to stand out. We can expect a function to be called, with the element passed as a parameter, when the button is pressed.

Let's start by defining our styles for the pressed button in a style sheet, as shown in Listing 7-7.

Listing 7-7. styles.css Pressed Button Styles: All Browsers

```
1  button.selected {
2    color: white;
3    background-color: blue;
4    border-color: blue;
5  }
```

---

[10]https://learn.jquery.com/using-jquery-core/css-styling-dimensions/

When the button is pressed, all we need to do is add a CSS class to the element to trigger the styles defined in the styles.css file. Now we need to implement the function that adds the "selected" class to this button in order to trigger the style rules defined in the style sheet:

```
1  function onSelected(selectedButton) {
2    selectedButton.className += ' selected';
3  }
```

What follows is a line to import the CSS file, our button element, *and* the function that, when called, triggers the previously defined style rules on the button:

```
1  <link rel="style sheet" href="styles.css">
2  <script src="button-handler.js"></script>
3  <button>demo button</button>
```

This approach has a few advantages. First, it demonstrates a separation of concerns. In other words, rules for display belong in style sheets, behavior in JavaScript files, and content in HTML files. This separation makes maintenance simpler and potentially less risky. It also ensures that if, for example, the styles are adjusted, the HTML and JavaScript files continue to be cached by the browser. If all this logic were jammed into a single HTML file, the entire file would have to be re-downloaded by the browser, regardless of the scope of the change.

Another advantage of tying these styles to a CSS class and defining this in an external style sheet is that these can be easily re-used for other purposes elsewhere in this document, or any other document. The idiomatic jQuery approach leaves us copying and pasting the same styles over and over again, since we are defining them inline.

And the second scenario? Remember, we want to increase the opacity of a box by 10% each time it is clicked. Again, we are given a function that will be called with the box element whenever it is clicked:

```
1  function onClicked(clickedBox) {
2    var currentOpacity = clickedBox.style.opacity ||
3      getComputedStyle(clickedBox, null).opacity;
4
5    if (currentOpacity > 0) {
6      clickedBox.style.opacity = currentOpacity - 0.1;
7    }
8  }]
```

Our optimized non-jQuery approach is a little more code, but it is much faster than the idiomatic jQuery solution.[11] Here, we are only utilizing the expensive call to getComputedStyle[12] when there is no style defined on the element's style property. getComputedStyle determines an element's actual style by examining not only the element's style property, but also by looking at any available style sheets. As a result, this operation can be a bit expensive, so we avoid it unless absolutely necessary.

Setting and Determining Element Visibility

Showing and hiding elements is a common problem in web development. These tasks may not be straightforward, but it's often even more complicated to determine, programmatically, whether an element is visible or not. Traditionally, element visibility is a confounding problem for developers to deal with. But it doesn't have to be this way. There are two ways to do handle element visibility: the way you've always done it (using jQuery) and the correct way (without jQuery). You'll see how inefficient jQuery is in this context, and how this illustrates why blind faith in this type of software library is dangerous.

---

[11]http://jsperf.com/jquery-css-vs-optimized-non-jquery-approach3
[12]www.w3.org/TR/DOM-Level-2-Style/css.html#CSS-CSSview-getComputedStyle

The Typical jQuery Approach

The upside of using jQuery to show, hide, and determine the visibility of an element is simplicity. As you'll find out soon, this is the *only* upside. But for now, let's focus on this advantage.

Hiding and showing elements with jQuery is almost always accomplished using the show() and hide() API methods, respectively. There's no real need to create a fragment of HTML to demonstrate these methods, so let's just dive into a couple code samples:

```
1  // hide an element
2  $element.hide();
3
4  // show it again
5  $element.show();
```

None of that code demands further elaboration. What *does* need further examination is the underlying code that actually carries out these operations. Unfortunately, both of these methods make use of window. getComputedStyle, a method discussed in the last section. In some cases, particularly with hide(), getComputedStyle() may be called multiple times. This has serious performance consequences. Why is all this processing power needed simply to hide or show a single DOM element? For the most part, all the clever and generally unnecessary code underneath these two commonly used API methods is in place solely to handle styling edge cases where it is otherwise difficult to show or hide a targeted element. As I said before, element visibility doesn't *have* to be a complex problem. We can avoid all the CPU cycles required by jQuery to hide and show elements simply by adopting a simpler approach. More on that in the next section, where I discuss the "native web approach" to this problem.

What if we need to figure out whether a specific element is hidden or not? Well, jQuery makes this really easy too:

```
1  // is the element visible?
2  $element.is(':visible');
3
4  // conversely, is the element hidden?
5  $element.is(':hidden');
```

jQuery has decided to invent a couple of new pseudo-classes to represent element visibility. Even the creator of jQuery, John Resig, went on at length about the usefulness of this new innovative jQuery concoction.[13] But just like show(), hide(), and the css() API methods, these two non-standard pseudo-classes are quite slow. Again, they delegate to window.getComputedStyle(), again, sometimes multiple times per invocation.

In the next section, I outline several non-jQuery methods of showing and hiding elements, as well as determining the visibility of an element. The performance differences between the native and the jQuery methods will be included as well, and the differences will be notable, to say the least.

The Native Web Approach

Ultimately, jQuery's long-standing approach to toggling element visibility was exceptionally complex, and this contributed to potentially crippling performance issues. After reframing the problem, it became clear that the simplest approach was the best and most efficient one. The jQuery 3.0 release notes even suggest instead using a class name that is tied to appropriate CSS to show or hide hide an element.

---

[13]http://ejohn.org/blog/selectors-that-people-actually-use/

The simplicity of hiding, showing, and evaluating the visibility of an element in jQuery is compelling. This is the part where you may expect me to say something like, "It is a bit more difficult to do all of this without jQuery," or, "There's an easy way to solve this problem without jQuery, but it requires use of bleeding-edge browsers." In reality, it is very easy to show, hide, and determine element visibility in any browser without jQuery. jQuery developers may want you to believe that these are complex problems to solve, and that you *need* jQuery to solve them, but none of this is true. In this section, I demonstrate some simple conventions that will result in simple solutions.

There are many ways to hide an element. Some of the more unconventional methods include setting the element's opacity to 0, or setting the position to "absolute" and positioning it outside the visible page. These and other similar approaches may be effective, but they are generally considered to be "kludge." As a result, using these methods is generally discouraged when attempting to hide an element. Please don't do this; there are better ways.

A more reasonable approach involves setting the element's display style property to "none". As you have already learned, there are a number of different ways to adjust an element's style. But you have also learned that the best approach is to define this style in an external style sheet. So, perhaps the best solution would be to define a custom CSS class or attribute in your style sheet, include a display: none style for this selector, and then add the associated class or attribute to this element when it needs to be hidden.

So, which should we choose? An attribute or a CSS class? Does it really matter? The W3C HTML5 specification defines a hidden Boolean attribute,[14] which, as you might expect, allows you to hide an element simply by adding this attribute to the element. Not only does this standardized attribute allow you to easily hide an element, it also enhances the semantics of your markup and provides a useful cue to *all* screen readers.[15] Yes, it even makes your elements more accessible. And because the hidden attribute is part of a formal specification, it isn't just a convention—it represents the standardized way to deal with element visibility.

At this point, you are probably checking to see which browsers support this attribute. Let me save you the trouble—not all of them. In fact, the hidden attribute wasn't first supported by Microsoft until Internet Explorer 11. Luckily, the polyfill for the standardized hidden attribute is *unbelievably simple and elegant*: just add the rule shown in Listing 7-8 to your global style sheet.

Listing 7-8. Polyfill for Standardized Hidden Attribute: All Browsers

```
1  [hidden] { display: none; }
```

■ **Making sure your element is always hidden** The native hidden attribute marks an element as "irrelevant," which does not always mean that the element will be invisible to the eye. For example, if an element has an explicitly declared display style, such as display: block, the native hidden attribute will *not* remove it from view. Furthermore, simply including the preceding "polyfill" for this attribute will not always ensure the element is hidden from view either. That is due to the rules of specificity, outlined in W3C's CSS2 specification.[16] Specificity determines which of several competing styles associated with an element "win." For example, if a display: block rule pointing to the same element with a higher specificity exists, the element will remain visible. If you want any element with a hidden attribute to *never* be visible, you must utilize the following rule in your style sheet:

```
1  [hidden] { display: none !important; }
```

---

[14]www.w3.org/TR/html5/editing.html#the-hidden-attribute
[15]www.html5accessibility.com/tests/hidden2013.html
[16]www.w3.org/TR/CSS2/cascade.html#specificity

Given the preceding one-line polyfill, you can hide *any* element in *any* browser with the following line of JavaScript:

```
1  element.setAttribute('hidden', '');
```

Hiding elements couldn't possibly be simpler, more elegant, or more performant. This approach is incredibly faster than jQuery's hide() API method. In fact, jQuery's hide() method is more than 25 times slower![17] There is *no* reason to continue using jQuery to hide elements.

Since the simplest and most performant method of hiding an element involves adding an attribute, you may not be surprised to learn that you can show the same element simply by *removing* that same attribute:

```
1  element.removeAttribute('hidden');
```

Because we're following this convention—add an attribute to hide and element and remove it to show the element again—determining the visibility of the element is simple. All we need to do is check the element for the existence of this attribute, which is a trivial operation in all notable browsers:

```
1  // the element is hidden if this returns true
2  element.hasAttribute('hidden');
```

Yes, it's really that easy.

Determining Width and Height of Any Element

Before I review how jQuery allows you to check the width and height of an element, and how you can easily do this without using a DOM abstraction, you need to understand some basic concepts. The most critical specification required to intelligently calculate the width and height of any element is the box model.[18]

Every element is a box. One more time: *every element is a box*. This is simple, yet very surprising for many web developers to hear. Once you get over the initial shock of this realization, the next step is to understand how an element's box is divided up. This is called the box model. Look at Figure 7-1, a drawing of the box model from the World Wide Web Consortium's CSS 2.1 specification.

As you can see, an element, which again is a *box*, is made up of four "layers": content, padding, border, and margin. Simply put, an element's content, padding, and border are used to determine its height and width. Margins are not considered to be part of an element's "dimensions"—they simply push other elements away instead of influencing the element's height and width. How you measure width and height largely depends on which of the first three layers you care about. Generally speaking, an element's dimensions can take into account a subset of these three layers—content and padding—or all three layers. jQuery takes a different approach and only considers the content dimensions. More on that next.

---

[17]http://jsperf.com/jquery-hide-vs-setattribute-hidden
[18]www.w3.org/TR/CSS21/box.html

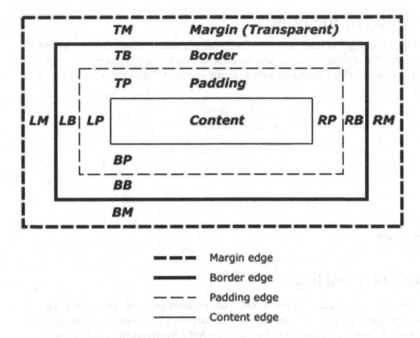

Figure 7-1. *The box model. Copyright 2015 W3C. License available at* www.w3.org/Consortium/Legal/2015/
copyright-software-and-document.

Examining an Element Using jQuery

Just as with the web API—described in the following section—there are many ways to discover the
dimensions of an element using jQuery's API. You may already be aware of some or even all of these
methods. What you may *not* be aware of is the poor performance associated with jQuery's built-in element
dimension methods—most developers are not. And why should you? The methods are so simple and
elegant, the possibility that you are paying a substantial penalty in terms of performance is not often a
concern. You probably trust that this critical library is not degrading the efficiency of your application in any
noticeable way. But you would be wrong.

The most visible API methods are width() and height(). Remember the box model diagram from
Figure 7-1? These two jQuery methods only measure the "content" portion of an element's box. This *sounds*
like a reasonable behavior, but it is not necessarily a complete representation, since content only accounts
for a portion of an element's actual width and height. Remember that margin is the only element of the box
model that does not directly affect the visible width and height of an element. Also remember that jQuery
isn't magic—it must delegate to the web API for *all* of its API methods. And the web API does not provide a
simple way to determine the dimensions of an element's content. So, jQuery must perform some unpleasant
operations in order to determine these values, sacrificing performance as a result. When I demonstrate how
to calculate the width and height of an element using the web API in the next section, I'll show you just how
relatively inefficient jQuery's other width and height API methods really are.

Options Natively Provided by the Browser

Although jQuery's width and height are popular methods, there is no similar pair of methods or properties to be found in any web specification. The appeal of these methods is likely tied to their suggestive names.

To better illustrate the code in this section, I'll start off with a simple element that takes up space in all four segments of the box model:

```
1  <style>
2  .box {
3    padding: 10px;
4    margin: 5px;
5    border: 3px solid;
6    display: inline-block;
7  }
8  </style>
9  <span class="box">a box</span>
```

Width and Height of Content + Padding

To obtain the width or height of the preceding box, only considering the content and padding values, we can use the clientWidth[19] and clientHeight[20] properties found on the Element interface. These are comparable to jQuery's innerWidth() and innerHeight() API methods, but the web API has significant performance advantages over jQuery's solution.[21] The native solution is about ten times faster!

These properties were first defined in the Cascading Style Sheet Object Model (CSSOM) View specification,[22] drafted by the W3C. As of mid-2016, the CSSOM spec is not yet a recommended standard—in fact, it is only a working draft. But these two Element properties, along with many of the other items represented in this specification, have been supported by browsers for a very long time. For example, the Element.clientWidth and Element.clientHeight properties are supported all the way back to Internet Explorer 6, yet they are only currently defined in this working draft spec. That seems a bit strange, doesn't it? Indeed it is, but the CSSOM spec is a special one. It exists mostly to codify and formally standardize long-standing CSS-related browser behaviors. Element.clientWidth and Element.clientHeight are two such examples, but you will see others in this section as well.

Listing 7-9 shows what clientWidth and clientHeight return on the <span> in our markup from earlier.

Listing 7-9. Find width/height of Content + Padding: Web API, Modern Browsers, and Internet Explorer 8

```
1  // returns 38
2  document.querySelector('.box').clientHeight;
3
4  // returns 55
5  document.querySelector('.box').clientWidth;
```

---

[19]www.w3.org/TR/cssom-view/#dom-element-clientwidth
[20]www.w3.org/TR/cssom-view/#dom-element-clientheight
[21]http://jsperf.com/innerheight-vs-element-clientheight
[22]www.w3.org/TR/cssom-view/

Note that the preceding return values may vary slightly between browsers, as default fonts and styling may also vary slightly between browsers. This will ultimately lead to a slight variance in the size of the element's content, which is to be expected.

There is something else at play here that you may not be aware of. Notice the `display: inline-block` style attached to our `<span>` element? Remove it and check the return values of `clientWidth` and `clientHeight` again. Without this style, both of these properties report a value of 0. By default, all browsers render `<span>` elements as `display: inline`, and inline elements will *always* report 0 as their `clientWidth` and `clientHeight`. Keep this in mind when using these properties. Note that floating a default inline element will *also* allow you to calculate width and height this way.

For comparison, jQuery's `width()` and `height()` methods return 35 and 18, respectively. Remember that these methods *only* consider the element's content, ignoring padding, border, and margin.

Width and Height of Content + Padding + Border

What if you need to include the border when reporting the width and height of an element? That is, content, padding, and border? Simple—use `HTMLElement.offsetWidth`[23] and `HTMLElement.offsetHeight`.[24] These properties have also long been implemented by browsers, but only first brought into a formal specification in the CSSOM View standard. Both properties are comparable to jQuery's `outerWidth()` and `outerHeight()` methods, as shown in Listing 7-10.

Listing 7-10. Find width/height of Content + Padding + Border: Web API, Modern Browsers, and Internet Explorer 8

```
1  // returns 44
2  document.querySelector('.box').offsetHeight;
3
4  // returns 61
5  document.querySelector('.box').offsetWidth;
```

As expected, these values are a bit larger than what `clientHeight` and `clientWidth` report since we are also taking border into account. In fact, each value is exactly 6 pixels larger. This is expected due to a border of 3 pixels on each side, defined in our `<style>` element.

Again, the returned values above may vary slightly between browsers due to the way browsers style element content. Also, `display: inline-block` is not needed for `offsetHeight` and `offsetWidth`—they will *not* report a zero height and width for inline elements.

There is a lot more to discuss regarding styling elements, but this book is about so much more. I've provided you with some of the critical concepts that will allow you to end your dependence on jQuery when facing other styling-related challenges going forward.

---

[23]www.w3.org/TR/cssom-view/#dom-htmlelement-offsetwidth
[24]www.w3.org/TR/cssom-view/#dom-htmlelement-offsetheight

CHAPTER 8

■ ■ ■

DOM Manipulation

One of the most confusing and misunderstood aspects of the web API pertains to DOM manipulation. I suspect you are already used to working with DOM elements through jQuery. But is it necessary to continue depending on a library in this regard? In this chapter, I show you how to create, update, and move elements and element content *without* any help from third-party code. You'll come to appreciate how easy it is to work with the DOM in virtually all browsers.

The DOM: A Central Component of Web Development

Most likely you've heard *about* the DOM. It's a common term in the world of web development. But maybe the DOM is still a mostly mysterious word to you. What exactly *is* the DOM, and why is it so important? How and why does jQuery abstract the DOM API away from developers?

As stated in one of the early W3C-maintained documents,[1] "The history of the Document Object Model, known as the DOM, is tightly coupled with the beginning of the JavaScript and JScript scripting languages." This model expresses an API, commonly implemented in JavaScript for use in web browsers, that allows programmatic access to an HTML document. In addition to working with attributes, selecting elements, and storing data, the DOM API also provides a way to create new content, remove elements, *and* move existing elements around the document. These specific aspects of the DOM API are the primary focus of this chapter.

jQuery Exists Because of the DOM API

Okay, it's not the *only* reason why jQuery was created, but it's certainly one of the reasons. John Resig, the creator of jQuery, famously called the DOM a "mess" in a 2009 presentation at Yahoo.[2] So this perhaps gives us some insight into one of the problems jQuery aims to solve. A few years before Resig's talk, jQuery 1.0 was released (2006), which included about 25 DOM-manipulation-specific methods. This accounted for about 17% of the entire API. Even as the API has grown to handle all aspects of the web API, DOM manipulation functions still account for 15%.

Sure, jQuery provides some elegant solutions to working with the DOM. But are they really necessary? Of course not! Is the DOM still "broken"? Not in my opinion. The DOM API may have some rough edges, but it is fairly easy to use and quite reliable. You *can* painlessly manipulate the DOM yourself without the help of jQuery.

---

[1] www.w3.org/2002/07/26-dom-article.html
[2] http://ejohn.org/blog/the-dom-is-a-mess/

© Ray Nicholus 2016
R. Nicholus, *Beyond jQuery*, DOI 10.1007/978-1-4842-2235-5_8

The DOM API Isn't Broken, It's Just Misunderstood

In Resig's talk at Yahoo, he said "Nearly every DOM method is broken in some way, in some browser." Although that is a bit hyperbolic, it may have had *some* truth to it back in 2009. The current age of browsers paints a much different picture, though. Browsers still have bugs, but this is true of all software, even jQuery.[3] The jQuery team already apparently knows that the library is no longer useful as a shield from browser bugs, as is evident in their responses to issues that appear to be browser-specific.[4]

One of the major goals of jQuery has always been to shield developers from the DOM API. Why? Because it historically *has* been a mess. It's also seen as a muddled path to follow when attempting to programmatically update a page's markup. This has a bit of truth to it, but only because many developers have not taken the time to learn the DOM API. As you'll see throughout this chapter, working with the DOM isn't as hard as you might think and is well supported throughout all popular browsers. It's hard to argue with the convenience offered by jQuery's API. You can even make better use of jQuery, should you continue to use it, once you have a better understanding of the underlying DOM API methods that jQuery itself relies on.

Moving and Copying Elements

In this first part, I'm going to focus on moving and copying existing elements. You'll learn how to insert elements anywhere in the DOM, change the order of adjacent elements, and clone an element. I'll demonstrate methods present on the Document,[5] Element,[6] and Node[7] interfaces, among others. You'll see how basic DOM operations have been executed with jQuery, followed by explanations and demonstrations of the same tasks utilizing the DOM API alone.

Moving Elements Around the DOM

I'm going to start this section out with one of my patented (pending) sample documents. In order to focus primarily on the functionality of the demonstrable methods, I'll keep this simple and straightforward. Admittedly, this results in a somewhat contrived example, but I feel it will easily allow us to compare and contrast jQuery with the DOM API in the context of DOM manipulation.

Our super-simple document consists of a few different categories and attributes of ice cream: flavors, types, and a section of unassigned types and flavors. This document represents some choices for customers of an ice cream shop. Using this markup, we're going to solve several "problems," first with jQuery, and then with the plain old DOM API.

The first challenge involves reordering the flavors and types in descending order, based on their popularity. Chocolate is the most popular flavor, followed by vanilla and strawberry. We'll have to change the order of the flavors list items to reflect their popularity, but the types list is already in the correct order.

Second, we really want to present our readers with the types of ice cream *first*, followed by the flavors. The current order, which includes *flavors* first, is known to be less than ideal, as our customers want to be informed of the types first before deciding on flavors.

Finally, we need to take the items in the "unassigned" section and assign them to the proper category. "Rocky road" is a flavor that is less popular than vanilla, but more popular than strawberry. And "gelato" is a type, also the least popular of the bunch:

```
1  <body>
2    <h2>Flavors</h2>
```

---

[3]https://github.com/jquery/jquery/issues
[4]https://github.com/jquery/jquery/issues/2679#issuecomment-152289474
[5]https://developer.mozilla.org/en-US/docs/Web/API/Document
[6]https://developer.mozilla.org/en-US/docs/Web/API/Element
[7]https://developer.mozilla.org/en-US/docs/Web/API/Node

```
3   <ul class="flavors">
4     <li>chocolate</li>
5     <li>strawberry</li>
6     <li>vanilla</li>
7   </ul>
8
9   <h2>Types</h2>
10  <ul class="types">
11    <li>frozen yogurt</li>
12    <li>custard</li>
13    <li>Italian ice</li>
14  </ul>
15
16  <ul class="unassigned">
17    <li>rocky road</li>
18    <li>gelato</li>
19  </ul>
20  </body>
```

After solving the problems described so far, our document should look like this:

```
1   <body>
2     <h2>Types</h2>
3     <ul class="types">
4       <li>frozen yogurt</li>
5       <li>Italian ice</li>
6       <li>custard</li>
7       <li>gelato</li>
8     </ul>
9
10    <h2>Flavors</h2>
11    <ul class="flavors">
12      <li>chocolate</li>
13      <li>vanilla</li>
14      <li>rocky road</li>
15      <li>strawberry</li>
16    </ul>
17
18    <ul class="unassigned">
19    </ul>
20  </body>
```

Moving Elements Using jQuery

In order to properly order the flavors, "vanilla" must be moved after "chocolate". To accomplish this, we must make use of jQuery's after() API method:

```
1   var $flavors = $('.flavors'),
2       $chocolate = $flavors.find('li').eq(0),
3       $vanilla = $flavors.find('li').eq(2);
4
5   $chocolate.after($vanilla);
```

99

For our second challenge, we have to move the "types" list *and* the heading (`<h2>`) for the "types" list before the "flavors" list. We can take advantage of the fact that this means the heading and list must be the first set of children inside the `<body>` element. First, we prepend the "types" heading to the `<body>` using the prependTo() method and then insert the "types" list after the newly moved heading, again using jQuery's after() method:

```
1  var $typesHeading = $('h2').eq(1);
2
3  $typesHeading.prependTo('body');
4  $typesHeading.after($('.types'));
```

Finally, we need to move the unassigned "rocky road" just above "strawberry" in the flavors list, and "gelato" to the end of the "types" list. For the first move, we can again use jQuery's after() method. For the second move, we will use the appendTo method on the "gelato" element to insert it as the last child in the "types" list:

```
1  var $unassigned = $('.unassigned'),
2      $rockyRoad = $unassigned.find('li').eq(0),
3      $gelato = $unassigned.find('li').eq(1);
4
5  $vanilla.after($rockyRoad);
6  $gelato.appendTo($('.types'));
```

None of the preceding solutions is particularly elegant or intuitive. It's certainly possible to come up with more attractive examples to solve these problems, but I would expect this attempt to be common among jQuery developers. We also could have made use of some of jQuery's proprietary pseudo-classes, such as :first and :last, but we already learned how inefficient those options are.

The DOM API's Solution to Reordering Elements

In order to make the proper adjustments to our ice cream store page *without* jQuery, I'm going to introduce two new DOM API methods. You'll also see a number of selectors and other DOM API methods previously discussed in Chapter 4. Surprisingly, *all* of the code in this section works in all modern browsers *and* Internet Explorer 8 as well! Before we start, the eye-rolling nature of this example ice cream store markup is not lost on me, but it allows me to succinctly demonstrate a number of DOM manipulation operations without getting bogged down in details unrelated to the problem at hand. That said, let's get started.

Remember that our first task is to move the "vanilla" element before the "strawberry" element. To accomplish this, we can make use of the insertBefore() method,[8] which was added to the Node interface as part of W3C's DOM Level 2 Core specification. This method, as you might imagine, allows us to move one element just before another in the DOM. And because this is available on the Node interface, we have the power to move anything in the DOM, even a Text or Comment node! Take a look at how we move this element—I'll explain what's going on immediately after the following code fragment:

```
1  var flavors = document.querySelector('.flavors'),
2      strawberry = flavors.children[1],
3      vanilla = flavors.children[2];
4
5  flavors.insertBefore(vanilla, strawberry);
```

[8] www.w3.org/TR/2000/REC-DOM-Level-2-Core-20001113/core.html#ID-952280727

At the top of the preceding code, I'm simply selecting elements needed by our move operation. The last line is the most important one. Since the `insertBefore()` method is defined on the Node object's prototype, we must call `insertBefore()` on an DOM object that implements this interface. In fact, this element *must* be a parent element of the Node we are moving. Since we are moving the "vanilla" `<li>` element, we can use its parent—the "flavors" `<ul>`.

The first parameter passed to `insertBefore()` is the element we want to relocate: the "vanilla" list item. The second parameter is the "reference node." This is the Node that will become the next sibling of our target element (the "vanilla" `<li>`) *after* the move operation. Since we want to move "vanilla" before "strawberry," the "strawberry" `<li>` is our reference node.

We've reordered our flavors, but we still need to move the flavors heading and list to the top of our document. We can easily accomplish this goal with the `insertBefore()` method as well:

```
1  var headings = document.querySelectorAll('h2'),
2      flavorsHeading = headings[0],
3      typesHeading = headings[1],
4      typesList = document.querySelector('.types');
5
6  document.body.insertBefore(typesHeading, flavorsHeading);
7  document.body.insertBefore(typesList, flavorsHeading);
```

■ **Note**   Regarding this line of code in the preceding code listing - `document.body.` `insertBefore(typesHeading, flavorsHeading)` - this behaves just like `$typesHeading.prependTo('body')` in the earlier jQuery code listing. Why? Because `flavorsHeading` happens to be the first child of `document.body`.

The meat of our logic is contained in the final two lines of the preceding code. First, we're moving the "types" `<h2>` to the top of our document. The parent of this heading is the `<body>` element, which we can easily select using `document.body`. Our target element is, of course, the "types" heading. We want to move this just before the "flavors" `<h2>`, so that becomes our reference element.

The second `insertBefore()` moves the `<ul>` of ice cream types after the recently moved heading. Again, `<body>` is our parent element. Since we need to move this list before the "flavors" heading, that is again our reference node.

Our final task is to move the unassigned elements into their respective lists. To accomplish this, we'll again make use of `insertBefore()`, but you'll also see a new method in action. The W3C DOM Level 1 specification, which is quite an old spec, first defined an `appendChild()` method on the Node interface.[9] This method will be of some use to us as we wrap up our exercise:

```
1  flavors.insertBefore(
2    document.querySelector('.unassigned > li'), strawberry);
3
4  document.querySelector('.types').appendChild(
5    document.querySelector('.unassigned > li'));
```

In the first statement, we're moving the "rocky road" element from the unassigned list into the flavors list. The flavors list is our parent element, as expected. The target is the first list item child of the unassigned list, which happens to be the "rocky road" `<li>`. And the reference node is the strawberry item in the flavors list, since we want to move "rocky road" before this element.

---

[9]www.w3.org/TR/REC-DOM-Level-1/level-one-core.html#ID-184E7107

We also want to move the unassigned "gelato" list item to the *end* of the types list. The simplest way to do this is to use appendChild(). As with the insertBefore() method, appendChild() expects to be called on the parent of the node we plan to move—the "types" list. The appendChild() method only takes one argument—the element that is to become the last child of the parent element. At this point, the "gelato" item is the first <li> child in the unassigned list, so we can use the same selector as used to locate the target element in our insertBefore() statement.

That was all surprisingly easy, wasn't it? The DOM API may not be as scary as many make it out to be!

Making Copies of Elements

To demonstrate the various ways to clone elements using jQuery and the DOM API, consider the following markup:

```
1  <ol class="numbers">
2    <li>one</li>
3    <li>two</li>
4  </ol>
```

The DOM API offers a method to clone the <ol> *and* its children, as well as a way to clone *only* <ol> and *not* any of its children/content. The former is called a *deep clone*, and the latter a *shallow clone*. jQuery *only* offers a way to deep clone.

In jQuery-land, we must make use of $.clone():

```
1  // deep clone: return value is an exact copy
2  $('.numbers').clone();
```

You can optionally pass Boolean parameters to the preceding clone() if you'd like jQuery to clone any data and event listeners on the element. But be warned that jQuery will only copy event listeners and data attached to the element via jQuery. Any listeners and data added outside of jQuery's API will be lost.

The DOM API provides a similarly named method, cloneNode(), available on the Node interface. It was first standardized as part of DOM Level 2 Core,[10] which became a W3C recommendation back in 2000. As a result, cloneNode() is supported in *any* browser. The next example is limited to Internet Explorer 8 and up (though this is hardly a problematic limitation) due to my use of querySelector():

```
1  // shallow clone: return value is an empty <ol class="numbers">
2  document.querySelector('.numbers').cloneNode();
3
4  // deep clone: return value is an exact copy of the tree
5  document.querySelector('.numbers').cloneNode(true);
```

In both cases, the element copies will contain *everything* defined in the markup, even the class names, and any other attributes such as inline styles. Event listeners are *not* included with the copy, nor are any properties exclusively set on the element's JavaScript object representation. In other words, cloneNode() copies *only* what you see: markup.

Whether you are using jQuery or the DOM API, the copy created by cloneNode() is *not* added to the document for you. You will need to do this yourself using one of the methods demonstrated earlier in this section.

---

[10]www.w3.org/TR/DOM-Level-2-Core/core.html#ID-3A0ED0A4

Composing Your Own Elements

Now that we've explored moving and coping elements, how about creating and removing them? You'll see how these common problems have been solved with jQuery, and how you can solve them just as easily with the DOM API. As with the previous section, all DOM API code here will work in all modern browsers, and most are supported in Internet Explorer 8 as well.

To best demonstrate all of the concepts outlined in this final section, I'll build upon the modified example document from the previous section that I used to demonstrate moving elements. Using jQuery and then the bare DOM API, I'll show you how to perform various operations on our example document, such as the following:

1. Add some new ice cream flavors.

2. Remove some existing types.

3. Make simple text adjustments to our document.

4. Read parts of the document to a string to allow it to be saved.

5. Create a new section to further classify our ice cream.

Creating and Deleting Elements

Suppose we have a couple new flavors to add to our list: pistachio and neapolitan. These of course belong in the "flavors" section. To accomplish this task, we'll need to create two new `<li>` elements with Text Nodes that contain the names of these two new flavors. It's fine to simply add these new flavors to the end of the list so that we can stay focused on creating the representative elements. We also want to remove the "gelato" type from the end of the list of types, since we no longer sell gelato ice cream.

Creating elements is pretty easy with jQuery, and due to chaining we can add both elements in two lines:

```
1  var $flavors = $('.flavors');
2
3  // add two new flavors
4  $('<li>pistachio</li>').appendTo($flavors);
5  $('<li>neapolitan</li>').appendTo($flavors);
```

Removing an element isn't very difficult either:

```
1  // remove the "gelato" type
2  $('.types li:last').remove();
```

Here we've made use of a CSS selector, partially proprietary. The last `<li>` beneath the element with a "types" CSS class is being removed from the document. This happens to be our "gelato" type. The :last pseduo-class is specific to jQuery and as such is not particularly performant. There *is* a native CSS pseduo-class we could use, which you will see in a moment, but many jQuery developers may not know that it exists, since the jQuery API provides this proprietary alternative as part of its documented API.

How can we achieve the same results with the DOM API? Depending on desired browser support, we may have several options. Although newer browsers *may* allow for more elegant options than older ones, this is not always the case, and these operations are all relatively simple in *all* modern browsers (and even older ones) without relying on jQuery.

We can add our two new flavors to the end of the "flavors" list in two total lines, just like the jQuery solution, although the lines are a *bit* longer:

```
1  var flavors = document.querySelector('.flavors');
2
3  // add two new flavors
4  flavors.insertAdjacentHTML('beforeend', '<li>pistachio</li>')
5  flavors.insertAdjacentHTML('beforeend', '<li>neapolitan</li>')
```

In the preceding code, I'm using the insertAdjacentHTML method[11] present on the Element interface prototype. While this method has likely existed in browsers for many years, it was only first standardized in the W3C's DOM Parsing and Serialization specification,[12] drafted in 2014.

What about removing "gelato" from our list of types? In the newest available browsers, we have the *most* elegant solution:

```
1  // remove the "gelato" type
2  document.querySelector('.types li:last-child').remove();
```

The preceding code is very similar to the jQuery solution, with a couple noticeable differences. First, I am of course using querySelector to locate the element to remove. Second, I'm making use of the :last-child CSS3 pseudo-class[13] selector. The remove() method, present on the ChildNode interface, is relatively new and only supported in Microsoft Edge, Chrome, Firefox, and Safari 7. It is not supported by any versions of Internet Explorer, nor is it available on Apple iOS browsers. This method was first defined by the WHATWG as part of its DOM living standard[14] and in particular is our limiting factor in terms of browser support.

Luckily, we have a solution that covers *all* modern browsers, which requires only a little more code:

```
1  var gelato = document.querySelector('.types li:last-child');
2
3  // remove the "gelato" type
4  gelato.parentNode.removeChild(gelato);
```

I've replaced ChildNode.remove() with Node.removeChild(), which has existed since DOM Level 1 Core,[15] so it is supported in all browsers. To remove a child node, of course, we need to access the parent first. Luckily, it's really easy to do this, as you learned in Chapter 4. In this instance, the code that limits us to modern browsers is the :last-child CSS3 pseudo-class, which isn't available in Internet Explorer 8.

To support IE8, you'll have to replace the selector with document.querySelectorAll('.types li')[3]. And if you don't want to hard-code the index of the gelato element, you'll have to move the result of the querySelectorAll() into a variable and access the last element in the returned collection by examining this variable's length property.

---

[11]https://w3c.github.io/
DOM-Parsing/#widl-Element-insertAdjacentHTML-void-DOMString-position-DOMString-text
[12]https://w3c.github.io/DOM-Parsing/
[13]www.w3.org/TR/css3-selectors/#last-child-pseudo
[14]https://dom.spec.whatwg.org/#dom-childnode-remove
[15]www.w3.org/TR/REC-DOM-Level-1/level-one-core.html#method-removeChild

Text Content

There are two workflows to address in terms of element text: updating and parsing. Although jQuery provides one specific method to accomplish both tasks, the DOM API offers two—both with different behaviors that accommodate different needs. In this section, I demonstrate jQuery's `text()` method, the native `textContent` property, and the native `innerText` property. You'll see how each of these differ as we make changes to our document of ice cream types and flavors and then output the resulting document as text.

First, let's examine jQuery's `text()` method, which allows us to both read and update text in a document. Notice that one of our types—"Italian ice"—starts with a capital letter. None of the other types or flavors shares this trait. Even though "Italian" is a proper adjective and normally *should* start with a capital "I," let's modify it to be consistent with the case of the rest of our types and flavors:

```
1  $('.types li').eq(1).text('italian ice');
```

As you probably already know, the text of an element can be updated simply by passing the new text as a parameter of the `text()` method. This is exactly what I have done in order to normalize the case of this type of ice cream. What would our modified document look like if we output it using jQuery's `text()` method? Like this:

```
 1  "
 2      Types
 3
 4          frozen yogurt
 5          italian ice
 6          custard
 7          gelato
 8
 9
10      Flavors
11
12          chocolate
13          vanilla
14          rocky road
15          strawberry
16
17  "
```

The quotation marks have been added to show where the output starts and ends. They are not part of the actual text. Notice that this output reflects the structure of our *markup*. This can be verified by examining the indentation of the text as well as the line breaks at the end of the document. The series of line breaks before the output ends account for the empty "unassigned" list. You'll see how this output mirrors the output of one of the two native text manipulation properties offered by the DOM API.

There are two common properties available on the DOM elements used to read and update text: `textContent` and `innerText`. There are notable advantages and disadvantages of both properties, but their presence allows for more flexibility in dealing with text than jQuery's `text()` method alone. Next, I compare and contrast these two properties against each other and jQuery's `text()` method, and it will be clear when you should choose one over the other.

Let's first examine `textContent`, which was added to the Node interface in W3C's DOM Level 3 Core).[16] This property allows element text to be read and updated in *all* modern browsers. Changing the text of our "Italian ice" list item to "italian ice" is just as simple as jQuery's `text()` method:

```
1  document.querySelectorAll('.types li')[1].textContent = 'italian ice';
```

---

[16]www.w3.org/TR/DOM-Level-3-Core/core.html#Node3-textContent

The textContent property not only matches the behavior of jQuery's text() method when writing text, it also functions *exactly* like jQuery when *reading* text as well. Take our previous example where we outputted our entire ice cream document after modifying the "Italian ice" type. The output from the DOM API's textContent property matches that of jQuery's text() *exactly*:

```
 1   "
 2       Types
 3
 4           frozen yogurt
 5           italian ice
 6           custard
 7           gelato
 8
 9
10       Flavors
11
12           chocolate
13           vanilla
14           rocky road
15           strawberry
16
17   "
```

As you can see, textContent outputs the text inside an element *and* its descendants formatted with the structure of the document markup in mind, just like jQuery's text().

The second available property, innerText, is available on the HTMLElement interface, though it is a bit strange in that it is not yet part of any formal web specification. However, it is supported by all versions of all browsers, except for Firefox, which didn't add support until version 45.[17] Even though innerText is not yet standardized, there is a rudimentary draft proposal[18] in place, created by Robert O'Callahan of Mozilla.

Changing "Italian ice" to "italian ice" using innerText is not much different than textContent or jQuery's text(), with the exception of the *addition* of Internet Explorer 8 support and *lack* of Firefox support for versions older than 45:

```
1   document.querySelectorAll('.types li')[1].innerText = 'italian ice';
```

So what happens if we attempt to output our document using innerText? You'll see that the result looks a bit different than the result garnered from textContent and jQuery's text():

```
 1   "Types
 2
 3   frozen yogurt
 4   italian ice
 5   custard
 6   gelato
 7   Flavors
 8
 9   chocolate
10   vanilla
11   rocky road
12   strawberry"
```

---

[17]https://developer.mozilla.org/en-US/Firefox/Releases/45
[18]https://rocallahan.github.io/innerText-spec/index.html

Initially, the preceding output may look a bit odd, but it actually makes perfect sense if you understand what it represents. I'd like you to paste the markup from the modified document listed earlier into a browser, copy the rendered result to your system's clipboard, and then paste it into a text editor. You'll notice that the pasted text is formatted identically to the output listed here. As the draft specification describes, innerText "return(s) the 'rendered text' of an element."

I was asked once "When dealing with reading element text, is there a general solution for using web APIs that is supported in all browsers?" Well, that depends on your requirements. If the behavior of textContent is appropriate and you only need modern browser support, then that is probably your best choice. But there are certainly instances when innerText is more appropriate, as previously mentioned. jQuery's text() behaves like textContent, so, if you want to mirror the behavior of jQuery and need to support all modern browsers including older versions of Firefox, that is another reason to favor textContent.

Rich Content

HTML is nothing more than text formatted per conventions defined by a set of web specifications. This reality is useful when we need to serialize or deserialize a document or a *portion* of a document. Deserialization of HTML may occur when receiving server-generated markup in response to an HTTP request. In this instance, the HTML in the response must be inserted into the DOM in an appropriate location. I'll demonstrate this specific scenario and talk about how this may be completed with the help of several methods available in the DOM API. And perhaps this server-generated markup must be returned to the server and persisted for later use after it is modified in some way. That, too, can be accomplished with the DOM API, and you'll see how in this final section.

jQuery provides a grand total of *one* method for reading and writing HTML. This is accomplished using the aptly named html() function. First, let's assume we've already received a string of HTML from our server and we need to insert it into our document. Keeping with the theme of this chapter, this markup represents an entirely new section for our ice-cream store page. We simply need to insert it after the existing sections. The markup from our server is simply a long string of HTML, such as "<h2>Containers</h2><ul><li>cone</li><li>cup</li></ul>". This string of HTML will be stored in a variable named container. Here you can see how this should be inserted at the end of our document using jQuery:

```
1  $('<div>').html(container).appendTo('body');
```

First, we are creating a new <div>, which is disconnected from the DOM, then we're setting the contents of this disconnected <div> to the HTML from our server, and finally this element is added to the end of our ice cream store page. After modifying our page in various ways, we now want to send the markup back to our server, which can also be accomplished using jQuery's html() method:

```
1  var contents = $('body').html();
2  // ...send `contents` to server
```

The jQuery-less DOM API route is a bit less elegant, but still very simple and widely supported. In order to read and write the same markup, we'll use the innerHTML property defined on the Element interface. This property, while supported in every browser imaginable, has only recently achieved standardization. innerHTML started as a Microsoft Internet Explorer proprietary extension, but is now part of the W3C DOM Parsing and Serialization specification.[19]

We can use innerHTML to add the server-generated HTML to the end of our page:

```
1  var div = document.createElement('div');
2  div.innerHTML = container;
3  document.body.appendChild(div);
```

[19]www.w3.org/TR/DOM-Parsing/#widl-Element-innerHTML

The createElement method of the Document interface is courtesy of W3C's DOM Level 1 Core[20] specification, which means it is supported in *any* browser. Reading the markup of our document back for persistence server-side also uses innerHTML, and it's just as elegant as jQuery's html() method:

```
1  var contents = document.body.innerHTML;
2  // ...send `contents` to server
```

The DOM API is a bit more flexible than jQuery in this instance; it provides a few more options. For example, the standardized Element.outerHTML property will take the reference element into account when reading or updating HTML. Conversely, innerHTML is only concerned with the descendents of the reference element. Had I used outerHTML in the "add a string" demonstration above, everything in the document *including* the <body> element would have been replaced with the new <div>-wrapped ice cream containers section. In the last DOM API example, where we read back the contents of the document, the <body> element would have been included in the stringified-html had we used outerHTML instead. Depending on your requirements, this may be desirable.

Though I certainly haven't demonstrated *all* the properties and methods provided by the DOM API, the point I am trying to make is that the browser already provides more than enough in terms of reasonable and intuitive native support for DOM manipulation.

---

[20]www.w3.org/TR/REC-DOM-Level-1/level-one-core.html#method-createElement

CHAPTER 9

■ ■ ■

AJAX Requests: Dynamic Data and Page Updates

AJAX, or Asynchronous JavaScript and XML, is a feature provided by the web API that allows data to be updated or retrieved from a server without reloading the entire page. This capability was absent from the browser initially. The time without this feature marked the infancy of the web, and with it came along a less-than-ideal user experience that resulted in a fair amount of redundant bytes circulated between client and server. The inefficiency of this primitive model was compounded by the fact that Internet bandwidth was extremely limited by today's standards. Back in 1999 when Microsoft first introduced XMLHTTP as an ActiveX control in Internet Explorer 5.0,[1] about 95% of Internet users were limited by a 56 Kbps or slower dial-up connection.[2]

XMLHTTP was a proprietary JavaScript object implemented in Microsoft's Internet Explorer browser, and it represented a huge leap in both web development technology and user experience. It was the first full-featured built-in transport for focused client/server communication that allowed for updates without replacing the entire page. Previously, the entire page had to be reloaded even if only a small segment of the data on the page had changed. The initial API for this new transport matches its modern-day standardized cousin: XMLHttpRequest. Essentially, this object allows a developer to construct a new transport instance, send a GET, POST, PUT, PATCH, or DELETE request to any endpoint (on the same domain), and then programmatically retrieve the status and message body of the server's response. Although the aging XMLHttpRequest will eventually be replaced by the Fetch API,[3] it has thrived unopposed and mostly unchanged for about 15 years.

Mastering the Concepts of AJAX Communication

It is critical to understand a few key concepts when dealing with AJAX communication:

1. Asynchronous operations.

2. HyperText Transfer Protocol, also know as HTTP.

3. JSON, URL encoding, and multipart form encoding.

4. The Same Origin Policy.

The first two items will be dealt with directly in this section, in addition to an introduction to web sockets (which are not as important as some other concepts, but still potentially useful). The last two in the list will be addressed later on in this chapter.

---

[1]https://blogs.msdn.microsoft.com/ie/2006/01/23/native-xmlhttprequest-object/
[2]www.websiteoptimization.com/bw/0403/
[3]https://fetch.spec.whatwg.org

© Ray Nicholus 2016
R. Nicholus, *Beyond jQuery*, DOI 10.1007/978-1-4842-2235-5_9

Async Is Hard

Based on my extensive experience with AJAX communication, along with observations of other developers struggling with this piece of the web API, the most attractive attribute of this feature is also its most confusing. JavaScript does not abstract asynchronous operations nearly as well as other more traditional languages, such as Java. On top of the historical lack of intuitive native support for tasks that occur out of band (such as AJAX requests), there are currently three different common ways to account for these types of asynchronous operations. These methods include callbacks, promises, and asynchronous functions. Although native support for asynchronous operations has improved over time, most developers still must explicitly deal with these types of tasks, which can be challenging due to the fact that it often requires all surrounding code to be structured accordingly. That often makes the software developer's job of accounting for asynchronous calls awkward and the resulting code complex. This, of course, adds risk and potentially more bugs to the underlying application.

Callbacks will be demonstrated in this chapter, as will promises. Both promises and callbacks are covered in much more detail in Chapter 11, along with asynchronous functions, a feature defined in the ECMAScript 2017 specification that aims to make dealing with asynchronous operations, such as AJAX requests, surprisingly easy. However, some developers don't have the luxury of using async functions (due to lack of current browser support as of 2016), so the reality of dealing with AJAX requests remains that you must embrace their asynchronous nature instead of hiding from it. This is quite mind-bending, initially. Even after you have successfully grasped this concept, expect frequent frustration in less-than-trivial situations, such as when dealing with nested asynchronous requests. If this is not already clear through previous experience, you may even come to realize this complexity as you complete this chapter. Still, this concept is perhaps the most important of all to master when working with AJAX requests.

HTTP

The primary protocol used to communicate between a browser and a server is, of course, HTTP, which stands for HyperText Transfer Protocol. Tim Berners-Lee, the father of the Web, created the first official HTTP specification[4] in 1991. This first version was designed alongside HTML and the first web browser with one method: GET. When a page was requested by the browser, a GET request would be sent, and the server would respond with the HTML that makes up the requested page, which the web browser would then render. Before AJAX was introduced as a complementary specification, HTTP was mostly limited to this workflow.

Though HTTP started with just one method—GET—several more were added over time. Currently, HEAD, POST, PUT, DELETE, and PATCH are all part of the current specification, version 2, which is maintained by the Internet Engineering Task Force (IETF) as RFC 7540.[5] GET requests are expected to have an empty message body (request payload), with a response that describes the resource referenced in the request URI (Universal Resource Indicator). It is a "safe" method, such that no changes to the resource should be made server-side as a result of handling this request. HEAD is very similar to GET, except it returns an empty message body. However, HEAD is useful in that it includes a response header—Content-Length— with a value equal the the number of bytes that would be transferred had the request been GET instead. This is useful to, for example, check the size of a file without actually returning the entire file. HEAD, as you might expect, is also a "safe" method.

DELETE, PUT, POST, and PATCH are not safe, in that they are expected to possibly change the associated resource on the server. Of these four "unsafe" methods, two of them—PUT and DELETE—are considered to be *idempotent*, which means that they will always produce the same result even though they are called multiple times. PUT is commonly used to replace a resource, whereas DELETE is, obviously, used to remove a resource. PUT requests are expected to have a message body that describes the updated resource content, and DELETE is *not* expected to have a payload. POST differs from PUT in that it will create a new resource. Finally, PATCH,

---

[4] www.w3.org/Protocols/HTTP/AsImplemented.html
[5] https://httpwg.github.io/specs/rfc7540.html

a relatively new HTTP request method,[6] allows a resource to be modified in very specific ways. The message body of this request describes exactly how the resource should be modified. PATCH differs from the PUT method in that it does not entirely replace the referenced resource.

All AJAX requests will use one of these methods to communicate dynamically with a server. Note that new methods such as PATCH may not be supported in older browsers. Later in this chapter, I go into more detail regarding proper use of these methods, and how the AJAX request specification can be used with these methods to produce a highly dynamic web application.

Expected and Unexpected Responses

An understanding of the protocol used to communicate between client and server is a fundamentally important concept. Part of this is, of course, *sending* requests, but the *response* to these requests is equally important. Requests have headers and optionally a message-body (payload), whereas responses are made up of three parts: the response message-body, headers, and a status code. The status code is unique to responses and is usually accessible on the underlying transport instance (such as XMLHttpRequest or fetch). Status codes are usually three digits and can be generally classified based on the most significant digit. 200-level status codes are indicative of success, 300 is used for redirects, while 400- and 500-level statuses indicate some sort of error. These are all formally defined in great detail in RFC 2616.[7]

Just as it is important to handle code exceptions with a try/catch block, it is equally important to address exceptional AJAX responses. Although 200-level responses are often expected, or at least desired, you must also account for unexpected or undesired responses, such as 400- and 500-level, or even responses with a status of 0 (which may happen if the request is terminated due to a network error or the server returns a completely empty response). I have observed that simply ignoring exceptional conditions appears to be common, and this is not limited to handling of HTTP responses. In fact, I am guilty of this myself.

Web Sockets

Web sockets are a relatively new web API feature compared to traditional AJAX requests. They were first standardized in 2011 by the IETF (Internet Engineering Task Force) in RFC 6455[8] and are currently supported by all modern browsers, with the exception of Internet Explorer 9. Web sockets differ from pure HTTP requests in a number of ways, most notably their lifetime. Whereas HTTP requests are normally very short lived, web socket connections are meant to remain open for the life of the application instance or web page. A web socket connection starts as an HTTP request, which is required for the initial handshake. But after this handshake is complete, client and server are free to exchange data at will in whatever format they have agreed upon. This web socket protocol allows for true real-time communication between client and server. Although web sockets are not explored in more depth in this chapter, I felt it was useful to at least mention them, because they *do* account for another method of JavaScript-initiated asynchronous communication.

Sending GET, POST, DELETE, PUT, and PATCH Requests

jQuery provides first-class support for AJAX requests through the appropriately named ajax() method. Through this method, you can send AJAX requests of any type, but jQuery also provides aliases for some standardized HTTP request methods—such as get() and post()—which save you a few keystrokes. The web API provides two objects, XMLHttpRequest and fetch, to send asynchronous requests of any type from browser to server. XMLHttpRequest is supported in all browsers, but fetch is relatively new and not supported in all modern browsers, though a solid polyfill is available which provides support for all browsers.

---

[6]https://tools.ietf.org/html/rfc5789
[7]www.w3.org/Protocols/rfc2616/rfc2616-sec10.html#sec10
[8]https://tools.ietf.org/html/rfc6455

A simple GET request to a server endpoint using jQuery, with a trivial response handler, looks something like this:

```
1  $.get('/my/name').then(
2    function success(name) {
3      console.log('my name is ' + name);
4    },
5    function failure() {
6      console.error('Name request failed!');
7    }
8  );
```

■ **Note**   The console object is not available in Internet Explorer 9 and older unless the developer tools are open.

In the preceding code, we are sending a GET request to the "/my/name" server endpoint and expecting a plaintext response containing a name value, which we are then printing to the browser console. If the request fails (such as if the server returns an error status code), the failure function is invoked. In this case, I'm making use of the promise-like object (or "thenable") that jQuery's ajax() method and its aliases return. jQuery provides several ways to deal with responses, but I will focus specifically on the one demonstrated before. Chapter 11 talks more about promises, which are a standardized part of JavaScript.

The same request, sent without jQuery and usable in all browsers, involves a bit more typing but is certainly not too difficult:

```
1  var xhr = new XMLHttpRequest();
2  xhr.open('GET', '/my/name');
3  xhr.onload = function() {
4    if (xhr.status >= 400) {
5      console.error('Name request failed!');
6    }
7    else {
8      console.log('my name is ' + xhr.responseText);
9    }
10 };
11 xhr.onerror = function() {
12   console.error('Name request failed!');
13 };
14 xhr.send();
```

onload is called when the request completes and some response has been received. It *may* be an error response, though, so we must confirm by looking at the response status code. onerror is called if the request fails at some very low level, such as due to a CORS error. The onload property is where we can easily set our response handler. From here, we can be sure the response has completed and then can determine whether the request was successful and get a handle on the response data. All of this is available on the instance of XMLHttpRequest we created and assigned to the xhr variable. From the preceding code, you may be a bit disappointed that the web API doesn't support promises like jQuery. That *was* true, up until the fetch API[9] was created by the WHATWG. The Fetch API provides a modern native replacement for the aging XMLHttpRequest transport, and it is currently supported by Firefox, Chrome, Opera, and Microsoft Edge, with Safari support likely on the horizon. Let's look at this same example using fetch:

---

[9]https://fetch.spec.whatwg.org

```
1   fetch('/my/name').then(function(response) {
2     if (response.ok) {
3       return response.text();
4     }
5     else {
6       throw new Error();
7     }
8   }).then(
9     function success(name) {
10      console.log('my name is ' + name);
11    },
12    function failure() {
13      console.error('Name request failed!');
14    }
15  );
```

The code not only embraces the promises specification, it also removes a lot of the boilerplate commonly seen with XMLHttpRequest. You'll see more examples of fetch throughout this chapter. Note that any of the previous examples are identical for HEAD requests, with the exception of the method specifier. You'll also notice that fetch returns a Promise, similar to jQuery's ajax(). The difference is that jQuery executes the error function when a non-success status code is executed. fetch only does this, like XMLHttpRequest, when a low-level network error occurs. But we can trigger our error function when the server returns a response with an error code by throwing an exception if the response is not "ok", via the ok property on the Response object passed to our first promise handler.

Many developers who learned web development through a jQuery lens probably think that this library is doing something magical and complex when you invoke the $.ajax() method. That couldn't be further from the truth. All the heavy lifting is done by the browser via the XMLHttpRequest object. jQuery's ajax() is just a wrapper around XMLHttpRequest. Using the browser's built-in support for AJAX requests isn't very difficult, as you'll see in a moment. Even cross-origin requests are not only simple without jQuery—you'll see how they are actually *easier* without jQuery.

Sending POST Requests

I've demonstrated how to GET information from a server endpoint using jQuery, XMLHttpRequest, and fetch. But what about some of the other available HTTP methods? Instead of GETting a name, suppose you would like to add a new name to the server. The most appropriate method for this situation is POST. The name to add will be included in our request payload, which is a common place to include this sort of data when sending a POST. To keep it simple, we'll send the name using a MIME type of text/plain (I cover more advanced encoding techniques later in this chapter). I'll omit response handling code here as well so we can focus on the key concepts:

```
1   $.ajax({
2     method: 'POST',
3     url: '/user/name',
4     contentType: 'text/plain',
5     data: 'Mr. Ed'
6   });
```

We're using jQuery's generic ajax() method, so we can specify various parameters, such as the request's Content-Type header. This will send a POST request with a plaintext body containing the text "Mr. Ed". We must explicitly specify the Content-Type in this case because jQuery will otherwise set this header to "application/x-www-form-urlencoded", which is not what we want.

The same POST request using XMLHttpRequest looks like this:

```
1  var xhr = new XMLHttpRequest();
2  xhr.open('POST', '/user/name');
3  xhr.send('Mr. Ed');
```

Sending this request without jQuery actually takes *fewer* lines of code. By default, the Content-Type is set to "text/plain" by XMLHttpRequest in this case,[10] so we don't need to mess with any request headers. We can conveniently pass the body of our request as a parameter to the send method, as illustrated before.

If your goal is to embrace the latest and greatest web standards, you can try sending this POST using fetch instead:

```
1  fetch('/user/name', {
2    method: 'POST',
3    body: 'Mr. Ed'
4  });
```

Sending this request looks similar to jQuery, but without a lot of the boilerplate. Like XMLHttpRequest, fetch intelligently sets the request Content-Type based on the request payload (in some cases), so we do not need to specify this request header.[11]

Sending PUT Requests

Whereas POST requests are often used to create a new resource, PUT requests typically replace an existing one. For example, PUT would be more appropriate for replacing information about an existing product. The URI of the request identifies the resource to be replaced with the new information located in the body. To simply illustrate sending a PUT request using jQuery, XMLHttpRequest, and fetch, I'll demonstrate updating a mobile phone number for an existing user record:

```
1  $.ajax({
2    method: 'PUT',
3    url: '/user/1',
4    contentType: 'text/plain',
5    data: //complete user record including new mobile number
6  });
```

This PUT request using jQuery looks almost identical to the previously illustrated POST, with the exception of the method property. This user is identified by their ID, which happens to be 1. You likely won't be surprised to see that sending a PUT with XMLHttpRequest is similar to the previous example as well:

```
1  var xhr = new XMLHttpRequest();
2  xhr.open('PUT', '/user/1');
3  xhr.send(/* complete user record including new mobile number */);
```

The Fetch API, as expected, provides the most concise approach:

```
1  fetch('/user/1', {
2    method: 'PUT',
3    body: //complete user record including new mobile number
4  });
```

---

[10]www.w3.org/TR/XMLHttpRequest#dom-xmlhttprequest-send
[11]https://fetch.spec.whatwg.org/#body-mixin

Sending DELETE Requests

DELETE requests are similar to PUTs in that the resource to be acted upon is specified in the request URI. The main difference, even though this is not clearly mandated by RFC 7231,[12] DELETE requests typically do *not* contain a message body. The IETF document refers to the possibility that a message body may in fact cause problems for the requestor:[13]

> A payload within a DELETE request message has no defined semantics; sending a payload body on a DELETE request might cause some existing implementations to reject the request.

This means that the only safe way to specify parameters, apart from the resource to be acted upon, is to include them as query parameters in the request URI. Other than this exceptional case, DELETE requests are sent in the same manner as PUTs. And like a PUT request, DELETE requests are idempotent. Remember that an *idempotent* request is one that behaves the same regardless of the number of times it is called. It would be quite surprising if multiple calls to delete the same resource resulted in, for example, removal of a different resource.

A request to remove a resource, using jQuery, looks like this:

```
1  $.ajax('/user/1', {method: 'DELETE'});
```

And the same simple request, using XMLHttpRequest, can be achieved with only two extra lines of code:

```
1  var xhr = new XMLHttpRequest();
2  xhr.open('DELETE', '/user/1');
3  xhr.send();
```

Finally, we can send this DELETE request natively in many modern browsers using the ever-so-elegant Fetch API (or in any browser with a polyfill for fetch (maintained on GitHub))[14]

```
1  fetch('/user/1', {method: 'DELETE'});
```

Sending this request with fetch is just as simple as $.ajax(); we can easily write the entire thing in one line without losing readability.

Sending PATCH Requests

As mentioned earlier, PATCH requests are relatively new on the HTTP scene and are used to update a *portion* of an existing resource. Take our previous PUT request example, where we only want to update a user's mobile phone number, but have to include all other user data in our PUT request as well. For small records, that may be fine, but for records of substantial size, it may be a waste of bandwidth. One approach may be to define specific endpoints for each part of the user's data, or identify the data to be updated based on URI query parameters, but that just clutters up our API. For this situation, it is best to use PATCH requests instead.

Let's revisit the PUT example where we need to update an existing user's mobile number, this time with PATCH. A jQuery approach—using a simple plaintext-based key-value message body to indicate the property to change along with the new property value—would look like this:

```
1  $.ajax({
2    method: 'PATCH',
```

---

[12]https://tools.ietf.org/html/rfc7231
[13]https://tools.ietf.org/html/rfc7231#section-4.3.5
[14]https://github.com/github/fetch

```
3    url: '/user/1',
4    contentType: 'text/plain',
5    data: 'mobile: 555-5555'
6  });
```

■ **Note**   If your underlying model is JSON, it is more appropriate to send a JSON Patch Document instead.[15] But we haven't talked much about JSON yet. I cover that later in this chapter.

Remember that we can use any format we choose for the body of the PATCH request to specify the data to update, as long as client and server are in agreement. If we prefer to use XMLHttpRequest, the same request looks like this:

```
1  var xhr = new XMLHttpRequest();
2  xhr.open('PATCH', '/user/1');
3  xhr.send('mobile: 555-5555');
```

For the sake of completeness, I'll show you how to send the exact same request using the Fetch API as well:

```
1  fetch('/user/1', {
2    method: 'PATCH',
3    body: 'mobile: 555-5555'
4  });
```

Encoding Requests and Reading Encoded Responses

In the preceding section, I touched on the simplest of all encoding methods—text/plain—which is the Multipurpose Internet Mail Extension (MIME) for unformatted text that makes up an HTTP request or response. The simplicity of plain text is both a blessing and a curse. That is, it is easy to work with, but it's only appropriate for very small and simple cases. The lack of any standardized structure limits its expressiveness and usefulness. For more complex (and more common) requests, there are more appropriate encoding types. In this section, I discuss three other MIME types: "application/x-www-form-urlencoded", "application/json", and "multipart/form-data". At the end of this section, you will be not only familiar with these additional encoding methods, you will also be able to understand how to encode and decode messages without jQuery, especially when sending HTTP requests and parsing responses.

URL Encoding

URL encoding can take place in the request's URL or in the message body of the request/response. The MIME type of this encoding scheme is "application/x-www-form-urlencoded", and data consists of simple key/value pairs. Each key and value is separated by an equal sign (=), while each pair is separated by an ampersand (&). But the encoding algorithm is much more than this. Keys and values may be further encoded, depending on their character makeup. Non-ASCII characters, along with some reserved characters, are replaced with a percent character (%) followed by the hex value of the character's associated byte. This is further defined in the HTML forms section of the W3C HTML5 specification.[16] This description is arguably a bit over-simplistic, but it's appropriate and comprehensive enough for the purposes of this chapter. If you'd like to learn more about the encoding algorithm for this MIME type, please have a look at the spec, though it is a bit dry and may take a few reads to properly parse.

---

[15]https://tools.ietf.org/html/rfc6902
[16]www.w3.org/TR/html5/forms.html%23application/x-www-form-urlencoded-encoding-algorithm

For GET and DELETE requests, URL-encoded data should be included at the end of the URI, since these request methods typically should not include payloads. For all other requests, the body of the message is the most appropriate place for your URL-encoded data. In this case, the request or response must include a `Content-Type` header of "application/x-www-form-urlencoded"—the MIME type of the encoding scheme. URL-encoded messages are expected to be relatively small, especially when dealing with GET and DELETE requests due to real-world URI length restrictions in place on browsers and servers.[17] Although this encoding method is more elegant than text/plain, the lack of hierarchy means that these messages are also limited in their expressiveness to some degree. However, child properties *can* be tied to parent properties using brackets. For example, a "parent" key that has a value of a set of child key/value pairs—"child1" and "child2"—can be encoded as "parent[child1]=child1val&parent[child2]=child2val". In fact, this is what jQuery does when encoding a JavaScript object into a URL-encoded string.

jQuery's API provides a function that takes an object and turns it into a URL-encoded string: `$.param`. For example, if we wanted to encode a couple simple key/value pairs into a URL-encoded string, our code would look like this:

```
1  $.param({
2    key1: 'some value',
3    'key 2': 'another value'
4  });
```

That line would produce a string of "key1=some+value&key+2=another+value". The specification for the application/x-www-form-urlencoded MIME type *does* declare that spaces are reserved characters that should be converted to the "plus" character. However, in practice, the ASCII character code is also acceptable. So, the same couple of key/value pairs can *also* be expressed as "key1=some%20value&key%202=another%20value". You'll see an example of this when I cover URL encoding with the web API.

If we wanted to create a new user with three properties—name, address, and phone—we could send a POST request to our server with a URL-encoded request body containing the information for the new user. The request would look like this with jQuery:

```
1  $.ajax({
2    method: 'POST',
3    url: '/user',
4    data: {
5      name: 'Mr. Ed',
6      address: '1313 Mockingbird Lane',
7      phone: '555-555-5555'
8    }
9  });
```

jQuery does admittedly make this relatively intuitive, as it allows you to pass in a JavaScript object describing the new user. There is no need to use the `$.param` method. As mentioned earlier, jQuery's `$.ajax()` API method assumes a `Content-Type` of "application/x-www-form-urlencoded", and it encodes the value of your `data` property to automatically to match this assumption. You don't have to think about encoding or encoding types at all in this case.

Even though the web API *does* require you to be conscious of the encoding type *and* it requires you encode your data before sending the request, these tasks are not overly complicated. I've already showed you how jQuery allows you to encode a string of text to "application/x-www-form-urlencoded"—using `$.param()`—and you can accomplish the same without jQuery using the `encodeURI()` and `encodeURIComponent()` methods available on global namespace. These methods are defined in the ECMAScript specification and have been available since the ECMA-262 3rd edition specification,[18] completed in 1999.

---

[17]http://stackoverflow.com/questions/417142/
what-is-the-maximum-length-of-a-url-in-different-browsers
[18]http://www.ecma-international.org/publications/files/ECMA-ST-ARCH/ECMA-
262%2C3rdedition%2CDecember1999.pdf

Both encodeURI() and encodeURIComponent() perform the same general task—URL encode a string. But they each determine *which* parts of the string to encode a bit differently, so they are tied to specific use cases. encodeURI() is meant to be used for a complete URL, such as *or* a string of key-value pairs separated by an ampersand (&), such as "first=ray&last=nicholus". However, encodeURIComponent() is meant to only be used on a single value that needs to be URL encoded, such as "Ray Nicholus" or "Mr. Ed". If you use encodeURIComponent() to encode the full URL listed earlier in this paragraph, then the colon, forward slashes, question mark, and ampersand will all be URL encoded, which is probably not what you want (unless the entire URL is itself a query parameter).

Looking back at the simple URL-encoding example with jQuery a little while back in this section, we can encode the same data with the web API using encodeURI():

```
1  encodeURI('key1=some value&key 2=another value');
```

A couple things about the output of encodeURI, which produces "key1=some%20value&key%202 =another%20value". First, notice that, while jQuery replaced spaces with the plus sign (+), encodeURI() (and encodeURI-Component) replace spaces with "%20". This is perfectly valid, but a notable difference. Second, whereas jQuery allows you to express the data to be encoded as a JavaScript object, encodeURI() requires you separate the keys from the values with an equals sign (=) and the key/value pairs with an ampersand (&). Taking this a bit further, we can duplicate the same POST request we sent earlier that adds a new name, first using XMLHttpRequest:

```
1  var xhr = new XMLHttpRequest(),
2      data = encodeURI(
3        'name=Mr. Ed&address=1313 Mockingbird Lane&phone=555-555-5555');
4  xhr.open('POST', '/user');
5  xhr.setRequestHeader('Content-Type', 'application/x-www-form-urlencoded');
6  xhr.send(data);
```

Another notable difference between the XMLHTTPRequest route and jQuery's $.ajax() is that we must set the request header's Content-Type header as well. jQuery sets it for us by default, and it is necessary to let the server know how to decode the request data. Luckily, XMLHttpRequest provides a method for setting request headers—the aptly named setRequestHeader().

We can gain some of the same benefits seen previously with the Fetch API, but we still need to do our own encoding. No worries—that can be accomplished without much trouble:

```
1  var data =
2    encodeURI('name=Mr. Ed&address=1313 Mockingbird Lane&phone=555-555-5555');
3    fetch('/user', {
4    method: 'POST',
5    headers: {'Content-Type': 'application/x-www-form-urlencoded'},
6    body: data
7  });
```

Just as with XMLHttpRequest, the Content-Type header must also be specified here, since the default Content-Type for fetch-initiated requests with a String body is also "text/plain". But, again, the Fetch API allows AJAX requests to be constructed in a more elegant and condensed form, similar to the solution that jQuery has provided for some time now. Fetch is supported in Firefox, Chrome, Opera, and Edge, there is an open case to add support to Safari.[19] In the near future, XMLHttpRequest will be an artifact of history, and fetch, which rivals jQuery's AJAX support, will be the AJAX transport of choice.

---

[19]https://bugs.webkit.org/show_bug.cgi?id=151937

JSON Encoding

JavaScript Object Notation, better known as JSON, is considered to be a "data-interchange language" (as described on json.org). If this obscure description leaves you a bit puzzled, don't feel bad—it's not a particularly useful summary. Think of JSON as a JavaScript object turned into a string. There *is* a bit more to explain, but this is a reasonable high-level definition in my opinion. In web development, this is particularly useful if a browser-based client wants to easily send a JavaScript object to a server endpoint. The server can, in turn, respond to requests from this client, also supplying JSON in the response body, and the client can easily convert this into a JavaScript object to allow easy programmatic parsing and manipulation. Although "application/x-www-form-urlencoded" requires that data be expressed in a flat format (or denote parent/child relationships using non-standard bracket notation), "application/json" allows data to be expressed in a hierarchical format. A key can have many sub-keys, and those sub-keys can have child keys as well. In this sense, JSON is more more expressive than URL-encoded data, which itself is more expressive and structured than plain text.

In case you are not already familiar with this common data format, let's represent a single user in JSON:

```
1  {
2    "name": "Mr. Ed",
3    "address": "1313 Mockingbird Lane",
4    "phone": {
5      "home": "555-555-5555"
6      "mobile": "444-444-4444"
7    }
8  }
```

Notice that JSON gives us the power to easily express sub-keys, a feature that is lacking with plaintext and URL-encoded strings. Mr. Ed has two phone numbers, and with JSON we can elegantly associate both numbers with with a parent "phone" property. Extending our AJAX example from the previous section, let's add a new name record to our server using jQuery, this time with a JSON-encoded payload:

```
1  $.ajax({
2    method: 'POST',
3    url: '/user',
4    contentType: 'application/json',
5    data: JSON.stringify({
6      name: 'Mr. Ed',
7      address: '1313 Mockingbird Lane',
8      phone: {
9        home: '555-555-5555',
10       mobile: '444-444-4444'
11     }
12   });
13 });
```

Notice that our code is looking a bit uglier than the previous URL-encoded example. Two reasons for this, one being that we must explicitly specify the Content-Type header via a contentType property, an abstraction that isn't really much help. Second, we must leave the comfortable and familiar jQuery API to convert our JavaScript object into JSON. Since jQuery provides no API method to accomplish this (which is odd since it *does* provide a way to convert a JSON string to an object - $.parseJSON()), we must make use of the JSON object, which has been standardized as part of the ECMAScript specification. The JSON object provides a couple of methods for converting JSON strings to JavaScript objects and back again. It first appeared in the ECMAScript 5.1 specification,[20] which means it is supported in Node.js as well as all modern browsers, including Internet Explorer 8. The JSON.stringify() method, used in the earlier jQuery POST example, takes the user record, which is represented as a JavaScript object, and converts it into a proper JSON string. This is needed before we can send the record to our server.

If you'd like to send a GET request that receives JSON data, you can do that quite simply using getJSON:

```
1  $.getJSON('/user/1', function(user) {
2      // do something with this user JavaScript object
3  });
```

What about sending the previous POST request without jQuery? First, with XMLHttpRequest:

```
1  var xhr = new XMLHttpRequest(),
2      data = JSON.stringify({
3        name: 'Mr. Ed',
4        address: '1313 Mockingbird Lane',
5        phone: {
6          home: '555-555-5555',
7          mobile: '444-444-4444'
8        }
9      });
10 xhr.open('POST', '/user');
11 xhr.setRequestHeader('Content-Type', 'application/json');
12 xhr.send(data);
```

No surprises with XHR. This attempt looks very similar to the URL-encoded POST request we sent in the last section, with the exception of stringifying our JavaScript object and setting an appropriate Content-Type header. As you have already seen, we must address the same issues whether we are using jQuery or not.

But sending a JSON-encoded request is only half of the required knowledge. We must be prepared to receive and parse a JSON response too. That looks something like this with XMLHTTPRequest:

```
1  var xhr = new XMLHttpRequest();
2  xhr.open('GET', '/user/1');
3  xhr.onload = function() {
4    var user = JSON.parse(xhr.responseText);
5    // do something with this user JavaScript object
6  };
7  xhr.send();
```

Notice that we're sending a GET request for user data and expecting our server to return this record in a JSON-encoded string. In the preceding code we're leveraging the onload function, which will be called when the request completes. At that point, we can grab the response body via the responseText property on our XHR instance. To turn this into a proper JavaScript object, we must make use of the other method on the JSON object—parse(). In modern browsers (except Internet Explorer), receiving JSON data with XMLHttpRequest is even easier:

```
1  var xhr = new XMLHttpRequest();
2  xhr.open('GET', '/user/1');
3  xhr.onload = function() {
4    var user = xhr.response;
```

---

[20]www.ecma-international.org/ecma-262/5.1/#sec-15.12

```
5    // do something with this user JavaScript object
6  };
7  xhr.send();
```

The preceding example assumes that the server has included a Content-Type header of "application/json". This lets XMLHttpRequest know what to do with the response data. It ultimately converts it to a JavaScript object and makes the converted value available on the response property of our XMLHttpRequest instance.

Finally, we can use the Fetch API to add this new user record to our server, again using a JSON-encoded request:

```
1  fetch('/user', {
2    method: 'POST',
3    headers: {'Content-Type': 'application/json'},
4    body: JSON.stringify({
5      name: 'Mr. Ed',
6      address: '1313 Mockingbird Lane',
7      phone: {
8        home: '555-555-5555',
9        mobile: '444-444-4444'
10     }
11   });
12 });
```

This is unsurprising and straightforward, but what about receiving a JSON-encoded response from our server? Let's send a simply GET request using fetch for a user record, with the expectation that our server will respond with a user record encoded as a JSON string:

```
1  fetch('/user/1').then(function(request) {
2      return request.json();
3  }).then(function(userRecord) {
4      // do something with this user JavaScript object
5  });
```

The Fetch API provides our promissory callback with a Request object.[21] Since we are expecting JSON, we call the json() method on this object, which itself returns a Promise. Note that the json() method is actually defined on the Body interface.[22] The Request object implements the Body interface, so we have access to methods on both interfaces here. By returning that promise, we can chain another promissory handler and expect to receive the JavaScript object representation of the response payload as a parameter in our last success callback. Now we have our user record from the server. Pretty simple *and* elegant! Again, if promises are still a bit murky, don't worry—I cover them in great detail later in Chapter 11.

Interestingly, ECMAScript 2016 provides the ability to use an alternate syntax that makes the above (any many other code example) even more elegant. Below, I've re-written the preceding example using "arrow functions":

```
1  fetch('/user/1')
2    .then(request => request.json())
3    .then(userRecord => {
4      // do something with this userRecord object
5    });
```

---

[21]https://fetch.spec.whatwg.org/#request-class
[22]https://fetch.spec.whatwg.org/#body

Arrow functions are out of scope for this book, but I thought it would be nice to point this out to readers who were not already aware of this language feature. Note that not all browsers support arrow functions, so you'll likely need to use a build-time compiler that converts these to "traditional" functions. Some JavaScript compilers include TypeScript, Closure Compiler, Babel, and Bublè. Some of these are mentioned later in the book, such as in Chapter 11.

Multipart Encoding

Another common encoding scheme, usually associated with HTML form submissions, is multipart/- form-data, also known as *multipart encoding*. The algorithm for this method of passing data is formally defined by the IETF in RFC 2388.[23] The use of this algorithm in the context of HTML forms is further described by the W3C in the HTML specification.[24] Non-ASCII characters in a multipart/form-data message do *not* have to be escaped. Instead, each piece of the message is split into fields, and each field is housed inside of a multipart boundary. Boundaries are separated by unique IDs that are generated by the browser, and they are guaranteed to be unique among all other data in the request, as the browser analyzes the data in the request to ensure a conflicted ID is not generated. A field in a multipart encoded message is often an HTML <form> field. Each field is housed inside of its own multipart boundary. Inside of each boundary is a header, where metadata about the field lives (such as its name/key), along with a body (where the field *value* lives).

Consider the following form:

```
1   <form action="my/server" method="POST" enctype="multipart/form-data">
2     <label>First Name:
3       <input name="first">
4     </label>
5
6     <label>Last Name:
7       <input name="last">
8     </label>
9
10    <button>Submit</button>
11  </form>
```

When the submit button is hit, any entered data will be submitted to the server. Let's say the user enters "Ray" into the first text input, and "Nicholus" into the second text input. After hitting submit, the request body may look something like this:

```
1   ----------------------------16865367459864164462127721994
2   Content-Disposition: form-data; name="first"
3
4   Ray
5   ----------------------------16865367459864164462127721994
6   Content-Disposition: form-data; name="last"
7
8   Nicholus
9   ----------------------------16865367459864164462127721994--
```

---

[23]www.ietf.org/rfc/rfc2388.txt
[24]www.w3.org/TR/html5/forms.html#multipart-form-data

The server knows how to find each form field by looking for the unique ID marking each section in the request body. This ID is included by the browser in the Content-Type header, which in this case is "multipart/form-data; boundary=—————————16865367459864164621 27721994". Notice that the MIME type of the message body is separated by the multipart boundary ID with a semicolon.

But HTML form submissions are not the *only* instance where we might want to encode our request message using the multipart/form-data MIME type. Since this MIME type is trivial to implement in all server-side languages, it is probably a safe choice for transmitting key/value pairs from client to server. But, above all else, multipart encoding is perfect for mixing key/value pairs with binary data (such as files). I talk more about uploading files in the next section.

So how can we send a multipart encoded request using jQuery's $.ajax() method? As you'll see shortly, it's ugly, and the layer of abstraction that jQuery normally provides is incomplete in this case, as you must delegate directly to the web API anyway. Continuing with some of the previous examples, let's send a new user record to our server—a record consisting of a user's name, address, and phone number:

```
1  var formData = new FormData();
2  formData.append('name', 'Mr. Ed');
3  formData.append('address', '1313 Mockingbird Lane');
4  formData.append('phone', '555-555-5555');
5
6  $.ajax({
7    method: 'POST',
8    url: '/user',
9    contentType: false,
10   processData: false,
11   data: formData
12 });
```

To send a multipart encoded AJAX request, we must send a FormData object that contains our key/value pairs, and the browser takes care of the rest. There is no jQuery abstraction here; you must make use of the web API's FormData directly. Note that FormData isn't supported in Internet Explorer 9. This lack of abstraction is a hole in jQuery's blanket, though FormData is relatively intuitive and quite powerful. In fact, you can pass it a <form> element, and key/value pairs will be created for you, ready for asynchronous submission to your server. Mozilla Developer Network has a great writeup on FormData.[25] You should read it for more details.

The biggest problem with sending MPE requests with jQuery is the obscure options that must be set to make it work. processData: false? What does that even mean? Well, if you don't set this option, jQuery will attempt to turn FormData into a URL-encoded string. As for contentType: false, this is required to ensure that jQuery doesn't insert its own Content-Type header. Remember from the section introduction that the browser *must* specify the Content-Type for you as it includes a calculated multipart boundary ID used by the server to parse the request.

The same request with plain old XMLHttpRequest contains no surprises and, quite frankly, isn't any less intuitive than jQuery's solution:

```
1  var formData = new FormData(),
2      xhr = new XMLHttpRequest();
3
4  formData.append('name', 'Mr. Ed');
5  formData.append('address', '1313 Mockingbird Lane');
6  formData.append('phone', '555-555-5555');
7
8  xhr.open('POST', '/user');
9  xhr.send(formData);
```

---

[25]https://developer.mozilla.org/en-US/docs/Web/API/FormData

In fact, using XHR results in *less* code, and we don't have to include nonsensical options such as contentType: false and processData: false. As expected, the Fetch API is even simpler:

```
1  var formData = new FormData();
2  formData.append('name', 'Mr. Ed');
3  formData.append('address', '1313 Mockingbird Lane');
4  formData.append('phone', '555-555-5555');
5
6  fetch('/user', {
7    method: 'POST',
8    body: formData
9  });
```

See? If you can look *Beyond jQuery*, just a bit, you'll find that the web API is not always as scary as some make it out to be. In this case, jQuery's API suffers from inelegance.

Uploading and Manipulating Files

Asynchronous file uploading, a topic that I have quite a bit of experience with,[26] is yet another example of how jQuery can often fail to effectively wrap the web API and provide users with an experience that justifies use of the library. This is indeed a complex topic, and though I can't cover everything related to file uploads here, I'll be sure to explain the basics and show how files can be uploaded using jQuery, XMLHttpRequest, and fetch both in modern browsers *and* ancient browsers. In this specific and somewhat unusual case, note that Internet Explorer 9 is excluded from the definition of "modern browsers." The reason for this will become clear soon.

Uploading Files in Ancient Browsers

Before we get into uploading files in older browsers, let's define a very important term for this section: *browsing context*. A browsing context can be a window or an iframe, for example. So if we have a window, and an iframe inside of this window, we have two browsing contexts: the parent window and the child iframe.

The *only* way to upload files in ancient browsers, including Internet Explorer 9, is to include an <input type="file"> element inside of a <form> and submit this form. By default, the server's response to this form submit replaces the current browsing context. When working with a highly dynamic single-page web application, this is unacceptable. We need to be able to upload files in older browsers and still maintain total control over the current browsing context. Unfortunately, there is no way to prevent a form submit from replacing the current browsing context. But we can certainly create a child browsing context where we submit the form and then monitor this browsing context to determine when our file has been uploaded by listening for changes.

This approach can be implemented quite easily, simply by asking the form to target an <iframe> in the document. To determine when the file has finished uploading, attach an "onload" event handler to the <iframe>. To demonstrate this approach, we'll need to make a few assumptions in order to make this relatively painless. First, imagine our primary browsing context contains a fragment of markup that looks like this:

```
1  <form action="/upload"
2        method="POST"
3        enctype="multipart/form-data"
4        target="uploader">
5
```

---

[26]http://fineuploader.com

```
6    <input type="file" name="file">
7
8  </form>
9
10  <iframe name="uploader" style="display: none;"></iframe>
```

Notice that the enctype attribute is set to "multipart/form-data". You may remember from the previous section that a form with file input elements must generate a multipart encoded request in order to properly communicate the file bytes to the server.

Second assumption: we are given a function—upload()—that is called when the user selects a file via the file input element. I'm not going to cover this specific detail now, since we haven't yet covered event handling. I discuss events in Chapter 10.

Okay, so how do we make this happen with jQuery? Like this:

```
1  function upload() {
2    var $iframe = $('IFRAME'),
3        $form = $('FORM');
4
5    $iframe.on('load', function() {
6      alert('file uploaded!')
7    });
8
9    $form.submit();
10  }
```

We *could* have accomplished a lot more with JavaScript/jQuery here if we needed to, such as setting the target attribute. If we were working with nothing more than a single file input element, we could have also dynamically created the form and moved the file input inside of it as well. But none of that was necessary since our markup contained everything we needed already. How much work and complexity has jQuery saved us from here? Let's take a look at the non-jQuery version for a comparison:

```
1  function upload() {
2    var iframe = document.getElementsByTagName('IFRAME')[0],
3        form = document.getElementsByTagName('FORM')[0]
4
5    iframe.onload = function() {
6      alert('file uploaded!');
7    }
8
9    form.submit();
10  }
```

jQuery hasn't done much at all for us. The web API solution is almost identical to the initial jQuery code. In both cases, we must select the iframe and form, attach an onload handler that does something when the upload has completed, and the submit the form. In both cases, our primary browsing context/window remains untouched. The server's response is buried in our hidden <iframe>. Pretty neat!

Uploading Files in Modern Browsers

There is a much more modern way to upload files asynchronously, and this is possible in all modern browsers, with the exception of Internet Explorer 9. The ability to upload files via JavaScript is possible due to the File API,[27] *and* XMLHttpRequest Level 2 (a small and non-breaking update to the original specification in terms of API).[28] Both of these elements of the web API are standardized by W3C specifications. jQuery does *nothing* to make uploading files easier. The modern native APIs that bring file uploading the browser are elegant, easy to use, and powerful. jQuery doesn't do much to attempt to provide a layer of abstraction here, and actually makes file uploading a bit awkward.

A typical workflow involves the following steps:

1. User selects one or more files via a <input type="file" multiple> element. Note that the multiple Boolean attribute allows the user to select multiple files, provided that the browser supports this attribute.

2. JavaScript is used to specify a "change" event listener, which is called when the user selects one or more files.

3. When the "change" listener is invoked, grab the file or files from the <input type="file"> element. These are made available as File objects,[29] which extend the Blob interface.[30]

4. Upload the File objects using your AJAX transport of choice.

Because we haven't covered events yet, assume a function exists that, when called, signals that our user has selected one or more files on the <input type="file"> that we are monitoring. The goal is to upload these files. And to keep this example focused and simple, *also* assume that the user is only able to select *one* file. This means our <input type="file"> element will *not* include a multiple Boolean attribute. File uploading in modern browsers (except in IE9) with jQuery can be accomplished, given the environment I just described, like this:

```
1  function onFileInputChange() {
2    var file = $('INPUT[type="file"]')[0].files[0];
3
4    $.ajax({
5      method: 'POST',
6      url: '/uploads',
7      contentType: false,
8      processData: false,
9      data: file
10   });
11 }
```

The preceding code will send a POST request to an "/uploads" endpoint, and the request body will contain the bytes of the file our user selected. Again we must use the obscure contentType: false option to ensure that jQuery leaves the Content-Type header alone so that it may be set by the browser to reflect the MIME type of the file. Also, processData: false is needed to prevent jQuery from encoding the File object, which would destroy the file we are trying to upload. We also could have included the file in a FormData object and uploaded that instead. This becomes a better option if we need to upload multiple files in a single request, or if we want to easily include other form data alongside the file or files.

---

[27]www.w3.org/TR/FileAPI/
[28]www.w3.org/TR/XMLHttpRequest2/
[29]www.w3.org/TR/FileAPI/#dfn-file
[30]www.w3.org/TR/FileAPI/#dfn-Blob

Without jQuery, using XMLHttpRequest, file uploading is actually much simpler:

```
1  function onFileInputChange() {
2    var file = document.querySelector('INPUT[type="file"]').files[0],
3        xhr = new XMLHttpRequest();
4
5    xhr.open('POST', '/uploads');
6    xhr.send(file);
7  }
```

As with the jQuery example, we're grabbing the selected File from the file input's files property, which is included as part of the File API, and sending it to our endpoint by passing it into the send() method, which supports Blobs as of XMLHttpRequest level 2.

File uploading is also possible with the Fetch API. Let's take a look:

```
1  function onFileInputChange() {
2    var file = document.querySelector('INPUT[type="file"]').files[0];
3
4    fetch('/uploads', {
5      method: 'POST',
6      body: file
7    });
8  }
```

Reading and Creating Files

Generally speaking, developers comfortable with jQuery often attempt to solve *all* of their front-end development problems with jQuery. They sometimes fail to see the web beyond this library. When developers become dependent on this safety net, it can often lead to frustration when a problem is not addressable through jQuery. This is the oppressive magic I wrote about in Chapter 1. You just saw how jQuery, at best, provides almost no help when uploading files. Suppose you want to read a file, or even create a new one or modify an existing one to be sent to a server endpoint? This is an area where jQuery has absolutely zero coverage. For reading files, you must rely on the FileReader interface,[31] which is defined as part of the File API. Creation of "files" browser-side requires use of the Blob constructor.[32]

The simplest FileReader example, which is sufficient for demonstration purposes here, is to read a text file to the console. Suppose a user selected this text file via a <input type"file">, and the text File object is sent to a function for output. The code required to read this file and output it to the developer tools console would involve the following code:

```
1  function onTextFileSelected(file) {
2    var reader = new FileReader();
3
4    reader.onload = function() {
5      console.log(reader.result);
6    }
7
8    reader.readAsText(file);
9  }
```

---

[31]www.w3.org/TR/FileAPI/#dfn-filereader
[32]www.w3.org/TR/FileAPI/#dfn-Blob

No jQuery needed or even possible to read files. And why would you need it? Reading files is pretty easy. Suppose you want to take the same text file and then append some text to the end of the file before uploading it to your server? Surprisingly, this is pretty easy too:

```
1  function onTextFileSelected(file) {
2    var modifiedFile = new Blob([file, 'hi there!'], {type: 'text/plain'});
3    // ...send modifiedFile to uploader
4  }
```

The modifiedFile here is a copy of the selected file with the text "hi there!" added to the end. This was accomplished in a grand total of one line of code.

Cross-domain Communication: an Important Topic

As more and more logic is offloaded to the browser, it is becoming common for web applications to pull data from multiple APIs, some of which exist as part of third-party services. A great example of this is a web application (like Fine Uploader)[33] that uploads files directly to an Amazon Web Services (AWS) Simple Storage Service (S3) bucket. Server-to-server cross-domain requests are simple and without restrictions. But the same is not true for cross-domain requests initiated from the browser. For the developer who wants to develop a web application that sends files directly to S3 from the browser, an obstacle lies in the way: the same-origin policy.[34] This policy places restrictions on requests initiated by JavaScript. More specifically, requests made by XMLHttpRequest between domains are prohibited. For example, sending a request to https://api.github.com from https://mywebapp.com is prevented by the browser because of the same-origin policy. While this restriction is in place for added security, this seems like a major limiting factor. How can you make legitimate requests from domain A to domain B without funneling them through a server on domain A first? The next two sections cover two specific approaches to accomplish this.

The Early Days (JSONP)

The same-origin policy prevents scripts from initiating requests outside the domain of their current browsing context. Although this covers AJAX transports such as XMLHttpRequest, elements such as <a>, <img>, and <script> are *not* bound by the same-origin policy. JavaScript Object Notation with Padding, or JSONP, exploits one of these exceptions to allow scripts to make cross-origin GET requests.

If you're not familiar with JSONP, the name may be a bit misleading. There is actually no JSON involved here at all. It's a very common misconception that JSON must be returned from the server when the client initiates a JSONP call, but that's simply not true. Instead, the server returns a function invocation, which is *not* valid JSON.

JSONP is essentially just an ugly hack that exploits the fact that <script> tags that load content from a server are not bound by the same-origin policy. There need to be cooperation and an understanding of the convention by both client and server for this to work properly. You simply need to point the src attribute of a <script> tag at a JSONP-aware endpoint and include the name of an existing global function as a query parameter. The server must then construct a string representation that, when executed by the browser, will invoke the global function, passing in the requested data.

Exploiting this JSONP approach in jQuery is actually pretty easy. Say we want to get user information from a server on a different domain:

```
1  $.ajax('http://jsonp-aware-endpoint.com/user/1', {
2    jsonp: 'callback',
```

---

[33]http://fineuploader.com
[34]https://developer.mozilla.org/en-US/docs/Web/Security/Same-origin_policy

```
3    dataType: 'jsonp'
4  }).then(function(response) {
5    // handle user info from server
6  });
```

jQuery takes care of creating the `<script>` tag for us and also creates and tracks a global function. When the global function is called after the response from the server is received, jQuery passes that to our response handler mentioned earlier. This is actually a pretty nice abstraction. Completing the same task without jQuery is certainly possible, but not as nice:

```
1  window.myJsonpCallback = function(data) {
2    // handle user info from server
3  };
4
5  var scriptEl = document.createElement('script');
6  scriptEl.setAttribute('src',
7    'http://jsonp-aware-endpoint.com/user/1?callback=myJsonpCallback');
8  document.body.appendChild(scriptEl);
```

Now that you have this newfound knowledge, I suggest you forget it and avoid using JSONP altogether. It's proven to be a potential security issue.[35] Also, in modern browsers, CORS is a much better route. And you're in luck: CORS is featured in the next sub-section. This explanation of JSONP serves mostly as a history lesson and an illustration of how jQuery *was* quite useful and important before the modern evolution of web specifications.

Modern Times (CORS)

CORS, short for Cross Origin Resource Sharing, is the more modern way to send AJAX requests between domains from the browser. CORS is actually a fairly involved topic and very commonly misunderstood even by seasoned web developers. Although the W3C specification[36] can be hard to parse, Mozilla Developer Network has a great explanation.[37] I'm only going to touch on a few CORS concepts here, but the MDN article is useful if you'd like to have a more detailed understanding of this topic.

With a reasonable understanding of CORS, sending a cross-origin AJAX request via JavaScript is not particularly difficult in modern browsers. Unfortunately, the process is *not* as easy in Internet Explorer 8 and 9. Cross-origin AJAX requests are only possible via JSONP in IE7 and older, and you are restricted to GET requests in those browsers (because this is an inherent limitation of JSONP). In all non-JSONP cases, jQuery offers zero assistance.

For modern browsers, all the work is delegated to server code. The browser does everything necessary client-side for you. In the most basic case, your code for a cross-origin AJAX request in a modern browser is identical to a same-origin AJAX request when using jQuery's `ajax()` API method, or when directly using the web API's `XMLHttpRequest` transport, and even with the Fetch API. So, I won't bother showing that here.

CORS requests can be divided up into two distinct types: simple and non-simple. Simple requests consist of GET, HEAD, and POST requests, with a Content-Type of "text/plain" or "application/x-www-form-urlencoded". Non-standard headers, such as "X-" headers, are not allowed in "simple" requests. These CORS requests are sent by the browser with an `Origin` header that includes the sending domain. The server must acknowledge that requests from this origin are acceptable. If not, the request fails. Non-simple requests consists of PUT, PATCH, and DELETE requests, as well as other Content-Types, such as "application/json". Also, non-standard headers, as you just learned, will mark a CORS request as "non-simple." In fact, even a GET or POST request can be non-simple if it, for example, contains non-standard request headers.

---

[35]http://security.stackexchange.com/a/23439
[36]www.w3.org/TR/cors/
[37]https://developer.mozilla.org/en-US/docs/Web/HTTP/Access_control_CORS

A non-simple CORS request must be "preflighted" by the browser. A preflight is an OPTIONS request sent by the browser before the underlying request is sent. If the server properly acknowledges the preflight, the browser will then send the underlying/original request. Non-simple cross-origin requests, such as PUT or POST/GET requests with an X-header (for example) could not be sent from a browser pre-CORS specification. So, for these types of requests, the concept of preflighting was written into the specification to ensure servers do not receive these types of non-simple cross-origin browser-based requests without explicitly opting in. In other words, if you don't want to allow these types of requests, you don't have to make any changes to your server. The preflight request that the browser sends first will fail, and the browser will never send the underlying request.

It is also important to know that cookies are *not* sent by default with cross-origin AJAX requests. You must set the withCredentials flag on the XMLHttpRequest transport. For example:

```
1  $.ajax('http://someotherdomain.com', {
2    method: 'POST',
3    contentType: 'text/plain',
4    data: 'sometext',
5    beforeSend: function(xmlHttpRequest) {
6      xmlHttpRequest.withCredentials = true;
7    }
8  });
```

jQuery offers somewhat of a leaky abstraction here. We must set the withCredentials property on the underlying xmlHttpRequest that jQuery manages. This can also be accomplished by adding a withCredentials property with a value of true to an xhrFields settings object. This is mentioned in the ajax method documentation, but it may be difficult to locate unless you know exactly where to look. The web API route is familiar, and, as expected, we must set the withCredentials flag in order to ensure cookies are sent to our server endpoint:

```
1  var xhr = new XMLHttpRequest();
2  xhr.open('POST', 'http://someotherdomain.com');
3  xhr.withCredentials = true;
4  xhr.setRequestHeader('Content-Type', 'text/plain');
5  xhr.send('sometext');
```

The Fetch API makes sending credentials with cross-origin AJAX requests simpler:

```
1  fetch('http://someotherdomain.com', {
2    method: 'POST',
3    headers: {
4      'Content-Type': 'text/plain'
5    },
6    credentials: 'include'
7  });
```

The credentials option used there ensures that any credentials, such as cookies, are sent along with the CORS request. Note that even for same-origin requests, fetch does not send cookies to the server endpoint by default. For same-origin requests, you must include a credentials: 'same-origin' option to ensure fetch sends cookies with the request. The default value of the credentials option is "omit", which is why fetch does not send cookies with any request by default.

jQuery actually becomes a headache to deal with when we need to send a cross-domain AJAX request in IE8 or IE9. If you're using jQuery for this purpose, you are truly trying to fit a square peg into a round hole. To understand why jQuery is a poor fit for cross-origin requests in IE9 and IE8, it's important to consider a couple low-level points:

1. Cross-origin AJAX requests in IE8 and IE9 can only be sent using the IE-proprietary XDomainRequest transport. I'll save the rant for why this was such a huge mistake by the IE development team for another book. Regardless, XDomainRequest is a stripped-down version of XMLHttpRequest and it *must* be used when making cross-origin AJAX requests in IE8 and IE9. There are significant restrictions restrictions imposed on this transport,[38] such as an inability to send anything other than POST and GET requests, and the lack of API methods to set request headers or access response headers.

2. jQuery's ajax() method (and all associated aliases) are just wrappers for XMLHttpRequest. It has a hard dependency on XMLHttpRequest. I mentioned this earlier in the chapter, but it's useful to point it out here again, given the context.

So, you need to use XDomainRequest to send the cross-origin request in IE8/9, but jQuery.ajax() is hard-coded to use XMLHttpRequest. That's a problem, and resolving it in the context of jQuery is not easy. Luckily, for those dead-set on using jQuery for this type of call, there are a few plug-ins that will "fix" jQuery in this regard. Essentially, the plug-ins must override jQuery's AJAX request sending/handling logic via the $.ajaxTransport() method.

Instead of wrestling with jQuery when attempting to send cross-origin AJAX requests in older browsers, stick with the web API. The following code demonstrates a simple way to determine whether you need to use XDomainRequest instead of XMLHttpRequest (use only if needed):

```
1  if (new XMLHttpRequest().withCredentials === undefined) {
2      var xdr = new XDomainRequest();
3      xdr.open('POST', 'http://someotherdomain.com');
4      xdr.send('sometext');
5  }
```

The native web not only provides a reasonable API for initiating AJAX requests, both with XMLHttpRequest and even more so with fetch, it sometimes is even *more* intuitive than jQuery in this context, especially when sending some cross-origin AJAX requests.

---

[38]http://blogs.msdn.com/b/ieinternals/archive/2010/05/13/xdomainrequest-restrictions-limita-tions-and-workarounds.aspx

CHAPTER 10

■ ■ ■

Browser Events

Reacting to changes on a page is a big part of modern web application development. Although this has always been possible to *some* degree with anchor links and form submit buttons, the introduction of an events system made it possible to write code that adjusts to user input without the need to reload or changing the current page. You can probably see how this complements the ability to send AJAX requests as well. Since Internet Explorer version 4 (with the introduction of Microsoft's Trident layout engine) and Netscape Navigator version 2 (along with the first JavaScript implementation), it has been possible to listen for DOM events in order to provide a more dynamic user experience in the browser. The first implementation of this model was quite limited. But as the browser evolved via standardization, so did the events system. Today, we have a fairly elegant native API for listening to and triggering both standardized DOM events *and* custom events. You'll see throughout this chapter how you can make use of events in modern browsers to accomplish various tasks.

While the *modern* Web provides a powerful and intuitive set of methods for working with events, this was not always the case. This unfortunate point in history, along with lack of parity between Internet Explorer and the rest of the browsers in terms of the events API, made jQuery a great library for dealing with events across all popular browsers. In addition to normalizing events, jQuery also provides additional help through its support for event delegation and one-time event listener binding. jQuery is no longer needed to normalize significant event API implementation differences between browsers, but it still provides added convenience through extra-useful features. In this chapter, I also show you how to mirror the most important event-related jQuery features simply by relying on the native web API.

Throughout the following sections, you'll learn how to create, trigger, and listen for standard browser events *and* custom events. The jQuery method will be compared to the native web API approach, and you'll feel much more comfortable dealing with events yourself without using jQuery as a crutch. At the very least, even if you decide to continue using jQuery for event handling in your projects, this chapter will give you a comprehensive understanding of the event system provided by the browser. I will be focusing primarily on modern browsers in this chapter, but a section at the end will include some useful information that will help you understand how the events API worked in ancient browsers, and how this differs from the modern system.

How Do Events Work?

Before I cover *using* events to solve common problems, I think it's prudent to first outline how browser events "work." This event system follows the publish-subscribe pattern at a basic level, but there is much more to browser events than this. For starters, there are multiple classifications of browsers events. The two broadest categories are referred to as "custom" and "native" (by me).

"Native" browser events can be further assigned to sub-groups, such as mouse events, keyboard events, and touch events (to name a few). Apart from event types, browser events also have a unique attribute: the process by which they are dispersed to registered listeners. In fact, there are two distinct ways that a browser event can be broadcast across a page. Individual listeners can affect these events in various ways as well. In addition to event *types*, I also explain event *propagation* in this section. After completing this first section,

© Ray Nicholus 2016
R. Nicholus, *Beyond jQuery*, DOI 10.1007/978-1-4842-2235-5_10

133

you will have a good understanding of the core concepts surrounding browser events. This will allow you to effectively follow the subsequent sections that outline more specific uses of the events API.

Event Types: Custom and Native

To start off my comprehensive coverage of browser events, I'll now introduce you to the two high-level categories that all events fit into: "custom" and "native." *Native* events are those defined in one of the official web specifications, such as those maintained by WHATWG or W3C. A listing of most events can be found in the DOM Level 3 UI Events specification[1] maintained by the W3C. Please note that this is *not* an exhaustive list; it only contains a subset of the events available today. Some of the native events include "click", a mouse event triggered by the browser when a DOM element is activated via a pointing device or keyboard. Another common event is "load", which is fired when an <img>, document, window, or <iframe> (among others) has successfully loaded. There are quite a few other native events available. A good resource that provides a list of all currently available native DOM events can be seen on the Mozilla Developer Network events page.[2]

Custom events are, as you might expect, non-standard events that are created to be specific to a particular application or library. They can be created on-demand to support dynamic event-based workflows. For example, consider a file upload library that would like to fire an event whenever an file upload has started, and then another when the file upload is finished. Just after (or perhaps just before) the upload commences, the library might want to fire an "uploadStart" event, and then "uploadComplete" once the file is successfully on the server. It can even fire an "uploadError" event if a file upload ends prematurely. There really aren't any native events that provide the semantics needed for this situation, so custom events are the best solution. Luckily, the DOM API does provide a way to trigger custom events. Although triggering custom events has been a bit inelegant in some browsers without a polyfill, that is changing. More on that later.

A custom event created and triggered without jQuery can be observed and handled using jQuery's event API. However, there is an interesting limitation associated with jQuery when dealing with custom events, something you won't find anywhere in the jQuery documentation. A custom event created and triggered with jQuery's event API *cannot* be observed and handled without also using jQuery's event API. In other words, custom events created by jQuery are entirely proprietary and non-standard. The reason for this is actually quite simple. Although it is possible for jQuery to trigger all event handlers on a specific element for a native DOM event, it is *not* possible to do the same for custom events, nor is it possible to query a specific HTML element for its attached event listeners. For this reason, *jQuery* custom events are only usable by *jQuery* custom event handlers.

There is one object that ties custom and native events together. This central object is the Event object,[3] which is described in a specification curated by the W3C. Every DOM event, custom or native, is represented by an Event object, which itself has a number of properties and methods useful for identifying and controlling the event. For example, a type property makes the name of the custom or native event available. A "click" event has a type of 'click' on its corresponding Event object. That same Event object instance will also contain, among others, a stopPropagation() method, which can be called to prevent the click event from being further broadcasted to other listeners on the page.

Event Propagation: Bubbling vs. Capturing

In the early days of the Web, Netscape provided one way to disperse events throughout the DOM—event capturing—while Internet Explorer provided a contrasting process—event bubbling. Before standardization, browsers essentially made their own proprietary choices when implementing features, which is what led to these two divergent approaches. This all changed in 2000 when the W3C drafted the DOM Level 2 Events Specification.[4] This document describes an event model that includes both event capturing *and* bubbling.

---

[1]www.w3.org/TR/DOM-Level-3-Events
[2]https://developer.mozilla.org/en-US/docs/Web/Events
[3]www.w3.org/TR/uievents/#h-event-interfaces
[4]www.w3.org/TR/DOM-Level-2-Events/

All browsers that adhere to this specification follow this process of distributing events across the DOM. Currently, all modern browsers implement DOM Level 2 Events. Ancient browsers, which only support event bubbling, are covered at the end of this chapter.

In all modern browsers, per the DOM Level 2 Events spec, When a DOM event is created, the capturing phase begins. Assuming the event is not canceled at some point after it is triggered, it starts at window, followed by document, and propagates downwards, ending with the element that triggered the event. After the capturing phase is complete, the bubbling phase commences. Starting with this target element, the event "bubbles" up the DOM, hitting each ancestor, until the event is cancelled or until it hits window again.

If the description regarding the progress of an event is still a bit confusing, let me try to explain with a simple demonstration. Consider the following HTML document:

```
1   <!DOCTYPE html>
2   <html>
3   <head>
4     <title>event propagation demo</title>
5   </head>
6   <body>
7     <section>
8       <h1>nested divs</h1>
9       <div>one
10        <div>child of one
11          <div>child of child of one</div>
12        </div>
13      </div>
14    </section>
15  </body>
16  </html>
```

Suppose the <div>child of child of one</div> element is clicked. The click event takes the following path through the DOM:

Capturing Phase

1. window

2. document

3. <html>

4. <body>

5. <section>

6. <div>one

7. <div>child of one

8. <div>child of child of one

Bubbling Phase

9. <div>child of child of one

10. <div>child of one

135

11. `<div>one`

12. `<section>`

13. `<body>`

14. `<html>`

15. `document`

16. `window`

So, when is it appropriate to focus on the capturing phase instead of the bubbling phase, or vice versa? The most common choice is to intercept events in the bubbling phase. One reason for the overwhelming focus on the bubbling phase is due to historical reasons. Before Internet Explorer 9, this was the *only* phase available. This is no longer an obstacle with the advent of standardization and modern browsers. In addition to lack of support for capturing in ancient browsers, jQuery *also* lacks support for this phase. This is perhaps yet another reason why it is not particularly popular, and bubbling is the default choice. But there is no denying that the concept of event bubbling is more intuitive than capturing. Envisioning an event that moves up the DOM tree, starting with the element that created the event, seems to be a bit more sensible than an event that *ends* with the event that created it. In fact, capturing is rarely discussed when describing the browser event model. Attaching a handler to the event bubbling phase is also the default behavior when using the web API to listen for events.

Even though the event bubbling phase is often preferred, there *are* instances where capturing is the better (or only) choice. There appears to be a performance advantage to utilization of the capturing phase. Because event capturing occurs *before* bubbling, this seems to make sense. Basecamp, a web-based project-management application, has made use of event capturing to improve performance in their project,[5] for example. Another reason to make use of the capturing phase: event delegation for "focus"[6] and "blur"[7] events. Although these events do not bubble, handler delegation is possible by hooking into the capturing phase. I cover event delegation in detail later in this chapter.

Capturing can also be used to react to events that have been cancelled in the bubbling phase. There are a number of reasons to cancel an event—that is, to prevent it from reaching any subsequent event handlers. Events are almost always cancelled in the bubbling phase. I discuss this a bit more later in this chapter, but for now imagine a click event cancelled by a third-party library in your web application. If you still need access to this event in another handler, you can register a handler on an element in the capturing phase.

jQuery has made the unfortunate choice of artificially bubbling events. In other words, when an event is triggered via the library, it calculates the expected bubbling path and triggers handlers on each element in this path. jQuery does not make use of the native support for bubbling and capturing provided by the browser. This certainly adds complexity and bloat to the library and likely introduces performance consequences as well.

Creating and Firing DOM Events

To demonstrate firing DOM events with and without jQuery, let's use the following HTML fragment:

```
1  <div>
2    <button type="button">do something</button>
3  </div>
4
5  <form method="POST" action="/user">
```

---

[5]https://signalvnoise.com/posts/3137-using-event-capturing-to-improve-basecamp-page-load-times
[6]www.w3.org/TR/uievents/#event-type-focus
[7]www.w3.org/TR/uievents/#event-type-blur

```
6    <label>Enter user name:
7      <input name="user">
8    </label>
9    <button type="submit">submit</button>
10 </form>
```

Firing DOM Events with jQuery

jQuery's events API contains two methods that allow DOM events to be created and propagated throughout the DOM: `trigger` and `triggerHandler`. The `trigger` method is most commonly used. It allows an event to be created and propagated to all ancestors of the originating element via bubbling. Remember that jQuery artificially bubbles all events, and it does *not* support event capturing. The `triggerHandler` method differs from `trigger` in that it only executes event handlers on the element in which it is called; the event is *not* bubbled to ancestor elements. jQuery's `triggerHandler` is different from `trigger` in some other ways as well, but the definition I have provided is sufficient for this section.

In the next few listings, I use jQuery's `trigger` method to:

1. Submit the form in two ways.

2. Focus the text input.

3. Remove focus from the input element.

Listing 10-1. Triggering DOM Events: jQuery

```
1  // submits the form
2  $('FORM').trigger('submit');
3
4  // submits the form by clicking the button
5  $('BUTTON[type="submit"]').trigger('click');
6
7  // focuses the text input
8  $('INPUT').trigger('focus');
9
10 // removes focus from the text input
11 $('INPUT').trigger('blur');
```

To be fair, there is a second way to trigger the same events with jQuery, by using aliases for these events defined in the library's API.

Listing 10-2. Another Way of Triggering DOM Events: jQuery

```
1  // submits the form
2  $('FORM').submit();
3
4  // submits the form by clicking the button
5  $('BUTTON[type="submit"]').click();
6
7  // focuses the text input
8  $('INPUT').focus();
9
10 // removes focus from the text input
11 $('INPUT').blur();
```

What if we want to click the button that appears before the form, but we don't want to trigger any click handlers attached to ancestor elements? Suppose the parent `<div>` contains a click handler that we do not want to trigger in this instance. With jQuery, we can use `triggerHandler()` to accomplish this, as shown in Listing 10-3.

Listing 10-3. Triggering DOM Events without Bubbling: jQuery

```
1  // clicks the first button - the click event does not bubble
2  $('BUTTON[type="button"]').triggerHandler('click');
```

Web API DOM Events

There are two or three ways to trigger the same events just demonstrated *without* using jQuery. It's good to have choices (sometimes). Anyway, the easiest way to trigger the preceding events using the web API is to invoke corresponding native methods on the target elements. Listing 10-4 shows code that looks very similar to Listing 10-2.

Listing 10-4. Triggering DOM Events: Web API, All Modern Browsers, and Internet Explorer 8

```
1   // submits the form
2   document.querySelector('FORM').submit();
3
4   // submits the form by clicking the button
5   document.querySelector('BUTTON[type="submit"]').click();
6
7   // focuses the text input
8   document.querySelector('INPUT').focus();
9
10  // removes focus from the text input
11  document.querySelector('INPUT').blur();
```

The preceding code is only limited to IE8 and newer due to use of `querySelector()`, but this is far more than sufficient given the current year and state of browser support. The `click()`, `focus()`, and `blur()` methods are available on all DOM element objects that inherit from `HTMLElement`.[8] The `submit()` method is available to `<form>` elements only, as it is defined on the `HTMLFormElement` interface.[9] The "click" and "submit" events bubble when they are triggered with these methods. Per the W3C specification,[10] "blur" and "focus" events do *not* bubble, but they are available to event handlers that are coded to make use of the capturing phase.

The preceding events can also be created by using either the `Event()` constructor or the `createEvent()` method available on document.[11] The former is supported in all modern browsers, with the exception of any version of Internet Explorer. In the next code demonstration, I show you how to programmatically determine whether the `Event` constructor is supported and then fall back to the alternative path for triggering events. Perhaps you are wondering why you would even need to trigger events using an approach different from the simple one outlined here. If you want to alter the default behavior of an event in some way, construction of an `Event` object is required. For example, in order to mimic the behavior of jQuery's `triggerHandler()` method and prevent an event from bubbling, we must pass a specific configuration property to our "click" event when constructing it. You will see this at the end of Listing 10-5, which demonstrates a second approach to triggering events.

---

[8]www.w3.org/TR/html5/dom.html#htmlelement
[9]www.w3.org/TR/html5/forms.html#the-form-element
[10]www.w3.org/TR/DOM-Level-2-Events/
[11]www.w3.org/TR/DOM-Level-3-Events/#widl-DocumentEvent-createEvent

Listing 10-5. Triggering DOM Events without Bubbling: Web API, All Modern Browsers

```
1  var clickEvent;
2
3  // If the `Event` constructor function is not supported,
4  // fall back to `createEvent` method.
5  if (typeof Event === 'function') {
6    clickEvent = new Event('click', {bubbles: false});
7  }
8  else {
9      clickEvent = document.createEvent('Event');
10     clickEvent.initEvent('click', false, true);
11 }
12
13 document.querySelector('BUTTON[type="button"]')
14 .dispatchEvent(clickEvent);
```

In the listing, when we must fall back to initEvent(), the second parameter is bubbles, which must be set to false if we do *not* want the event to bubble. The third parameter, which is set to true, indicates that this event is indeed cancelable. In other words, any default browser actions associated with this event may be prevented using the preventDefault() method on the Event object. I'll explain canceling events a bit more later on in this chapter. The Event constructor provides a more elegant way to set this and other options using a set of object properties. Once Internet Explorer 11 is dead and buried, we can focus exclusively on the Event constructor and forget initEvent() ever existed. But until then, the preceding check will allow you to choose the proper path if you must construct an event with special configuration options.

Creating and Firing Custom Events

Remember that custom events are those that are not standardized as part of an accepted web specification, such as those maintained by the W3C and the WHATWG. Let's imagine a scenario where we are writing a third-party library that handles adding and removing items from a gallery of images. When our library is integrated into a larger application, we need to provide a simple way to notify any listeners when an item is added or removed by our library. In this case, our library will wrap the gallery of images so we can signal a removal or addition simply by triggering an event that can be observed by an ancestor element. There aren't any standardized DOM events that are appropriate here, so we'll need to create our own event, a *custom* event. The custom event associated with removing an image will be aptly named "image-removed", and will need to include the ID of the removed image.

jQuery Custom Events

Let's first fire this event using jQuery. We'll assume that we already have a handle on an element controlled by our library. Our event will be triggered by this particular element:

```
1  // Triggers a custom "image-removed" element,
2  // which bubbles up to ancestor elements.
3  $libraryElement.trigger('image-removed', {id: 1});
```

This looks identical to the code used to trigger native DOM events, and it is. jQuery has a simple, elegant, and consistent API for triggering events of all types. But there is a problem here—the code that listens for this event, outside of our jQuery library, *must* also use jQuery to observe this event. This is a limitation of jQuery's custom event system. It matters little if the user of our library is using some other library or even if the user does not want to use jQuery outside of this library. Perhaps it is not clear to our user that jQuery *must* be used to listen for this event. They are forced to rely on jQuery and jQuery alone to accept messages from our library.

Firing Custom Events with the Web API

Triggering custom events with the web API is exactly like triggering native DOM events. The difference here is with *creating* custom events, although the process and API are still quite similar.

```
1  var event = new CustomEvent('image-removed', {
2    bubbles: true,
3    detail: {id: 1}
4  });
5  libraryElement.dispatchEvent(event);
```

Here, we can easily create our custom event, trigger it, and ensure it bubbles up to ancestor elements. So, our "image-removed" event is observable outside of our library. We've also passed the image ID in the detail property of the event payload. More on accessing this data later on. But there's a problem here: this will *not* work in any version of Internet Explorer. Unfortunately, as I mentioned in the last section, Explorer does not support the Event constructor. So, we must fall back to the following approach for cross-browser support:

```
1  var event = document.createEvent('CustomEvent');
2  event.initCustomEvent('image-removed', false, true, {id: 1});
3  libraryElement.dispatchEvent(event);
```

Instead of creating an 'Event,' as we did when attempting to trigger a native DOM event in Internet Explorer in the previous section, we must instead create a 'CustomEvent.' This exposes an initCustomEvent() method, which is defined on the CustomEvent interface. This special method allows us to pass custom data along with this event, such as our image ID.

The preceding code currently (as of mid-2016) works in all modern browsers, but this *may* change in the future once the CustomEvent constructor is supported in all browsers. It *may* be removed from any future browser version. To make our code future proof and still ensure it works in Internet Explorer, we need to use the check for the existence of the CustomEvent constructor, just as we did with the Event constructor in the previous section:

```
1  var event;
2
3  // If the `CustomEvent` constructor function is not supported,
4  // fall back to `createEvent` method.
5  if (typeof CustomEvent === 'function') {
6    event = new CustomEvent('image-removed', {
7      bubbles: true,
8      detail: {id: 1}
9    });
10  }
11  else {
12    event = document.createEvent('CustomEvent');
13    event.initCustomEvent('image-removed', false, true, {
14      id: 1
15    });
16  }
17
18  libraryElement.dispatchEvent(event);
```

After Internet Explorer fades into obsolesce and Microsoft Edge takes its place, you can use the `CustomEvent` constructor exclusively, and the preceding code will no longer be needed at all.

Listening (and Un-listening) to Event Notifications

Triggering events is *one* important part of passing messages around the DOM, but these events provide more value with corresponding listeners. In this section, I cover handling DOM and custom events. You may already be familiar with the process of registering event observers with jQuery, but I'll demonstrate how this is done first so that the differences are apparent when relying exclusively on the web API.

A `window` resize event handler may be important to make adjustments to a complex application as the view of your page is changed by the user. This "resize" event, which is triggered on the `window` when the browser is resized by the user, will provide us with a good way to demonstrate registering and unregistering event listeners.

jQuery Event Handlers

jQuery's on API method provides everything necessary to observe both DOM and custom events triggered on an element:

```
1  $(window).on('resize', function() {
2    // react to new window size
3  });
```

If, at some point in the future, we no longer care about the size of the window, we can remove this handler using jQuery's appropriately named `off` handler, but that is less straightforward than adding a new listener. We have two options:

1. Remove *all* resize event listeners (easy).

2. Remove only our resize event listener (a bit harder).

Let's look at option 1 first:

```
1  // remove all resize listeners - usually a bad idea
2  $(window).off('resize');
```

The first option is quite simple, but we run the risk of causing problems for other code on the page that still relies on window resize events. In other words, option 1 is usually a poor choice. That leaves us with option 2, which requires that we store a reference to our handler function and provide that to jQuery so it can unbind only our listener. So, we will need to rewrite our event listener call from before such that we can easily unregister our listener later:

```
1  var resizeHandler = function() {
2    // react to new window size
3  };
4
5  $(window).on('resize', resizeHandler);
6
7  // ...later
8  // remove only our resize handler
9  $(window).off('resize', resizeHandler);
```

Binding an event listener to a specific element and then removing it later when it is no longer needed is usually sufficient, but we may have a situation where an event handler is only ever needed once. After it is first executed, it can and should be removed. Perhaps we have an element that, once clicked, changes state in such a way that subsequent clicks are not prudent. jQuery provides a one API method for such cases:

```
1  $(someElement).one('click', function() {
2    // handle click event
3  });
```

After the attached handler function is executed, the click event will no longer be observed.

Observing Events with the Web API

Since the beginning of time (almost), there have been two simple ways to attach an event handler to a specific DOM element, and both can be considered "inline." The first, shown in Listing 10-6, involves including the event handler function as the value of an attribute of the element in the document markup:

Listing 10-6. Inline Event Handler: Web API, All Browsers

```
1  <button onclick="handleButtonClick()">click me</button>
```

There are a couple problems with this approach. First, it requires a global handleButtonClick() function. If you have a number of buttons or other elements that require specific click handler functions, you will end with a cluttered and messy global namespace. Global variables and functions should always be limited to prevent conflicts and uncontrolled access to internal logic. This type of inline event handler is a step in the wrong direction for that reason.

A second reason why this is bad: it requires mixing your JavaScript and HTML in the same file. Generally speaking, that is discouraged because it goes against the principle of separation of concerns. That is, content belongs in HTML files, and behavior belongs in JavaScript files. This isolates the code such that changes are potentially less risky, and caching is improved as changes to JavaScript do not invalidate the markup files, and vice versa.

Another way to register for the same click event requires attaching a handler function to the element's corresponding event property:

```
1  buttonEl.onclick = function() {
2    // handle button click
3  };
```

Although this approach is slightly better than the HTML-based event handler, since we are not forced to bind to a global function, it is still a non-optimal solution. You cannot specify an attribute-based event handler *and* an element property handler for the same event on the same element. The last specified handler will effectively remove any other inline event handler on the element for a given event type. In fact, only one total inline event handler may be specified for a given event on a given element. This is likely a big issue for modern web applications, as it is quite common for multiple uncoordinated modules to exist on the same page. Perhaps more than one of these modules needs to attach an event handler of the same type to the same element. With inline event handlers, this simply is not possible.

Since Internet Explorer 9, an addEventListener() method has been available on the EventTarget interface. All Element objects implement this interface, as does Window (among other DOM objects). The EventTarget interface first appeared in the W3C DOM Level 2 Events specification,[12] and the addEventListener() method was part of this initial version of the interface. Registering for custom and

---

[12]www.w3.org/TR/DOM-Level-2-Events/

DOM events is possible with this method, and the syntax is very similar to jQuery's on() method. Continuing with the button example:

```
1  buttonEl.addEventListener('click', function() {
2    // handle button click
3  });
```

This solution does not suffer from any of the issues that plague inline event handlers. There is no required binding to global functions. You may attach as many different click handlers to this button element as you like. The handler is attached purely with JavaScript, so it may exist exclusively in a JavaScript file. In the previous section, I reminded you how a "resize" event was bound to the window with jQuery. The same handler using the modern web API looks like this:

```
1  window.addEventListener('resize', function() {
2    // react to new window size
3  });
```

This looks a *lot* like our example of binding to the same event with jQuery, with the exception of a longer event binding method (on() versus addEventListener()). You may be glad to know that an appropriately named web API method exists to un-bind our handler, should we need to do this at some point. The EventTarget interface also defines a removeEventListener() method. The removeEventListener() method differs from jQuery's off in one notable way: there is no way to remove *all* event listeners of a given type from a particular element. Perhaps this is a good thing. So, in order to remove our window "resize" handler, we must structure our code like so:

```
1  var resizeHandler = function() {
2    // react to new window size
3  };
4
5  window.addEventListener('resize', resizeHandler);
6
7  // ...later
8  // remove only our resize handler
9  window.removeEventListener('resize', resizeHandler);
```

Remember the one-time click handler we created with jQuery's one API method? Does something similar exist in the web API? Good news: yes! Bad news: It's a fairly new addition (added to the WHATWG's DOM living standard (https://dom.spec.whatwg.org/#interface-eventtarget). As of mid-2016, only Firefox offers support, but it's an exciting feature:

```
1  someElement.addEventListener('click', function(event) {
2    // handle click event
3  }, { once: true });
```

For better cross-browser support, especially since there isn't any elegant way to programmatically determine support for listener options, use this instead:

```
1  var clickHandler = function() {
2    // handle click event
3    // ...then unregister handler
4    someElement.removeEventListener('click', clickHandler);
5  };
6  someElement.addEventListener('click', clickHandler);
```

After the attached handler function is executed, the click event will no longer be observed, just like jQuery's one() method. There *are* more elegant ways to solve this problem, but this solution makes use of only what you have learned so far in this book. You may discover a more elegant method after completing this book, especially after reading about JavaScript utilities.

Controlling Event Propagation

I've showed you how to fire and observe events in the last couple sections, but sometimes you need to do more than just create or listen for events. Occasionally, you need to either influence the bubbling/capturing phase or even attach data to an event in order to make it available to subsequent listeners.

As a contrived example (but possibly realistic in a very twisted web application piloted by project managers who have no understanding of the web), suppose you were asked to prevent users from selecting any text or images on an entire page. How can you accomplish that? Perhaps by interfering with some mouse event, somehow. But which event, and how? Perhaps the event to concentrate on is "click". If this was your first guess, you were close, but not quite correct.

According to the W3C DOM Level 3 Events specification, the "mousedown" event[13] starts a drag or text selection operation as its *default* action. So, we must prevent the *default* action of a "mousedown" event. We can prevent text and image selection/dragging across the entire page using jQuery *or* the pure web API by simply registering a "mousedown" event listener on window and calling the preventDefault() method on the Event object that is passed to our handler once our handler is executed:

```
1  $(window).on('mousedown', function(event) {
2    event.preventDefault();
3  });
4
5  // ...or...
6  $(window).mousedown(function(event) {
7    event.preventDefault();
8  });
```

preventing a default event action - web API - modern browsers

```
1  window.addEventListener('mousedown', function(event) {
2    event.preventDefault();
3  });
```

The jQuery approach is almost identical to the one that only relies on the native web API. Either way, we've satisfied the requirements: no text or images can be selected or dragged on our page.

This is probably a good time to start discussing the Event object. Earlier, an Event instance is passed to our event handler function when it is executed by jQuery or the browser. The native Event interface is defined in the W3C DOM4 specification.[14] When a custom or native DOM event is created, the browser creates an instance of Event and passes it to each registered listener during the capturing and bubbling phases.

The event object passed to each listener contains a number of properties that, for instance, describe the associated event, such as:

- The event type (click, mousedown, focus)
- The element that created the event

---

[13]www.w3.org/TR/DOM-Level-3-Events/#event-type-mousedown
[14]www.w3.org/TR/dom/#interface-event

- The current event phase (capturing or bubbling)

- The current element in the bubbling or capturing phase

There are other, similar properties, but that list represents a good sampling of the more notable ones. In addition to properties that describe the event, there are also a number of methods that allow the event to be controlled. One such method is preventDefault(), as I just demonstrated. But there are others, which I will cover shortly.

jQuery has its own version of the Event interface (of course).[15] According to jQuery's docs, their event object "normalizes the event object according to W3C standards." This was potentially useful for ancient browsers. But for modern browsers, not so much. For the most part, with the exception of a few properties and methods, the two interfaces are very similar.

The next two examples demonstrate how to prevent a specific event from reaching other registered event handlers. In order to prevent a click event from reaching any event handler on subsequent DOM nodes, simply call stopPropagation() on the passed Event object. This method exists in both the jQuery Event interface *and* the standardized web API Event interface:

```
1  $someElement.click(function(event) {
2      event.stopPropagation();
3  });
4
5  // ...or...
6
7  $someElement.on('click', function(event) {
8      event.stopPropagation();
9  });
```

Using jQuery, you can stop an event from bubbling with stopPropagation(), but you *cannot* stop the event during the capturing phase, unless of course you defer to the web API, as shown in Listing 10-7.

Listing 10-7. Stop a Click Event from Propagating: Web API, Modern Browsers

```
1  // stop propagation during capturing phase
2  someElement.addEventListener('click', function(event) {
3      event.stopPropagation();
4  }, true);
5
6  // stop propagation during bubbling phase
7  someElement.addEventListener('click', function(event) {
8      event.stopPropagation();
9  });
```

The web API is capable of stopping event propagation in either the capturing *or* the bubbling phase. But stopPropagation() does not stop the event from reaching any subsequent listeners on the *same* element. For this task, the stopImmediatePropagation() event method is available, which stops the event from reaching any further handlers, whether they are registered on the current DOM node or subsequent nodes. Again, jQuery (Listing 10-8) and the web API (Listing 10-9) share the same method name, but jQuery is restricted to the bubbling phase, as always.

---

[15]https://api.jquery.com/category/events/event-object/

Listing 10-8. Stop a Click Event from Reaching Any Other Handlers: jQuery

```
1  $someElement.on('click', function(event) {
2      event.stopImmediatePropagation();
3  });
```

Listing 10-9. Stop a Click Event from Reaching Any Other Handlers: Web API, Modern Browsers

```
1  someElement.addEventListener('click', function(event) {
2      event.stopImmediatePropagation();
3  });
```

Note that both jQuery and the web API offer a shortcut to prevent an event's default action *and* to prevent the event from reaching handlers on subsequent DOM nodes. You can effectively call both event.preventDefault() and event.stopPropagation() by returning false in your event handler.

Passing Data to Event Handlers

Sometimes the standard data associated with an event is not enough. Event handlers may need more specific information about the event they are handling. Remember the "uploadError" custom event I detailed earlier? This is triggered from a library embedded on a page, and the "uploadError" event exists to provide information to listeners outside of the library about a failed file upload. Suppose the file upload library we are using is attached to a container element, and our application wraps this container element and registers an "uploadError" event handler. When a particular file upload fails, this event is triggered, and our handler displays an informational message to the user. In order to customize this message, we need the name of the failed file. The upload library can pass the file's name to our handler in the Event object.

First, let's review how data is passed to event handlers with jQuery:

```
1  // send the failed filename w/ an error event
2  $uploaderElement.trigger('uploadError', {
3    filename: 'picture.jpeg'
4  });
5
6  // ...and this is a listener for the event
7  $uploaderParent.on('uploadError', function(event, data) {
8    showAlert('Failed to upload ' + data.filename);
9  });
```

jQuery makes the object passed to the trigger() function available to any event listeners via a second parameter passed to the handler. With this, we can access any properties on the passed object.

To achieve the same result with the web API, we would make use of CustomElement and its built-in ability to handle data:

```
1  // send the failed filename w/ an error event
2  var event = new CustomEvent('uploadError', {
3    bubbles: true,
4    detail: {filename: 'picture.jpeg'}
5  });
6  uploaderElement.dispatchEvent(event);
7
8  // ...and this is a listener for the event
```

```
9   uploaderParent.addEventListener('uploadError', function(event) {
10    showAlert('Failed to upload ' + event.detail.filename);
11  });
```

This is not as succinct as the jQuery solution, but it works, at least in all modern browsers other than IE. For a more cross-browser solution, you can rely on the old custom event API, as demonstrated earlier. I'll focus only on the old API in the following demonstration, but I encourage you to read about a more future-proof method of creating CustomEvent instances covered earlier:

```
1   // send the failed filename w/ an error event
2   var event = document.createEvent('CustomEvent');
3   event.initCustomEvent('uploadError', true, true, {
4     filename: 'picture.jpeg'
5   });
6   uploaderElement.dispatchEvent(event);
7
8   // ...and this is a listener for the event
9   uploaderParent.addEventListener('uploadError', function(event) {
10    showAlert('Failed to upload ' + event.detail.filename);
11  });
```

In both cases, the data attached to the CustomEvent is available to our listeners via a standardized detail property.[16] With the CustomEvent constructor, this data is provided on a detail property of the object passed when creating a new instance. The detail property on this object matches the detail property on the CustomEvent object available to our listeners, which is nice and consistent. Our listeners still have access to this same detail property when setting up our "uploadError" event using the old event creation API, but it is buried in a sea of parameters passed to initCustomEvent(). In my experience, anything more than two parameters is confusing and non-intuitive. This is not an uncommon preference, which may explain why the more modern CustomEvent constructor only mandates two parameters, the second being an object where all custom even configuration and data is provided.

Event Delegation: Powerful and Underused

There have been multiple occasions where I have danced around and entirely avoided a very important topic: event delegation. Simply put, *event delegation* involves attaching a single event handler to a top-level element with the intention of handling events that bubble up from descendant elements. The event handler logic in this top-level element may contain code paths that differ based on the event target element (the element that first received the event). But why do this? Why not simply attach specific event handlers directly to the appropriate elements?

One reason that has been discussed ad nauseam is potential performance benefits of delegated event handlers. CPU cycles are saved by binding a single event handler that is responsible for monitoring events on many descendant elements, as opposed to querying each element and attaching a dedicated handler function to each element directly. This theory makes a lot of sense, and of course it's true. But how much time in terms of CPU cycles is really saved here? I suppose the answer to that question is: it depends. It depends on how many elements you intend to monitor, for one.

---

[16]https://dom.spec.whatwg.org/#dom-customevent-detail

It's hard to imagine a common scenario where delegated event handling is both desirable and detrimental to performance. The practice has caught on, partially for the expected performance reasons, and also due to the ability to centralize event handling code to one specific root element instead of spreading it out across the DOM. Take React, for example. React is a JavaScript library that focuses specifically on the "view" portion of a typical Model View Controller web application. In terms of event handling, React has implemented an interesting abstraction:[17]

> React doesn't actually attach event handlers to the nodes themselves. When React starts up, it starts listening for all events at the top level using a single event listener.

In other words, all event handlers attached to elements with React are promoted to a single delegated event handler on a common parent element. Perhaps you still don't see an instance where delegated event handlers are appropriate. In the rest of this section, I focus on a simple example that demonstrates the power of event delegation.

Suppose you have a list filled with list items, each with a button that removes an item from the list. You *could* attach a click handler to each individual list item's button. But doesn't it seem like the wrong approach to loop over all of the button elements and attach the very same click handler function to each? You may argue that this is not unreasonable, and even easy to accomplish. But what if new items can be added to this list dynamically after the initial page load? Now attaching a new event handler to each new list item, after it is added, becomes less appealing.

The best solution here is to use event delegation. In other words, attach one click handler to the list element. When any of the delete buttons inside of the list item elements is clicked, the event will bubble up to the list element. At this point, your one event handler will be hit, and you can easily determine, by inspecting the event object, which list item was clicked and respond appropriately by removing the associated list item. In this section, we're using some text to make our delete buttons more accessible, as well as close/remove icons from the Ionicons site[18] to enhance the appearance of our buttons.

The HTML for such a list may look something like this:

```
1  <link href="http://code.ionicframework.com/ionicons/2.0.1/css/ionicons.min.css"
2        rel="stylesheet">
3  <ul id="cars-list">
4      <li>Honda
5          <button>
6              <span>delete</span>
7              <span class="ion-close-circled"></span>
8          </button>
9      </li>
10     <li>Toyota
11         <button>
12             <span>delete</span>
13             <span class="ion-close-circled"></span>
14         </button>
15     </li>
16     <li>Kia
17         <button>
18             <span>delete</span>
19             <span class="ion-close-circled"></span>
```

[17]https://facebook.github.io/react/docs/interactivity-and-dynamic-uis.html#under-the-hood-autobinding-and-event-delegation
[18]http://ionicons.com

```
20        </button>
21      </li>
22      <li>Ford
23        <button>
24          <span>delete</span>
25          <span class="ion-close-circled"></span>
26        </button>
27      </li>
28  </ul>
```

With jQuery, we can use the click alias to attach a click handler to the <ul> and delete the appropriate car list item by inspecting the event object:

```
1  $('#cars-list').on('click', 'button', function() {
2       $(this).closest('li').remove();
3  });
```

But wait, we didn't have to examine the event object at all! jQuery provides a nice feature here by setting the event handler function's context (this) to the click element target. Note that this click event might target the "delete" span element *or* the "x" icon, depending upon which of these elements is selected by our user. In either case, we are *only* interested in clicks on the <button> or its children. jQuery ensures that our event handler will only be called if this is true, and at that point we can use jQuery's closest() method to find the associated <li> and remove it from the DOM, as shown in Listing 10-10.

Listing 10-10. Delegated Event Handling: Web API, All Modern Browsers (with closest Shim)

```
1  document.querySelector('#cars-list')
2    .addEventListener('click', function(event) {
3      if (event.target.closest('BUTTON')) {
4        var li = event.target.closest('LI');
5        li.parentElement.removeChild(li);
6      }
7    });
```

The above pure web API solution is a bit more verbose than jQuery's API (ok, it's a *lot* more verbose). But it shows how to accomplish a few common goals *without* jQuery:

1. Attach a click event handler to an element.

2. Examine an Event object to focus on events triggered only by one of our <button> elements.

3. Remove the <li> associated with the clicked delete button.

We're making use of Element.closest here to easily find the parent <li> and determine if the event target's parent is indeed a <button>, all without explicitly dealing with the fact that the event target may be multiple levels beneath the <button> or <li>. Since Element.closest is not supported in Internet Explorer, Microsoft Edge (at least, as of version 13), or older versions of iOS Safari and Android, you'll need to make use of the shim demonstrated in Chapter 4 if you require solid cross-browser support.

This may all seem a bit inelegant compared to jQuery, and that may indeed be true. But remember, the mission of this book isn't necessarily about compelling you to eschew jQuery or any other library, but rather to show you how to solve the same problems by yourself *without* the aid of third-party dependencies. The knowledge gained from these exercises and demonstrations will empower you as a web developer by offering insight into the web API and allow you to make better decisions when deciding if your project will benefit from some outside help. And perhaps you will elect to pull in small and focused shims (such as the `Element.closest` polyfill demonstrated earlier) instead of depending on a large library like jQuery.

Handling and Triggering Keyboard Events

Keyboard events are, as you might expect, native DOM events triggered by the browser when a user presses a key on their keyboard. Just like all other events, keyboard events go through both a capturing and a bubbling phase. The target element is the one that is focused when the key is pressed. You may be wondering why I have dedicated a special section exclusively to keyboard events. As you'll see shortly, key events are a bit different than the other DOM and custom events discussed earlier. Plus, keyboard events *can* be a bit trickier to handle than the other DOM events.

This is mostly due to mostly misunderstood multiple keyboard event types *and* the confusing array of event properties used to identify keys with varying browser support. Fear not—after this section, you'll have a pretty good understanding of keyboard events. You'll fully comprehend when to use the three types of keyboard events, how to identify the pressed key, and even how to put this knowledge to use to solve real problems.

Three Types of Keyboard Events

Each key on your keyboard is *not* a separate event type. Instead, a keyboard-triggered action is attached to one of three possible keyboard-specific event types:

1. keydown

2. keyup

3. keypress

The browser triggers a "keydown" event before a pushed key is released. It may fire repeatedly if the key is held down, and is triggered for *any* key on the keyboard (even Shift/Ctrl/Command/other). Though some keys will *not* trigger multiple "keydown" events when held, such as Shift/Command/Option/Function. jQuery provides a keydown alias in its API to handle these events:

```
1  $(document).keydown(function(event) {
2    // do something with this event
3  });
```

And the same event can be handled (for the web API and modern browsers) without jQuery using trusty old `addEventListener()`:

```
1  document.addEventListener('keydown', function(event) {
2    // do something with this event
3  });
```

After a key (any key) in the down position is released, the browser fires a "keyup" event. The logic for handling this event is identical to "keydown"—just replace "keydown" with "keyup" in the code samples just given. In fact, the same is true for the "keypress" event, which is the the final keyboard event type. The "keypress" event is *very* similar to "keydown"—it is also triggered when a pressed key is in the down position. The only difference is that "keypress" events are only fired for printable characters. For example, pressing the "a," "Enter," or "1" keys will trigger a "keypress" event. Conversely, "Shift," "Command," and the arrow keys will *not* result in a "keypress" event.

Identifying Pressed Keys

Suppose we are building a modal dialog. If a user of our dialog presses the "Esc" key, we would like to close the dialog. In order to accomplish this, we need to do a few things:

1. Listen for "keydown" events on the document.

2. Determine if the "keydown" event corresponds to the "Esc" key.

3. If the "keydown" event *is* the result of pressing "Esc," close the modal dialog.

If we are using jQuery, our code will look something like this:

```
1 $(document).keydown(function(event) {
2   if (event.which === 27) {
3     // close the dialog...
4   }
5 });
```

The number 27 corresponds to the ESC key's key code.[19] We can make use of the same key code without jQuery (for the web API and modern browsers) by also looking at the which property on the KeyboardEvent that our handler receives:

```
1 document.addEventListener('keydown', function(event) {
2   if (event.which === 27) {
3     // close the dialog...
4   }
5 });
```

But the web API is beginning to advance beyond jQuery in this respect. The UI Events Specification,[20] maintained by the W3C, defines a *new* property on KeyboardEvent: key.[21] When a key is pressed, the KeyboardEvent (in supported browsers) will contain a key property with a value that corresponds to the exact key pressed (for printable characters) *or* a standardized string that describes the pressed key (for non-printable characters). For example, if the "a" key is pressed, the key property on the corresponding KeyboardEvent will contain a value of "a". In our case, the Esc key is represented as the string "Escape". This value, along with the key values for other non-printable characters, are defined in the DOM Level 3 Events specification,[22] also maintained by W3C. If we are able to use this key property, our code will look like Listing 10-11.

Listing 10-11. Closing a Modal Dialog on Esc: Web API, All Modern Browsers Except Safari

```
1 document.addEventListener('keydown', function(event) {
2   if (event.key === 'Escape') {
3     // close the dialog...
4   }
5 });
```

---

[19]https://lists.w3.org/Archives/Public/www-dom/2010JulSep/att-0182/keyCode-spec.
html#fixed-virtual-key-codes
[20]www.w3.org/TR/uievents/
[21]www.w3.org/TR/uievents/#widl-KeyboardEvent-key
[22]www.w3.org/TR/DOM-Level-3-Events-key/

At the moment, Safari is the *only* modern browser *without* support for this KeyboardEvent property. This will likely change as the WebKit engine evolves. In the meantime, you may want to consider sticking with the which property until Safari is brought up-to-date.

Making an Image Carousel Keyboard Accessible with the Web API

One important benefit of mastering keyboard events: accessibility. An accessible web application is one that can be easily used by those with varying requirements. Perhaps the most common accessibility consideration involves ensuring that those without the ability to use a pointing device can completely and effectively navigate the web application. This requires, in some cases, listening for keyboard events and responding appropriately.

Suppose you are building an image carousel library. An array of image URLs is passed to the carousel, the first image rendered in a full-screen modal dialog, and the user can move to the next or previous image by clicking buttons on either side of the current image. Making it possible to cycle through the images with the keyboard allows those without the ability to use a pointing device to use the carousel. It also adds convenience to the carousel for those who simply don't *want* to use a mouse or trackpad.

Just to keep this simple, let's say our image gallery HTML template looks like this:

```
1  <div class="image-gallery">
2    <button class="previous" type="button">Previous</button>
3    <img>
4    <button class="next" type="button">Next</button>
5  </div>
```

And JavaScript to cycle through the images when a button is clicked looks like this (for modern browsers):

```
1  // assuming we have an array of images in an `images` var
2  var currentImageIndex = 0;
3  var container = document.querySelector('.image-gallery');
4  var updateImg = function() {
5    container.querySelector('IMG').src =
6      images[currentImageIndex];
7  };
8  var moveToPreviousImage = function() {
9    if (currentImageIndex === 0) {
10     currentImageIndex = images.length - 1;
11   }
12   else {
13     currentImageIndex--;
14   }
15   updateImg();
16 };
17 var moveToNextImage = function() {
18   if (currentImageIndex === images.length - 1) {
19     currentImageIndex = 0;
20   }
21   else {
22     currentImageIndex++;
23   }
24   updateImg();
25 };
26
```

```
27  updateImg();
28
29  container.querySelector('.previous')
30    .addEventListener('click', function() {
31      moveToPreviousImage();
32    });
33
34  container.querySelector('.next')
35    .addEventListener('click', function() {
36      moveToNextImage();
37    });
```

If we want to allow our users to move though the set of images with the left and right arrow keys, we can attach keyboard event handlers to the left and right arrows and delegate to the existing moveToPreviousImage() and moveToNextImage() functions as appropriate:

```
1   // add this after the block of code above:
2   document.addEventListener('keydown', function(event) {
3     // left arrow
4     if (event.which === 37) {
5       event.preventDefault();
6       moveToPreviousImage();
7     }
8     // right arrow
9     else if (event.which === 39) {
10      event.preventDefault();
11      moveToNextImage();
12    }
13  });
```

The addition of event.preventDefault() ensures that our arrow keys *only* change the image in this context instead of providing any undesired default actions, such as scrolling the page. In our example, it's not clear when our carousel is no longer in use, but we would likely provide some mechanism to close the carousel. Once the carousel is closed, don't forget to use removeEventListener() to unregister the keydown event handler. You'll need to refactor the event listener code such that the logic is moved into a standalone function. This will make it easy to unregister the keydown handler by passing removeEventListener() the 'keydown' event type as the first parameter, and the event listener function variable as the second. For more information on using removeEventListener(), check out the earlier section on observing events.

Determining When Something Has Loaded

The following questions may occur to you as a web developer at one point or another:

- When have all elements on the page fully loaded and rendered with applied styles?

- When has all static markup been placed on the page?

- When has a particular element on the page fully loaded? When has an element failed to load?

153

The answer to all of these questions lies in the browser's native event system. The "load" event,[23] defined in the W3C UI Events specification, allows us to determine when an element or page has loaded. There are some other related events, such as "DOMContentLoaded" and "beforeunload". I discuss both of those as well in this section.

When Have All Elements on the Page Fully Loaded and Rendered with Applied Styles?

To answer this particular question, we can rely on the "load" event fired by the window object. This event will be fired after:

1. All markup has been placed on the page.

2. All style sheets have been loaded.

3. All <img> elements have loaded.

4. All <iframe> elements have fully loaded.

jQuery provides an alias for the "load" event, similar to many other DOM events:

```
1  $(window).load(function() {
2    // page is fully rendered
3  });
```

But you can (and should) use the generic on() method instead and pass in the name of the event - "load" - especially since the load() alias is deprecated and was subsequently removed in jQuery 3.0. Here's the same listener without the deprecated alias:

```
1  $(window).on('load', function() {
2    // page is fully rendered
3  });
```

The web API solution looks almost exactly like the preceding jQuery code. We're making using of addEventListener(), which is available to all modern browsers, and passing the name of the event followed by a callback to be invoked when the page has been loaded:

```
1  window.addEventListener('load', function() {
2    // page is fully rendered
3  });
```

But why might we care about this event? Why is it important to know when the page has entirely loaded? The most common understanding of the load event is that it should be used to determine when it is safe to perform DOM manipulation. This is technically true, but waiting for the "load" event is probably unnecessary. Do you really need to ensure all images, style sheets, and iframes have loaded before operating on the document? Probably not.

---

[23]www.w3.org/TR/uievents/#event-type-load

When Has All Static Markup Been Placed on the Page?

Another question we can ask here: when is the earliest point at which I can safely operate on the DOM? The answer to this and the question in this heading here is the same: wait for the browser to fire the "DOMContentLoaded" event. This event fires after all markup has been placed on the page, which means it often occurs much sooner than "load".

jQuery provides a "ready" function that mirrors the behavior of the native "DOMContentLoaded". But under the covers, it delegates to "DOMContentLoaded" itself in modern browsers. Here's how you have been determining when a page is ready for interaction with jQuery:

```
1  $(document).ready(function() {
2    // markup is on the page
3  });
```

You may even be familiar with the shorthand version:

```
1  $(function() {
2    // markup is on the page
3  });
```

Because jQuery just makes use of the browser's native "DOMContentLoaded" event in modern browsers to feed its ready API method, we can build our own ready using "DOMContentLoaded" with addEventListener():

```
1  document.addEventListener('DOMContentLoaded', function() {
2    // markup is on the page
3  });
```

Note that you will likely want to ensure your script that registers the "DOMContentLoaded" event handler is placed before any style sheet <link> tags, since loading these style sheets will block any script execution and prolong the "DOMContentLoaded" event until the defined style sheets have completely loaded.

When Has a Particular Element on the Page Fully Loaded? When Has It Failed to Load?

In addition to window, load events are associated with a number of elements, such as <img>, <link>, and <script>. The most common use of this event outside of window is to determine when a specific image has loaded. The appropriately named "error" event is used to signal a failure to load an image (or a <link> or <script>, for example).

jQuery, as you might expect, has aliases in its API for the "load" and "error" events, but these are both deprecated and were subsequently removed from the library in jQuery 3.0. So to determine if an image has loaded, or has failed to load with jQuery, we should simply rely on the on() method. And our code would look something like this:

```
1  $('IMG').on('load', function() {
2    // image has successfully loaded
3  });
4
5  $('IMG').on('error', function() {
6    // image has failed to load
7  });
```

155

There is a one-to-one mapping between the event names used in jQuery and those used in the browser's native event system. As you might expect, jQuery relies on the browser's "load" and "error" events to signal success and failure, respectively. So, the same end can be reached without jQuery by registering for these events with addEventListener():

```
1  document.querySelector('IMG').addEventListener('load', function() {
2    // image has successfully loaded
3  });
4
5  document.querySelector('IMG').addEventListener('error', function() {
6    // image has failed to load
7  });
```

As we've seen many times before, the syntax between jQuery and the web API here for modern browsers is strikingly similar.

Preventing a User from Accidentally Leaving the Current Page

Imagine yourself as a user (we can't always be the developer). You're filling out a (long) series of form fields. It takes ten minutes to complete the form, but you're finally done. And . . . then . . . you . . . accidentally . . . close . . . the browser tab. All your work is gone! Replace "filling out a form" with "writing a document" or "drawing a picture." Regardless of the situation, it's a tragic turn of events. As a developer, how can you save your users from this mistake? Can you? You can!

The "beforeunload" event is fired on the window just before the current page is unloaded. By observing this event, you can force the user to confirm that they really to want to leave the current page, or close the browser, or reload the page. They will be presented with a confirm dialog, and if they select Cancel, they will remain safely on the current page.

In jQuery-land, you can observe this event using the on API method and return a message for the user to be displayed in the confirm dialog:

```
1  $(window).on('beforeunload', function() {
2    return 'Are you sure you want to unload the page?';
3  });
```

Note that not every browser will display this specific message. Some will always display a hard-coded message, and there is nothing that jQuery can do about this.

The web API approach is similar, but we must deal with a small difference in implementation of this event between various browsers:

```
1  window.addEventListener('beforeunload', function(event) {
2    var message = 'Are you sure you want to unload the page?';
3    event.returnValue = message;
4    return message;
5  });
```

Some browsers accept the return value of the handler function as the text to display to the user, whereas others take a more non-standard approach and require this message be set on the event's returnValue property. Still, this isn't much of a hoop to jump through. It's pretty simple either way.

A History Lesson: Ancient Browser Support

This final section in the events chapter is where I describe a time when jQuery *was* a required library for web applications. This section applies to ancient browsers only. Back when it was common to support Internet Explorer 8, the web API was a bit of a mess in *some* instances. This was especially true when dealing with the browser's event system. In this section, I discuss how you can manage, observe, and fire events in ancient browsers. Because ancient browsers are becoming less important to worry about, all of this serves as more of a history lesson than a tutorial. Please keep that in mind when reading this section, as it is not intended to be a comprehensive guide to event handling in super-old browsers.

The API for Listening to Events Is Non-standard

Take a look at the following code snippet that registers for a click event:

```
1  someElement.attachEvent('onclick', function() {
2    // do something with the click event...
3  });
```

You'll notice two distinct differences between this and the modern browser approach:

1. We are relying on attachEvent instead of addEventListener.

2. The click event name includes a prefix of "on".

The attachEvent() method[24] is proprietary to Microsoft's Internet Explorer. In fact, it is still technically supported up until (and including) Internet Explorer 10. attachEvent() was never part of any official standard. Unless you must support IE8 and older, avoid using attachEvent() entirely. The W3C standardized addEventListener() provides a more elegant and comprehensive solution for observing events.

Perhaps you're wondering how you can programmatically use the correct event-handling method based on the current browser's capabilities. If you're developing apps exclusively for modern browsers, this isn't a concern. But if, for some reason, you must target ancient browsers such as IE8 (or older), you can use the following code to register for an event in *any* browser:

```
1  function registerHandler(target, type, callback) {
2    var listenerMethod = target.addEventListener
3          || target.attachEvent,
4
5        eventName = target.addEventListener
6          ? type
7          : 'on' + type;
8
9    listenerMethod(eventName, callback);
10 }
11
12 // example use
13 registerHandler(someElement, 'click', function() {
14   // do something with the click event...
15 });
```

---

[24]https://msdn.microsoft.com/en-us/library/ms536343(VS.85).aspx

And if you want to *remove* an event handler in an ancient browser, you must use detachEvent() instead of removeEventListener(). detachEvent() is another non-standard proprietary web API method. If you're looking for a cross-browser way to remove an event listener, try this out:

```
1  function unregisterHandler(target, type, callback) {
2    var removeMethod = target.removeEventListener
3         || target.detachEvent,
4
5        eventName = target.removeEventListener
6          ? type
7          : 'on' + type;
8
9    removeMethod(eventName, callback);
10 }
11
12 // example use
13 unregisterHandler(someElement, 'click', someEventHandlerFunction);
```

Form Field Change Events Are a Minefield

Very old versions of Internet Explorer have some serious change-event deficiencies. Here are the two big ones that you may come across (if you haven't already):

1.   Change events in old versions of IE do *not* bubble.

2.   Checkboxes and radio buttons *may* not trigger a change event at all in old versions of IE.

Keep in mind that the second issue was *also* reproducible when using jQuery with IE7 and 8 for quite a long time. As far as I can tell, current versions of jQuery do properly address this issue. But this is yet another reminder that jQuery is not without its own bugs.

To solve the change event issue, you must attach a change handler *directly* to *any* form field that you'd like to monitor, since event delegation is not possible. In order to tackle the checkbox and radio buttons conundrum, your best bet may be to attach a click handler directly to radio/checkbox fields (or attach the handler to a parent element and make use of event delegation) instead of relying on the change event to occur at all.

■ **Note**   Generally, the enter key will fire a click event (for example on a button). In other words, click events are not only fired by a pointing device. For accessibility reasons, activating an element via the keyboard will also trigger a click event. In the case of a checkbox or radio button input element, the "enter" key will not activate the form field. Instead, "spacebar" key is required to activate a checkbox or radio button and trigger a click event.

The Event Object Is Also Non-standard

Some properties of the Event object instance are a bit different in older browsers. For example, although the target of an event in modern browsers can be found by checking the target property of the Event instance, IE8 and older contain a different property for this element: srcElement. The relevant portion of a cross-browser event handler function may look like this:

```
1  function myEventHandler(event) {
2    var target = event.target || event.srcElement
3    // ...
4  }
```

In modern browsers, the event.target will be truthy, which short-circuits the conditional evaluation just given. But in IE8 and older, the Event object instance will not contain a target property, so the target variable will be the value of the srcElement property on the Event.

In terms of controlling your events, the stopPropagation() method is *not* available on an Event object instance in IE8 and older. If you want to stop an event from bubbling, you must instead set the non-standard cancelBubble property on the Event instance. A cross-browser solution looks like this:

```
1  function myEventHandler(event) {
2    if (event.stopPropgation) {
3        event.stopPropagation();
4    }
5    else {
6        event.cancelBubble = true;
7    }
8  }
```

IE8 and older also do not have a stopImmediatePropagation() method. There isn't much that can be done to work around this limitation. However, I personally don't see lack of this method as a big problem. Using stopImmediatePropagation() seems like a code smell to me since the behavior of this call is completely dependent on the order that multiple event handlers are attached to the element in question.

The important takeaway for this chapter: events are pretty simple to work with in modern browsers without jQuery, but if you are unlucky enough to support Internet Explorer 8 or older, consider using the cross-browser functions demonstrated here, or pull in a reliable events library for more complex event handling requirements.

CHAPTER 11

■ ■ ■

Mastering Asynchronous Tasks

I would expect most web developers to be aware of the concept of asynchronous operations. In fact, I've already demonstrated some such tasks in earlier chapters. Admittedly, when this concept appeared previous to this chapter, I elected to avoid exploring in much detail. That is precisely the goal of this chapter—to cover the intricacies, challenges, and importance of async tasks in the world of web development. Although jQuery provides adequate support for managing async tasks, I'll show you how limited jQuery is in this context, how the web API is advancing far past jQuery, and how jQuery has failed to correctly implement an essential async task-management pattern.

Just so we are all on the same page throughout this chapter, let's be clear about the precise definition of the central topic here. An *asynchronous call* is one that is processed out-of-band. Still not clear? Sorry, let's try again. An *asynchronous call* is one that does not immediately return the requested result. Hmm, that's still a bit vague, isn't it? Okay, how about: an *asynchronous call* is one that makes your code much more difficult to manage and evolve. That last one is tongue-in-cheek, but it is likely a real opinion held by many (and rightfully so).

My inability to describe async tasks in a manner that can be easily understood by everyone is partially my fault, but it suggests just how hard it may be to actually *manage* these types of operations with JavaScript. In my experience, proper use and management of asynchronous operations is one of the more frustrating tasks that web developers face. If the definitions I've provided don't suffice, perhaps some real-world examples will clear things up.

So what are some actual examples of async tasks? Where might we come across this concept in everyday web development? There are actually quite a few operations that are asynchronous by nature. For example:

1. Handling responses to AJAX requests.

2. Reading files or blobs of data.

3. Requesting user input.

4. Passing messages between browsing contexts.

The most common async task involves AJAX requests. Client/server communication is understandably asynchronous. When you send a request to a server endpoint from the browser using `XMLHttpRequest` or `fetch`, the server may respond in milliseconds, or perhaps even seconds after the request has been initiated. The point is, after you send the request, your application doesn't simply freeze until the request has returned. Code continues to execute. The user continues to be able to manipulate the page. So you must register a function that is invoked by the browser once the server has properly responded to your request.

There is no telling exactly when the function purposed with handling the server response will be executed, and that's "okay." Your application and code must be structured to account for the fact that this data will not be available until some unknown point in the future. Indeed, some logic may depend on this response, and your code will need to be written accordingly. Managing a single request or asynchronous operation may not be particularly difficult. But at scale, with a number of requests and other async tasks in progress concurrently, or a series of async tasks that depend on each other, this becomes mighty hairy.

© Ray Nicholus 2016
R. Nicholus, *Beyond jQuery*, DOI 10.1007/978-1-4842-2235-5_11

In a general sense, APIs benefit from support of async operations. Consider a library that executes a provided function when a user chooses a file to be uploaded. This function can prevent a file from being uploaded by returning `false`. But what if the function must delegate to a server endpoint to determine whether the file is valid? Perhaps the file must be hashed client-side and then the server must be checked to ensure a duplicate file does not exist. This accounts for two asynchronous operations: reading the file (to generate a hash) and then contacting the server to check for duplicates. If the library doesn't provide support for this type of task in its API, integration is limited to some degree.

Another example: a library maintains a list of contacts. The user is given the ability to delete a contact via a `<button>`. It is quite common to display a confirm dialog before *actually* deleting the contact. Our library provides a function that is called before the delete operation occurs and allows it to be ignored if the function returns `false`. If you want a confirm dialog that stops execution of your code before the user responds, you *could* use the browser's built-in confirm dialog and then return `false` if the user elects to cancel the operation, but the native confirm dialog is barebones and ugly. It isn't an ideal choice for most projects, so you will need to provide your own styled dialog, which will be non-blocking. In other words, the library will need to account for the asynchronous nature of waiting for a user to decide if they are *really sure* that the file should be deleted forever. These are just two examples of how important it may be to consider async support when building an API, but there are many more.

This chapter deals with both traditional and some relatively new methods for dealing with async calls, but I also cover another solution that can probably be classified as "bleeding edge." The reason for inclusion of a new specification in this chapter is to provide you with an indication of how important dealing with the asynchronous nature of the web has become, and how the maintainers of JavaScript are doing their best to make a traditionally difficult concept to manage much easier.

Callbacks: the Traditional Approach for Controlling Async Operations

The most familiar way to provide support for asynchronous tasks is via a system of callback functions. Let's take the the contacts list library example and apply a callback function to account for the fact that a `beforeDelete` handler function may need to ask the user to confirm the contact removal, which is an async operation (assuming we don't rely on the built-in `window.confirm()` dialog). Our code may look something like this:

```
1 contactsHelper.register('beforeDelete', function(contact, callback) {
2   confirmModel.open(
3     'Delete contact ' + contact.name + '?',
4     function(result) {
5       callback({cancel: result.cancel});
6     });
7 });
```

When the user clicks the delete button next to a contact, the function passed to the the "beforeDelete" handler is invoked. The contact to be deleted is passed to this function, along with a callback function. If the delete operation is to be ignored, an object with a `cancel` property set to `true` must be passed into this callback. Otherwise, the `callback` will be invoked with a `false` value for the `cancel` property. The library will "wait" for this call before attempting to delete the contact. Note that this "waiting" does not involve blocking the UI thread, so all other code can continue to execute.

I'm assuming there is a modal dialog component with an open function that displays a delete confirm dialog to the user. The result of the user's input is passed into another callback function supplied to the open function. If the user clicks the Cancel button on this dialog, the `result` object passed to this particular callback function will contain a `cancel` property with a value of `true`. At that point, the callback function passed to the "beforeDelete" callback function will be invoked, indicating that the file to be deleted should *not* in fact be deleted.

Notice how the preceding code depends on a number of varying conventions—a number of *non-standard* conventions. In fact, there aren't *any* standards associated with callback functions. The value or values passed to the callback are part of a contract defined by the supplier of the function. In this case, the conventions are similar enough between the modal callback and the "beforeDelete" callback, but that may not always be the case. Although callbacks are a simple and well-supported way to account for async results, some of the problems with this approach may already be clear to you.

Node.js and the Error-First Callback

I haven't spent a lot of time discussing Node.js, but it has come up periodically throughout this book. The non-browsers section of Chapter 3 goes into a *bit* of detail about this surprisingly popular server-side JavaScript-based system. Node.js has long relied on callbacks to support asynchronous behavior across APIs. In fact, it has has popularized a very specific type of callback system: the "error-first" callback. This particular convention is *very* common throughout the Node.js landscape and can be found as part of the API in many major libraries, such as Express,[1] Socket.IO,[2] and request.[3] It is arguably the most "standard" of all the various callback systems, though of course there is no *real* standard, just conventions, though some conventions are more popular than others.

Error-first callbacks require, as you might expect, an error to be passed as the first parameter to a supplied callback function. Usually, this error parameter is expected to be an Error object. The Error object has always been part of JavaScript, starting with the first ECMAScript specification published back in 1997. The Error object can be thrown in exceptional situations or passed around as a standard way to describe an application error. With error-first callbacks, an Error object can be passed as the first parameter to a callback if the related operation fails in some way. If the operation succeeds, null should be passed as the first parameter instead. This makes is easy for the callback function itself to determine the status of the operation. And if the related task did *not* fail, subsequent arguments are used to supply relevant information to the callback function.

Don't worry if this is not entirely clear to you. You'll see error-first callbacks in action through the rest of this section, and that error-first callbacks are the most elegant way to either signal an error or deliver the requested information when supporting an asynchronous task via a system of callbacks.

Solving Common Problems with Callbacks

Let's look at a simple example of a module that asks the user for their email address (which is an asynchronous operation):

```
1  function askForEmail(callback) {
2    promptForText('Enter email:', function(result) {
3        if (result.cancel) {
4           callback(new Error('User refused to supply email.'));
5        }
6        else {
7           callback(null, result.text);
8        }
9    })
10 }
11
12 askForEmail(function(err, email) {
13   if (err) {
```

---

[1] http://expressjs.com
[2] http://socket.io
[3] www.npmjs.com/package/request

```
14        console.error('Unable to get email: ' + err.message);
15    }
16    else {
17        // save the `email` with the user's account record
18    }
19 });
```

Can you figure out the flow of the preceding code? An error-first callback is passed in as the sole parameter when invoking the function that ultimately asks our user for their email address. If the user declines to provide one, an Error with a description of the situation is passed as the first parameter to our error-first callback. The callback logs this and moves on. Otherwise, the err argument is null, which signals to the callback function that we did indeed receive a valid response from our user—the email address—which is contained in the second argument to the error-first callback.

Another practical use of callbacks is to handle the result of an AJAX request. Since the very first version of jQuery, it has been possible to supply a callback function to be invoked when an AJAX request succeeds. Chapter 9 demonstrates GET requests with jQuery (among others). Here's an alternate version of the first GET request:

```
1 $.get('/my/name', function (name) {
2    console.log('my name is ' + name);
3 });
```

The second parameter is a success callback function, which jQuery will call with the response data if the request succeeds. But this example only handles success. What if the request fails? Yet another way to write this *and* account for both success and failure is to pass an object that contains the URL, success, and failure callback functions:

```
1 $.get({
2    url: '/my/name',
3    success: function(name) {
4        console.log('my name is ' + name);
5    },
6    error: function() {
7        console.error('Name request failed!');
8    }
9 });
```

The same section in the AJAX requests chapter demonstrates making this call without jQuery. This solution for all browsers also relies on callbacks to signal success and failure:

```
1  var xhr = new XMLHttpRequest();
2  xhr.open('GET', '/my/name');
3  xhr.onload = function() {
4    if (xhr.status >= 400) {
5        console.error('Name request failed!');
6    }
7    else {
8        console.log('my name is ' + xhr.responseText);
9    }
10 };
11 xhr.onerror = function() {
12    console.error('Name request failed!');
```

164

```
13  };
14  xhr.send();
```

The onload callback is invoked if the request has been sent a response from the server. Conversely, the onerror callback is used if the request cannot be sent, or if the server fails to respond. Callbacks certainly seem to be a reasonable way to register for the result of an asynchronous task. And this is indeed true for simple cases. But a system of callbacks becomes less appealing for more complex scenarios.

Promises: an Answer to Async Complexity

Before I discuss an alternative to callbacks, perhaps it would be prudent to first point out some of the issues associated with a dependence on callbacks to manage async tasks. The first fundamental flaw in the callback system described in the preceding section is evident in every method or function signature that supports this convention. When invoking a function that utilizes a callback to signal success or failure of an asynchronous operation, you must supply this callback as a method parameter. Any input values used by the method must also be passed as parameters. In this case, you are now passing input values and managing the method's output all through method parameters. This is a bit non-intuitive and awkward. This callback contract also precludes any return value. Again, all work is done via method parameters.

Another issue with callbacks: there is no standard, only conventions. Whenever you find yourself needing to invoke a method that executes some logic asynchronously and expects a callback to manage this process, it *may* expect an error-first callback, but it may *not*. And how can you possibly know? Since there is no standard for callbacks, you are forced to refer to the API documentation and pass the appropriate callback. Perhaps you must interface with multiple libraries, all of which expect callbacks to manage async results, each relying on different callback method conventions. Some may expect error-first callbacks. Others may include an error or status flag elsewhere when invoking the supplied callback. Some may not even account for errors at all!

Perhaps the biggest issue with callbacks becomes apparent when they are forced into non-trivial use. For example, consider a few asynchronous tasks that must run sequentially, each subsequent task depending on the result from the previous. To demonstrate such a scenario, imagine you need to send an AJAX request to one endpoint to load a list of user IDs and then a request must be made to a server to load personal information for the first user in the list. After this, the user's info is presented on-screen for editing, and finally the modified record is sent back to the server. This whole process involves four asynchronous tasks, with each task depending on the result of the previous. How would we model this workflow with callbacks? It's not pretty, but it might look something like this:

```
1   function updateFirstUser() {
2     getUserIds(function(error, ids) {
3       if (!error) {
4         getUserInfo(ids[0], function(error, info) {
5           if (!error) {
6             displayUserInfo(info, function(error, newInfo) {
7               if (!error) {
8                 updateUserInfo(id, info, function(error) {
9                   if (!error) {
10                    console.log('Record updated!');
11                  }
12                  else {
13                    console.error(error);
14                  }
15                });
16              }
```

```
17            else {
18                console.error(error);
19                }
20            });
21        }
22        else {
23            console.error(error);
24            }
25        });
26    }
27    else {
28        console.error(error);
29    }
30    });
31 }
32
33 updateFirstUser();
```

Code like the preceding is commonly referred to as *callback hell*. Each callback function must be nested inside of the previous one in order to make use of its result. As you can see, the callback system does not scale very well. Let's look at another example that further confirms this conclusion. This time, we need to send three files submitted for a product in three separate AJAX requests to three separate endpoints concurrently. We need to know when all requests have completed and whether one or more of these requests failed. Regardless of the outcome, we need to notify our user with the result. If we are stuck using error-first callbacks, our solution is a bit of a brain-teaser:

```
1  function sendAllRequests() {
2    var successfulRequests = 0;
3
4    function handleCompletedRequest(error) {
5      if (error) {
6        console.error(error);
7      }
8      else if (++successfulRequests === 3) {
9        console.log('All requests were successful!');
10     }
11   }
12
13   sendFile('/file/docs', pdfManualFile, handleCompletedRequest);
14   sendFile('/file/images', previewImage, handleCompletedRequest);
15   sendFile('/file/video', howToUseVideo, handleCompletedRequest);
16 }
17
18 sendAllRequests();
```

That code isn't *awful*, but we had to create our own system to track the result of these concurrent operations. What if we had to track more than three async tasks? Surely there must be a better way!

The First Standardized Way to Harness Async

The flaws and inefficiencies associated with relying on callback conventions often prompt developers to look for other solutions. Surely some of problems, and the boilerplate common to this async handling approach, can be solved by and packaged into a more standardized API. The Promises specification defines an API that achieves this very goal, and so much more.

Promises have been publicly discussed on the JavaScript front for some time. The first instance of a Promise-like proposal (that I am able to locate) was created by Kris Kowal. Dating to mid-2011, it describes "Thenable Promises".[4] A couple lines from the introduction provide a good glimpse into the power of promises:

> An asynchronous promise loosely represents the eventual result of a function. A resolution can either be "fulfilled" with a value or "rejected" with a reason, corresponding by analogy to synchronously returned values and thrown exceptions respectively.

This loose proposal was, in part, used to form the Promises/A+ specification.[5] This specification has a number of implementations, many of which can be seen in various JavaScript libraries, such as bluebird,[6] Q,[7] and rsvp.js.[8] But perhaps the more important implementation appeared in the ECMA-262 6th Edition specification.[9] Remember from Chapter 3 that the ECMA-262 standard defines the JavaScript language specification. The 6th edition of this spec was officially completed in 2015. At the time of writing, the Promise object defined in this standard is available natively in all modern browsers, with the exception of Internet Explorer. Luckily, many lightweight polyfills are available to fill in this gap.

Using Promises to Simplify Async Operations

So what exactly are promises? You could read through the ECMAScript 2015 or A+ specifications, but like most formal language specifications, these are both a bit dry and perplexing. First and foremost, a promise, in the context of ECMAScript, is an object used to manage the result of an asynchronous operation. It smoothes all the rough edges in a complex application left by traditional convention-based callbacks.

Now that the overarching goal of promises is clear, let's take a deeper look at this concept. The first logical place to start exploring promises in more depth is through Domenic Denicola's "States and Fates" article).[10] From this document, we learn that promises have three states:

1. *Pending*: The initial state, before the associated operation has concluded

2. *Fulfilled*: The associated operation monitored by the promise has completed without error

3. *Rejected*: The associated operation has reached an error condition

Domenic goes on to define a term that groups both the "fulfilled" and "rejected" states: *settled*. So, a promise is initially pending, and then it is settled once it has concluded.

---

[4]https://github.com/kriskowal/uncommonjs/blob/ea03e6d40430318b1d9821a181f3961bbf02eb12/promises/specification.md
[5]https://github.com/promises-aplus/promises-spec
[6]https://github.com/petkaantonov/bluebird
[7]https://github.com/kriskowal/q
[8]https://github.com/tildeio/rsvp.js
[9]www.ecma-international.org/ecma-262/6.0/#sec-promise-objects
[10]https://github.com/domenic/promises-unwrapping/blob/master/docs/states-and-fates.md

There are also two distinct "fates" defined in this document:

1. *Resolved*: A promise is resolved when it is fulfilled or rejected, *or* when it has been redirected to follow another promise. An example of the latter condition can be seen when chaining asynchronous promise-returning operations together. (More on that soon.)

2. *Unresolved*: As you might expect, this means that the associated promise has not yet been resolved.

If you can understand these concepts, you are very close to mastering promises, and you will find working with the API defined in the A+ and ECMA-262 specifications much easier.

The Anatomy of a Promise

A JavaScript promise is created simply by constructing a new instance of an A+ compliant `Promise` object, such as the one detailed in the ECMAScript 2015 specification. The `Promise` constructor takes one argument: a function. This function itself takes *two* arguments, which are both functions that give the promise a resolved "fate" (as described in the preceding section). The first of these two function arguments is a "fulfilled" function. This is to be called when the associated asynchronous operation completes successfully. When the "fulfilled" function is invoked, a value related to the completion of the promissory task should be passed. For example if a `Promise` is used to monitor an AJAX request, the server response may be passed to this "fulfilled" function once the request completes successfully. When a `fulfilled` function is called, the promise assumes a "fulfilled" state, as described earlier.

The second argument passed to the `Promise` constructor's function parameter is a "reject" function. This should be called when the promissory task has failed for some reason, and the reason describing the failure should be passed into this rejected function. Often, this will be an `Error` object. If an exception is thrown inside of the `Promise` constructor, this will automatically cause the "reject" function to be invoked with the thrown `Error` passed as an argument. Going back to the AJAX request example, if the request were to fail, the "reject" function should be called, passing either a string description of the result, or perhaps the HTTP status code. When a `reject` function is called, the promise assumes a "rejected" state, described in number 3 of the list of promise states given earlier.

When a function returns a `Promise`, the caller can "observe" the result a couple of different ways. The most common way to handle a promissory return value is to call a `then` method on the promise instance. This method takes two parameters, both functions. The first functional parameter is invoked if the associated promise is fulfilled. As expected, if a value is associated with this fulfillment (such as a server response for an AJAX request), it is passed to this first function. The second function parameter is invoked if the promise fails in some way. You may omit the second parameter if you are only interested in fulfillment (though it is generally unsafe to assume your promise will succeed). Additionally, you may specify a value of `null` or `undefined`, or any value that is not considered to be "callable"[11] as the first argument if you are only interested in promise rejection. An alternative to this, which also lets you focus exclusively on the error case, is to call the `catch` method on the returned `Promise`. This `catch` method takes one argument: a function that is invoked when/if the associated promise errors.

The ECMAScript 2015 `Promise` object includes several other helpful methods, but one of the more useful non-instance methods is `all()`, which allows you to monitor many promises at once. The `all` method returns a new `Promise` that is fulfilled if all monitored promises are fulfilled, or rejects as soon as one of the monitored promises is rejected. The `Promise.race()` method is very similar to `Promise.all()`, the difference being that the `Promise` returned by `race()` is fulfilled immediately when the first monitored `Promise` is fulfilled. It does not wait for all monitored `Promise` instances to be fulfilled first. One use for `race()` could also apply to AJAX requests. Imagine you were triggering an AJAX request that persisted the same data to multiple redundant endpoints. All that is important is the success of one request, in which case `Promise.race()` is more appropriate and much more efficient than waiting for all requests to complete with `Promise.all()`.

---

[11]`www.ecma-international.org/ecma-262/6.0/#sec-iscallable`

Simple Promise Examples

If the previous section isn't enough to properly introduce you to JavaScript promises, a few code examples should push you over the edge. Earlier, I provided a couple code blocks that demonstrated handling of async task results using callbacks. The first one outlined a function that prompts the user to enter an email address in a dialog box—an asynchronous task. An error-first callback system was used to handle both successful and unsuccessful outcomes. The same example can be rewritten to make use of promises:

```
1   function askForEmail() {
2     return new Promise(function(fulfill, reject) {
3       promptForText('Enter email:', function(result) {
4           if (result.cancel) {
5             reject(new Error('User refused to supply email.'));
6           }
7           else {
8             fulfill(result.text);
9           }
10      });
11    });
12  }
13
14  askForEmail().then(
15    function fulfilled(emailAddress) {
16      // do something with the `emailAddress`...
17    },
18    function rejected(error) {
19      console.error('Unable to get email: ' + error.message);
20    }
21  );
```

In the preceding example rewritten to support promises, our code is much more declarative and straightforward. The askForEmail() function returns a Promise that describes the result of the "ask the user for email" task. When calling this function, we can intuitively handle both a supplied email address and an instance where the email is not provided by following a codified standard. Notice that we are still assuming that the promptForText() function API is unchanged, but the code can be simplified even further if this function also returns a promise:

```
1   function askForEmail() {
2     return promptForText('Enter email:');
3   }
4
5   askForEmail().then(
6     function fulfilled(emailAddress) {
7       // do something with the `emailAddress`...
8     },
9     function rejected(error) {
10      console.error('Unable to get email: ' + error.message);
11    }
12  );
```

If promptForText() returns a Promise, it *should* pass the user-entered email address to the fulfilled function if an address is supplied, or a descriptive error to the rejected function if the user closes the dialog without entering an email address. These implementation details are not visible above, but based on the Promise specification, this is what we can expect.

The other example in the callbacks section demonstrates the onload and onerror callbacks provided by XMLHttpRequest. Just to recap, onload is called when the request completes (regardless of the server response status code), and onerror is invoked if the request fails to complete for some reason (such as due to CORS or other network issues). As Chapter 9 mentions, the Fetch API brings a replacement for XMLHttpRequest that makes use of the Promise specific to signal the result of an AJAX request. I'll dive into a more complex example that makes use of fetch shortly, but first, let's write a wrapper around the XMLHttpRequest call from the callbacks section that presents a more elegant interface using promises:

```
1  function get(url) {
2    return new Promise(function(fulfill, reject) {
3      var xhr = new XMLHttpRequest();
4      xhr.open('GET', url);
5      xhr.onload = function() {
6        if (xhr.status >= 400) {
7          reject('Name request failed w/ status code ' + xhr.status);
8        }
9        else {
10          fulfill(xhr.responseText);
11        }
12      }
13      xhr.onerror = function() {
14        reject('Name request failed!');
15      }
16      xhr.send();
17    });
18  }
19
20  get('/my/name').then(
21    function fulfilled(name) {
22      console.log('Name is ' + name);
23    },
24    function rejected(error) {
25      console.error(error);
26    }
27  );
```

Although the Promise-wrapped XMLHttpRequest doesn't simplify that code much, it gives us a great opportunity to generalize this GET request, which makes it more reusable. Also, our code that uses this new GET request method is easy to follow and magnificently readable and elegant. Both the success and failure conditions are a breeze to account for, and the logic required to manage this is wrapped away inside the Promise constructor function. Of course, we could have created a similar approach without Promise, but the fact that this async task-handling mechanism is an accepted JavaScript language standard makes it all the more appealing.

The same exact AJAX request logic can more elegantly make use of the Promise API (for Firefox, Chrome, Opera, and Edge) by relying on the Fetch API:

```
1  function get(url) {
2    return fetch(url).then(
3      function fulfilled(response) {
4        if (response.ok) {
```

```
5          return response.text();
6        }
7        throw new Error('Request failed w/ status code ' + response.status);
8      }
9    );
10  }
11
12  get('/my/name').then(
13    function fulfilled(name) {
14      console.log('Name is ' + name);
15    },
16    function rejected(error) {
17      console.error(error);
18    }
19  );
```

Here we've been able to simplify the GET name request much more with the help of promises *and* fetch. If the server indicates a non-successful status in its response, or if the request fails to send at all, then the rejected handler will be hit. Otherwise, the fulfilled function handler is triggered with the text of the response (the user name). A lot of the boilerplate that plagues the XHR version has been avoided entirely.

Fixing "Callback Hell" with Promises

Earlier, I demonstrated one of the many issues with callbacks that presents itself in a non-trivial situation where consecutive dependent async tasks are involved. That particular example required retrieving all user IDs in the system, followed by retrieval of the user information for the first returned user ID, and then displaying the info for editing in a dialog, followed by a callback to the server with the updated user information. This accounts for four separate but interdependent asynchronous calls. The first attempt to handle this made use of several nested callbacks, which resulted in a pyramid-style code solution—*callback hell*. Promises are an elegant solution to this problem, and callback hell is avoided entirely due to the ability to chain promises. Take a look at a rewritten solution that makes use of the Promise API:

```
1   function updateFirstUser() {
2     getUserIds()
3       .then(function(ids) {
4         return getUserInfo(ids[0]);
5       })
6       .then(function(info) {
7         return displayUserInfo(info);
8       })
9       .then(function(updatedInfo) {
10        return updateUserInfo(updatedInfo.id, updatedInfo);
11      })
12      .then(function() {
13        console.log('Record updated!');
14      })
15      .catch(function(error) {
16        console.error(error);
17      });
18  }
19
20  updateFirstUser();
```

That is quite a bit easier to follow! The flow of the async operations is probably apparent as well. Just in case it isn't, I'll walk you through it. I've contributed a fulfilled function for each of the four then blocks to handle specific successful async operations. The catch block at the end will be invoked if any of the async calls fails. Note that catch is *not* part of the A+ Promise specification, though it *is* part of the ECMAScript 2015 Promise spec.

Each async operation—getUserIds(), getUserInfo(), displayUserInfo(), and updateUserInfo()— returns a Promise. The fulfilled value for each async operation's returned Promise is made available to the fulfilled function on the subsequently chained then block. No more pyramids, no more callback hell, and a simple and elegant way to handle a failure of any call in the process.

Monitoring Multiple Related Async Tasks with Promises

Remember the callbacks example from the start of this section that illustrated one approach to handling three separate AJAX requests to three separate endpoints concurrently? We needed to know when all requests completed *and* whether one or more of them failed. The solution wasn't ugly, but it was verbose and contained a fair amount of boilerplate that could become cumbersome should we find ourselves in this situation often. I surmised that there must be a better solution to this problem, and there is! The Promise API allows for a much more elegant solution, particularly with the all method, which allows us to easily monitor all three asynchronous tasks and react when they all complete successfully, or when one fails. Take a look at the rewritten Promise-ified code:

```
1  function sendAllRequests() {
2    Promise.all([
3      sendFile('/file/docs', pdfManualFile, handleCompletedRequest),
4      sendFile('/file/images', previewImage, handleCompletedRequest),
5      sendFile('/file/video', howToUseVideo, handleCompletedRequest)
6    ]).then(
7      function fulfilled() {
8        console.log('All requests were successful!');
9      },
10     function rejected(error) {
11       console.error(error);
12     }
13   )
14 }
15
16 sendAllRequests();
```

The preceding solution assumes sendFile() returns a Promise. With this being true, monitoring these requests becomes much more intuitive and lacks almost all the boilerplate and ambiguity from the callbacks example. Promise.all takes an array of Promise instances and returns a new Promise. This new returned Promise is fulfilled when all the Promise objects passed to all are fulfilled, or it is rejected if *one* of these passed Promise objects is rejected. This is *exactly* what we are looking for, and the Promise API provides this support to us natively.

jQuery's Broken Promise Implementation

Almost all the code in this chapter has focused exclusively on the support for async tasks that is native to JavaScript. The rest of this chapter is going follow a similar pattern. This is mostly due to the fact that jQuery simply doesn't provide much in terms of powerful async support. The ECMA-262 standard is far ahead of jQuery in this regard. But because this book aims to explain much of the web API and JavaScript to those coming from a jQuery-centric perspective, I feel it is important to at least *mention* jQuery in this section, since it *does* have support for promises—but this support has been, unfortunately, broken and completely non-standard in all released versions of jQuery up until June of 2016. While the problems with promises have been fixed in jQuery 3.0, promises have suffered from some notable deficiencies in the library for quite some time.

There have been *at least* two serious bugs in jQuery's promise implementation. Both of these deficiencies made promises non-standard and frustrating to work with. The first related to error handling. Suppose an Error is thrown inside of a promise's fulfilled function handler, part of a first then block. To catch this sort of issue, it is customary to register a rejected handler on a subsequent then block, chained to the first then block. Remember that each then block returns a *new* promise. Your code may look something like this:

```
1  someAsyncTask
2    .then(
3      function fulfilled() {
4        throw new Error('oops!');
5      }
6    )
7    .then(null, function rejected(error) {
8      console.error('Caught an error: ' + error.message);
9  });
```

Using the ECMA-262 Promise API, the preceding code will print an error log to the console that reads "Caught an error: oops!" But if the same pattern is implemented using jQuery's deferred construct,[12] the error will *not* be caught by the chained rejected handler. Instead, it will remain uncaught. Valerio Gheri goes into much more detail in his article on the subject.[13] I'll leave it to you to read further if you are interested in more specifics regarding the issues with jQuery's promise error handling and won't spend more time on this here.

The second major issue with jQuery's promise implementation is a break in the expected order of operations. In other words, instead of observing the expected execution order of code alongside promise handlers, jQuery changes the order of execution to match the order in which the code appears in the executable source. This is an overly simplistic explanation, and if you'd like to read more, take a peek at Valera Rozuvan's "jQuery Broken Promises Illustrated" article.[14] The lesson here is simple - avoid jQuery's promise implementation, unless you are using a very recent version (3.0+). It has been non-standard and deficient for many years.

Native Browser Support

As mentioned earlier, the Promise API is standardized as part of ECMA-262 6th edition. As of this writing, all modern browsers, with the exception of Internet Explorer, implement promises natively. A number of Promises/A+ libraries are available (such as RSVP.js, Q, and Bluebird), but I prefer a small and focused polyfill to bring promises to non-compliant browsers (Internet Explorer). For this, I highly recommend the small and effective "es6-promise"[15] polyfill by Stefan Penner.

---

[12]https://api.jquery.com/jquery.deferred/
[13]https://thewayofcode.wordpress.com/2013/01/22/
javascript-promises-and-why-jquery-implementation-is-broken/
[14]http://valera-rozuvan.github.io/nintoku/jquery/promises/jquery-broken-promises-illustrated
[15]https://github.com/stefanpenner/es6-promise

Async Functions: Abstraction for Async Tasks

The TC39 group that standardized promises in ECMA-262 6th edition worked on a related specification that builds upon the existing Promise API. The async functions specification,[16] also known as async/await, will be part of the 8th edition of the ECMAScript specification in 2017. At the writing of this chapter, it is currently sitting in stage 4, which is the last stage in the TC39 specification acceptance process.[17] This means async functions are complete and ready to be associated with a future formal edition of JavaScript. There seems to be a lot of momentum and excitement surrounding async functions (and rightfully so).

Async functions provide several features that make handling async operations incredibly easy. Instead of getting lost in a sea of conventions or async-specific API methods, they allow you to treat asynchronous code as if it were completely synchronous. This lets you use the same traditional constructs and patterns for *asynchronous* code that you have already been using for your *synchronous* code. Need to catch an error in an asynchronous method call? Simply wrap it in a try/catch block. Want to return a value from an async function? Go ahead, return it! The elegance of async functions is a bit surprising at first, and web development will benefit enormously once they become more commonly used and understood.

The Problem with Promises

The Promise API provides a refreshing break from callback hell and all the other inelegance and inefficiency associated with callback-based async task-handling conventions. But promises don't mask the process of handling async. Promise merely provide us with a more elegant API—an API that makes managing async a bit easier than the alternatives that came before it. Let's look at two code samples—one that deals with two very similar tasks—one synchronous, the other asynchronous:

```
1   function handleNewRecord(record) {
2     try {
3       var savedRecord = saveRecord(record);
4       showMessage('info', 'Record saved! ' + savedRecord);
5     }
6     catch(error) {
7       showMessage('error', 'Error saving!' + error.message);
8     }
9   }
10
11  handleNewRecord({name: 'Ray', state: 'Wisconsin'});
```

■ **Note** The implementation of showMessage() has been left out as it is not important to the example code. It is intended to illustrate a commonly used approach to dealing with success and errors by displaying a message to the user.

In the preceding code, we're given a record of some type, which is then "saved" with the help of the saveRecord function. In this case, the operation is synchronous, and the implementation doesn't rely on an AJAX call or some other out-of-band processing. Because of this, we're able to use familiar constructs to handle the result of the call to saveRecord. When saveRecord is called, we expect a return value that represents the saved record. At that point, we may inform a user that the record was saved, for example. But if saveRecord fails unexpectedly—say it throws an Error—we have that covered too. A traditional try/catch block is all that is needed to account for such a failure. This is a basic pattern that virtually all developers are familiar with.

---

[16]https://tc39.github.io/ecmascript-asyncawait/
[17]https://tc39.github.io/process-document/

But suppose the saveRecord function *was* asynchronous. Suppose it did delegate to a server endpoint from the browser. Our code, using promises, would have to change to look something like this instead:

```
1  function handleNewRecord(record) {
2    saveRecord(record).then(
3      function fulfilled(savedRecord) {
4        showMessage('info', 'Record saved! ' + savedRecord);
5      },
6      function rejected(error) {
7        showMessage('error', 'Error saving!' + error.message);
8      }
9    );
10 }
11
12 handleNewRecord({name: 'Ray', state: 'Wisconsin'});
```

That code, rewritten to use promises due to the async nature of saveRecord, isn't terribly difficult to follow or write, but it's a notable departure from the familiar var savedRecord = try/catch block from the previous example. The burden of directly depending on the Promise API becomes even clearer as we run into more promissory functions throughout our project. Instead of simply using familiar patterns, we are continually forced to *think* about async. We must treat our async code completely differently from our synchronous code. That's unfortunate. If only we could handle async tasks without thinking about the async part. . . .

Async Functions to the Rescue

The primary asset that async functions bring to the table is the almost total abstraction they offer—so much so that asynchronous promissory tasks *appear* to be completely synchronous. It seems like magic at first. There are some things to be aware of, lest you get sucked up in the magic and become frustrated when an async function's dependency on promises leaks through the abstraction.

Let's start with a really simple and somewhat contrived example (don't worry, we'll work up to the *real* examples from the promises section soon). First, here's the saveRecord example that we recently discussed, written to make use of async functions:

```
1  async function handleNewRecord(record) {
2    try {
3      var savedRecord = await saveRecord(record);
4      showMessage('info', 'Record saved! ' + savedRecord);
5    }
6    catch(error) {
7      showMessage('error', 'Error saving!' + error.message);
8    }
9  }
10
11 handleNewRecord({name: 'Ray', state: 'Wisconsin'});
```

Did we just assign the result of an asynchronous operation to a variable *without* using a then block *and* handle an error by wrapping that call in a try/catch block? Why, yes we did! That code looks almost *exactly* like the initial example where we called a completely synchronous saveRecord function. Under the covers, this is all promises, but there's no trace of a then or even a catch block.

Earlier, I demonstrated how to prevent "callback hell" with the help of the `Promise` API. The solution presented in that section is certainly a vast improvement over the traditional callback-based approach, but the code is still a bit unfamiliar, and of course we are clearly forced to explicitly deal with the fact that we are invoking a number of interdependent asynchronous calls. Our code must be structured to account for this reality. Not so with async functions:

```
1   async function updateFirstUser() {
2     try {
3       var ids = await getUserIds(),
4           info = await getUserInfo(ids[0]),
5           updatedInfo = await displayUserInfo(info);
6
7       await updateUserInfo(updatedInfo.id, updatedInfo);
8       console.log('Record updated!');
9     }
10    catch(error) {
11      console.error(error);
12    }
13  }
14
15  updateFirstUser();
```

The preceding code is markedly more succinct and elegant than the earlier version that relied on direct use of promises. But what about the code in the next part of the promises section? This is the one where I converted the callback example that sent, managed, and monitored three files submitted for a product in three separate AJAX requests to three separate endpoints concurrently. I made use of the `Promise.all` method to simplify the code. Well, we can simplify that even further with some help from async functions.

But remember, as of the writing of this chapter, async functions are still an ECMA-262 proposal. It is not part of any formal specification *yet* (though it will be very soon). As with many proposals, async functions have changed a bit since the initial version of the proposal. In fact, this initial version included some syntactic sugar to make it even easier and more elegant to monitor an array of promissory functions. Let's look at a rewrite of the concurrent async tasks example, using the initial async functions proposal:

```
1   async function sendAllRequests() {
2     try {
3       // This is no longer valid syntax - do not use!
4       await* [
5         sendFile('/file/docs', pdfManualFile, handleCompletedRequest),
6         sendFile('/file/images', previewImage, handleCompletedRequest),
7         sendFile('/file/video', howToUseVideo, handleCompletedRequest)
8       ];
9       console.log('All requests were successful!');
10    }
11    catch(error) {
12      console.error(error);
13    }
14  }
15
16  sendAllRequests();
```

At one point early on in the development of the async functions proposal, await* was included as an alias for Promise.all(). Sometime after April 2014, this was removed from the proposal, apparently to avoid confusion with a keyword in the "generators" specification in the ECMAScript 6th edition standard. The yield* keyword in the generators spec resembles await* in appearance, but the two do not share similar behaviors. So, it was removed from the proposal. The appropriate way to monitor a number of concurrent promissory functions with async functions requires making use of Promise.all():

```
1  async function sendAllRequests() {
2    try {
3      await Promise.all([
4        sendFile('/file/docs', pdfManualFile, handleCompletedRequest),
5        sendFile('/file/images', previewImage, handleCompletedRequest),
6        sendFile('/file/video', howToUseVideo, handleCompletedRequest)
7      ]);
8      console.log('All requests were successful!');
9    }
10   catch(error) {
11     console.error(error);
12   }
13 }
14
15 sendAllRequests();
```

It's perhaps unfortunate that we still must make some direct use of promises in this one specific case, even when utilizing async functions, but this doesn't negatively impact the readability or elegance of the solution. But it's true, async functions aren't perfect—you still have to define functions as async, and you still must include the await keyword before a function that returns a promise, but the syntax is *much* simpler and more elegant than the bare Promise API. You can use familiar and traditional patterns to handle both async and non-async code. That's a pretty clear win to me. This is one of many ways in which specifications are evolving quite rapidly, building upon each other, and outpacing the progression of jQuery.

Browser Support

Sadly, async functions are not natively supported in *any* browsers as of August 2016. But this is to be expected as this proposal is just that, a proposal—it is not part of any formal JavaScript standard *yet*. That doesn't mean you must wait for browser adoption before using async functions in your project. Since async functions offer new keywords, a polyfill is not the appropriate solution. Instead, you will have to make use of a tool that compiles your async functions at build time into something that browsers can understand.

There are many such tools that are able to compile async function syntax into cross-browser JavaScript. Babel is one such tool, and a number of Babel plug-ins exist to accomplish this task. Discussing Babel or any other JavaScript compilation tool is beyond the scope of this book, but I can tell you that most plug-ins seems to compile async functions to ECMAScript 2015 generator functions. Generator functions must then be compiled down into ECMAScript 5 code if the project is browser based (since generator functions are not natively supported in all modern browsers). Type Script is another JavaScript compilation tool that performs many of the same tasks as Babel but also supports a number of non-standard language features. Type Script currently offers native support for async functions, but only in browsers that natively support generator functions. That limitation may very well be relaxed in a future release.

The Future of Standardized Async Task Handling

When I began writing this chapter, I intended to dedicate two entire sections to a couple additional ECMA-262 proposals. These proposals—Asynchronous Iterators[18] and Observable[19]—were created to further enhance JavaScript async task handling. I initially planned to dedicate a section to each of these proposals, complete with copious code examples, but I ultimately decided against it for a few reasons. First, these proposals are still fairly immature. Asynchronous Iterators is a stage 2 proposal, and Observable is only at stage 1. It didn't seem appropriate to include these proposals in a book when they could very well change in unexpected ways at some point during the process. Even worse, one or both proposals could be withdrawn. And no complete implementations of either proposal exist at the moment. That makes it difficult to actually create runnable code when attempting to demonstrate the benefits of these concepts. Even though Async Functions is also a proposal, it *did* make the cut due to its momentum in the JavaScript community and its advanced stage 4 status.

Asynchronous Iterators aim to make it simple use familiar looping constructs, such as a for loop, to iterate over a collection of items produced by an asynchronous operation. Each item in this collection is not immediately available after the invocation of the function. Instead, as the loop executes, logic inside of the asynchronous function progressively loads new items asynchronously. An intuitive example in the proposal repository[20] demonstrates how this new concept allows us to use a for loop to print out lines in a file. The process of reading the file is asynchronous, and our for loop only attempts to read each subsequent line as the for loop requests it. If the loop terminates,
so does the file reader. This proposal pairs Async Functions with ECMAScript 2015 Generator Functions. Although I did cover Async Functions in this chapter, I intentionally left out Generator Functions. Generator Functions are indeed useful for handling async tasks, but their use in this scenario is fairly low-level and awkward—not appropriate for this particular book, due to the explicit complexity associated with use of this language feature.

Observables are a bit better understood. A number of implementations of this pattern already exist, both in JavaScript and other languages. RxJS[21] is perhaps the most well-known Observable implementation, though it remains to be seen if this is a "standard" implementation, since the Observable proposal is just that—a proposal. Observables provide a standardized method for sifting through and focusing on specific data points in a stream of data. An example in the proposal repository[22] demonstrates use of Observables that monitor all browser keyboard events to focus on a specific combination of keys in this stream of events.

Although Async Iterators and Observables may be part of the future of JavaScript async task handling, I've already demonstrated a number of available APIs that can be used *today*. You no longer have to rely on conventions or proprietary solutions that are tied to a specific library. JavaScript continues to evolve to standardize intuitive solutions for complex operations. Support for asynchronous tasks is just one of many such examples.

---

[18]https://tc39.github.io/proposal-async-iteration/
[19]https://tc39.github.io/proposal-observable/
[20]https://github.com/tc39/proposal-async-iteration
[21]https://github.com/ReactiveX/rxjs
[22]https://github.com/zenparsing/es-observable

■ ■ ■

Common JavaScript Utility Functions

Here in chapter 12, I plan to match jQuery's utility functions[1] against the native APIs defined in the ECMAScript specification. Most of the code in this chapter will work both in the browser and on the server (with the notable exception of DOMParser and any references to window or document in examples). In modern browsers, jQuery is unnecessary most of the time. But even where jQuery saves a few keystrokes, it's important to be able to roll your own utility function, even if you do choose to pull in a library for some of the more complex and lesser-supported features. After all, understanding how jQuery works its magic makes you a more complete and effective software developer.

jQuery may provide other utility functions not detailed in this chapter, but I cover all of the "important" ones. First, I demonstrate and explain how functions that jQuery provides to work with strings, dates, XML, and JSON can be duplicated without any external libraries. Next, I move on to code that is useful for inspecting variable types. For example, determining if a value is an Object, Array, Function, or some specific primitive value. Don't worry, I elaborate on primitive values a bit, just in case you are not completely familiar with each of the primitive value types available in JavaScript. jQuery does provide functions to detect value types. I go over those and show you how the same type checking (and more) can be performed with vanilla JS.

I also explain manipulating, creating, and traversing objects, along with arrays. Finally, we'll figure out functions together—that is, how to perform various important and common operations on JavaScript functions sans jQuery. After this chapter is complete, you'll feel much more comfortable working with JavaScript objects, functions, arrays, and primitives yourself, without any "outside" help.

Working with Dates, Text, XML, and JSON

This first section considers duplicating the behavior of jQuery's Date and string helper functions in plain old vanilla JavaScript. But not *just* run-of-the-mill strings—JSON and XML too. Although jQuery makes it pretty easy to perform simple, common tasks with dates and strings, you'll see shortly how unnecessary this library is in this context.

---

[1]https://api.jquery.com/category/utilities/

© Ray Nicholus 2016
R. Nicholus, *Beyond jQuery*, DOI 10.1007/978-1-4842-2235-5_12

Dates

jQuery doesn't really focus much on dates, although perhaps it could have contributed some valuable utility functions to make some of the more useful Date prototype methods more reliable cross-browser. For example, Date.prototype offers a number of methods that can be used to format a specific date according to a specific locale, such as Date.prototype.toLocaleString() and Date.prototype.toLocateDateString(). Though this is well supported for the *current* locale, the ability to pass a variable locale has spotty browser support at the moment. Furthermore, these same methods allow a date to be formatted according to a specific set of requirements. Say you want the current month to be printed using its full name (instead of a number or an abbreviation). Simply pass an options object (the second parameter) to toLocaleString() as {month: 'long'}. But this too is not well supported across even modern browsers.

No, jQuery doesn't help us with any real Date-related problems in JavaScript. Instead, it only provides a single method to return the number of milliseconds since the Unix epoch (00:00:00 UTC, 1 January, 1970). Suppose the current time is midnight on 4 June, 2016. What if we were to call this utility function provided by jQuery to obtain the number of milliseconds since the Unix epoch? What would the code look like?

```
1 var currentTime = $.now();
```

The same value can be obtained without jQuery in *any* browser with just a few more characters:

```
1 var currentTime = new Date().getTime();
```

The currentTime variable in both code blocks is identical (assuming both lines are executed at the exact same point in time). The getTime() method has been available on Date.prototype since the very first version of the ECMAScript specification[2] 1st edition%2C June 1997.pdf). But if we depend only on modern browsers, the same exact call can be made without jQuery even more elegantly:

```
1 var currentTime = Date.now();
```

The now() function was added to the Date object in the 5.1 edition of the ECMAScript spec.[3] In fact, recent versions of jQuery connect $.now() directly to Date.now().[4] The same level of succinctness and convenience is available today without jQuery. But even if you are unfortunate enough to require support for ancient browsers (perhaps in a legacy web application that simply won't die), the same behavior is possible with only a minuscule amount of additional finger work, as you have already seen.

Converting JSON into a JavaScript Object

In version 1.4.1 of jQuery, an API method was introduced that parsed a JSON string, converting it into the appropriate JavaScript representation (String, Number, Boolean, Object, or Array). 1.4.1 was released in 2010, a year after Internet Explorer 8 was released (which was able to parse JSON strings natively). However, IE7 was still in use, as was IE6 to some degree, neither of which was able to easily convert JSON into JavaScript. jQuery's parseJSON() method aimed to make this task possible in all supported browsers. Consider the following simple JSON string:

```
1 {
2   "name": "Ray",
3   "id": 123
4 }
```

---

[2] www.ecma-international.org/publications/files/ECMA-ST-ARCH/ECMA-262%2C
[3] www.ecma-international.org/ecma-262/5.1/#sec-15.9.4.4
[4] https://github.com/jquery/jquery/blob/2.2.4/src/core.js#L453

The preceding JSON string is made available to our code as a `jsonString` variable, which is, of course, a string. This JSON string can be turned into a JavaScript object using jQuery's `$.parseJSON()` method:

```
1  var user = $.parseJSON(jsonString);
2
3  // prints "Ray"
4  console.log(user.name);
5
6  // prints 123
7  console.log(user.id);
```

Although `$.parseJSON()` certainly does provide an elegant way to turn a JSON string into a proper JavaScript value, it has been a completely unnecessary abstraction for many years now. All modern browsers and all versions of Node.js (as well as Internet Explorer 8, as mentioned before) include support for the JSON object, first included in ECMAScript 5.1.[5] Here's the exact same solution without jQuery:

```
1  var user = JSON.parse(jsonString);
2
3  // prints "Ray"
4  console.log(user.name);
5
6  // prints 123
7  console.log(user.id);
```

jQuery even hands all JSON string parsing work off to `JSON.parse()` if the browser supports the JSON object. In addition to parsing a JSON string, the native JSON object can also convert a JavaScript value into a string, via the `stringify()` method. There is no such abstraction included in jQuery's API, nor has there ever been.

For browsers older than and including Internet Explorer 7, there has always been at least one way to parse JSON strings without access to a native method. The most common approach involves using the native `eval()` function to parse the JSON string into a JavaScript value. Although this *does* work, it is widely known to be a bad idea due to the security implications of using `eval()`. Blindly parsing a string into a JavaScript value using `eval()` requires executing the underlying code. With a user-supplied string, this can lead to disastrous consequences. To combat this reality, Douglas Crockford created a library in 2007—json.js[6]—also delegates to `eval()` but only after verifying that the string to evaluate is "safe". Regardless, none of this is needed anymore due to the fact that browsers without support for JSON are not widely used.

Converting an XML String into a Document

Similar to `$.parseJSON()` for converting a JSON string into a JavaScript representation, jQuery also defines a `parseXML()` method in its public API. jQuery's `$.parseXML()` turns an XML string into a document. This gives you the ability to query the document using jQuery's selector API just as you would an HTML document. For example, consider an application that makes a request directly to a Microsoft Azure REST API endpoint. If the URL includes an invalid query parameter, the Azure service will respond with the following XML string in the response:[7]

```
1  <?xml version="1.0" encoding="utf-8"?>
2  <Error>
3    <Code>InvalidQueryParameterValue</Code>
```

---

[5]www.ecma-international.org/ecma-262/5.1/#sec-15.12
[6]https://github.com/douglascrockford/JSON-js/blob/master/json2.js
[7]https://msdn.microsoft.com/en-us/library/azure/dd179382.aspx

```
4    <Message>Value for one of the query parameters specified in the request URI is\
5    invalid.</Message>
6    <QueryParameterName>popreceipt</QueryParameterName>
7    <QueryParameterValue>33537277-6a52-4a2b-b4eb-0f905051827b</QueryParameterValue>
8    <Reason>invalid receipt format</Reason>
9   </Error>
```

I chose an Azure response for this section as I distinctly remember dealing with parsing an XML string browser-side when integrating the "upload to Azure" feature into Fine Uploader, which had to parse the response, and report the error code and message for display and logging.[8]

Let's say we wanted to do the same—extract the <Code> and the <Message> portions of the error message. We certainly *could* parse the string ourselves, using regular expressions, but that's hardly an ideal approach. Converting the XML string into a proper document is the goal, and this is easily doable with jQuery:

```
1    // assuming we have the above XML string assigned to a var
2    var errorDocument = $.parseXML(azureErrorXmlString);
3
4    // code = "InvalidQueryParameterValue"
5    var code = $(errorDocument).find('Code').text();
6
7    // message = "Value for one of the query parameters..."
8    var message = $(errorDocument).find('Message').text();
```

Note that jQuery does in fact give us back a document as the return value of $.parseXML(), so if we want to use jQuery's API to parse the document, we must wrap it ourselves.

You may be happy to know that we can do all of this, very easily, in all modern browsers without jQuery:

```
1    // assuming we have the above XML string assigned to a var
2    var errorDocument = new DOMParser()
3      .parseFromString(azureErrorXmlString, 'application/xml');
4
5    // code = "InvalidQueryParameterValue"
6    var code = errorDocument.querySelector('Code').textContent;
7
8    // message = "Value for one of the query parameters..."
9    var message = errorDocument.querySelector('Message').textContent;
```

Although the same solution is admittedly much less elegant in ancient browsers, that really isn't a concern in the current day. The DOMParser interface is defined as part of the W3C DOM Parsing and Serialization specification,[9] which was first drafted in 2012 and is still listed as a "draft" as of mid-2016. But the behavior described in that document has been implemented in all modern browsers for some time now. This particular specification is meant to standardize behaviors that have already been implemented across a wide range of browsers, similar to the CSS Object Model specification.[10]

Perhaps you are saying to yourself, "Why must I include a XML MIME type (application/xml)?" jQuery's parseXML() method does *not* require this to be included. The answer is simple and already may be obvious based on the generic name of the native parser. DOMParser was not solely created to parse XML strings. Although this is currently the most widely supported document type, there is also support for parsing SVG

---

[8]https://github.com/FineUploader/fine-uploader/blob/6aa179f7b009cb80376b997975a7acf3
5cc72635/client/js/azure/util.js#L78
[9]www.w3.org/TR/DOM-Parsing/
[10]https://www.w3.org/TR/cssom-1/

strings into SVG elements (image/svg+xml) *and* support for parsing HTML (text/html). The latter two document types are supported in all modern browsers, with the exception of Internet Explorer 9. DOMParser is much more powerful than any single offering in jQuery's API, and it has the potential to be expanded to support additional types in the future.

String Manipulation

It's surprising that a seemingly important and common string manipulation task—trimming the whitespace from the beginning and end of a line of text—was not natively supported as a JavaScript method until ECMAScript 5.1.[11] Internet Explorer 9 is the oldest browser to implement the String.prototype.trim() method defined in this spec. The late arrival of trim() explains one primary reason why jQuery has offered its own trim() method since version 1.0. The next three listings compare the jQuery API method, the String.protoype.trim() native method, and a workaround for ancient browsers:

Listing 12-1. Trim a String: jQuery

```
1  // trimmed = 'some name'
2  var trimmed = $.trim(' some name ');
```

Listing 12-2. Trim a String: JavaScript, Modern Browsers

```
1  // trimmed = 'some name'
2  var trimmed = (' some name ').trim();
```

Listing 12-3. Trim a String: JavaScript, All Browsers

```
1  // trimmed = 'some name'
2  var trimmed = (' some name ').replace(/^\s+|\s+$/g, '');
```

The workaround for browsers that don't natively implement String.prototype.trim() requires resorting to a regular expression. The preceding workaround is included in Fine Uploader in one of its many cross-browser utility methods (which was needed as the library has supported browsers as old as Internet Explorer 6 in the past.[12]

$.trim() is the *only* string-related convenience method provided by jQuery. You can read more about other string manipulation and parsing methods provided by JavaScript on the Mozilla Developer Network page dedicated to the String interface.[13] But this will *not* be the last time we dive into strings in this chapter.

What Kind of Value Is This?

The ECMAScript language specification for JavaScript defines two general data types: Object and primitive. As of the 7th edition of the standard, there are exactly six primitive data types: null, undefined, Boolean, Number, String, and Symbol. As far as the non-primitive types, Object is one, and all other such types inherit from Object. There are *many* complex JavaScript types that inherit from Object. Array and Function are two such examples. Some types are easier than others to reliably identify, but all values *can* be identified without the aid of a third-party library. Yet even if you already rely on such a library, this section will help you understand some of the logic your library may use in order to determine JavaScript value types. And since this book is focused on developers who are already familiar with jQuery and its collection of convenience API methods, expect me to mostly focus on the existing solutions provided by jQuery as I show you how to identify value types in JavaScript.

---

[11]www.ecma-international.org/ecma-262/5.1/#sec-15.5.4.20
[12]https://github.com/FineUploader/fine-uploader/blob/537a86bf3d6edd8068e66422a605b392dc8d0 b1e/client/js/util.js#L292
[13]https://developer.mozilla.org/en-US/docs/Web/JavaScript/Reference/Global_Objects/String

Primitives

jQuery contributes two API methods that may be used to resolve primitive values: $.isNumeric() and
$.type(). The type() API method provides the most useful and expected behavior. It will return a single-
word (lowercase) string that identifies the JavaScript type of a provided value. For example:

```
1   // true
2   $.type(3) === 'number';
3
4   // true
5   $.type('3') === 'string';
6
7   // true
8   $.type(null) === 'null';
9
10  // true
11  $.type(undefined) === 'undefined';
12
13  // true
14  $.type(false) === 'boolean';
15
16  // true (only supported in Chrome, Firefox, and Safari)
17  $.type(Symbol('mysymbol')) === 'symbol';
```

jQuery's type() method will also produce expected results for uncommon values, such as the following:

```
1   // true
2   $.type(new Number(3)) === 'number';
3
4   // true
5   $.type(new String('3')) === 'string';
6
7   // true
8   $.type(new Boolean(false)) === 'boolean';
```

Although it is perfectly legal to create a String, Number, or Boolean using a constructor function, it
is unusual, and this practice provides no real benefit. It can also make comparison difficult between two
primitives constructed this way. For example:

```
1   // both are true
2   3 === 3;
3   3 == 3;
4
5   // all are false
6   3 === new Number(3);
7   new Number(3) === new Number(3);
8   new Number(3) == new Number(3);
9
10
11  // both are true
12  'string' === 'string';
13  'string' == 'string';
```

```
14
15   // all are false
16   'string' === new String('string');
17   new String('string') === new String('string');
18   new String('string') == new String('string');
19
20
21   // both are true
22   false === false;
23   false == false;
24
25   // all are false
26   false === new Boolean(false);
27   new Boolean(false) === new Boolean(false);
28   new Boolean(false) == new Boolean(false);
```

In fact, a Boolean created with the Boolean constructor always evaluates to true in a conditional unless the valueOf() method is called on the Boolean instance.[14] How very intuitive!

So, how can we make the same primitive type comparisons without jQuery? The fact is that these operations are trivial in *all* browsers (both modern and ancient). Take a look:

```
1    // true
2    typeof 3 === 'number';
3
4    // true
5    typeof '3' === 'string';
6
7    // true
8    typeof undefined === 'undefined';
9
10   // true
11   typeof false === 'boolean';
12
13   var someVal = null;
14   // true
15   someVal === null;
16
17   // true (only supported in Chrome, Firefox, and Safari)
18   typeof Symbol('mysymbol') === 'symbol';
```

In all cases, except for one, we can make use of the typeof keyword to provide the exact same result as jQuery's type() method. typeof has been part of the language since the very first version of JavaScript. However, one small quirk has existed since this first version as well, which can be seen when evaluating null with the typeof keyword:

```
1    // false
2    typeof null === 'null';
3
4    // 'object'
5    typeof null;
```

[14]www.ecma-international.org/ecma-262/5.1/#sec-15.6.4.3

As you can see, typeof thinks null is an Object, strangely enough. This is largely considered to be a mistake in the initial implementation of JavaScript that has remained in place for backward-compatibility reasons. But another explanation is provided by the ECMAScript-262 language specification. The definition of a null value[15] is described as a "primitive value that represents the intentional absence of any object value." In that respect, it may arguably be appropriate to call this type an "object". This theory makes even more sense when we look at the result of typeof NaN, which evaluates to "number". Surely if the antithesis of Number evaluates to "number", it stands to reason that the antithesis of Object would evaluate to "object". Speaking in terms of consistency, this makes perfect sense (at least to me). Feel free to form your own opinion though. Regardless, this behavior will likely never change, as proposals to fix this have been rejected in the past.[16]

What about jQuery's $.isNumeric() method? Well, it is a bit bizarre, or at least it may *appear* that way initially. Take a look:

```
1  // all true
2  $.isNumeric(3);
3  $.isNumeric('3');
4
5  // all false
6  $.isNumeric(NaN);
7  $.isNumeric(Infinity);
```

In other words, if a value is indeed a Number or can be coerced into a Number, then jQuery's isNumeric() will return true. And by "coerced," I mean that a string such as "3" can be easily converted to a proper Number by, for example, passing it into parseInt(). Also, this string can be evaluated as a proper Number for the purposes of comparison with another value by using a double equal sign (==) which will convert the string to a Number as part of the comparison operation. Furthermore, values that are indeed Numbers but are not typically thought of as "numbers" (such as NaN and Infinity) result in a false return value when passed into $.isNumeric(). Achieving the same behavior sans jQuery involves a bit of thought (and perhaps Googling). But the solution can be found after realizing that we need to make two determinations when evaluating our value:

1. Is it NaN?

2. Is it a finite value?

Granted, it is unlikely that most will reach the point where it is clear that these two specific questions must be answered, but the fact remains that this is indeed what we need to determine. Luckily, there are two methods defined in the language that have been present since the first version that will allow us to easily mimic the behavior of jQuery's isNumeric():

```
1  function isNumeric(maybeNumber) {
2    return !isNaN(parseFloat(maybeNumber))
3           && isFinite(maybeNumber);
4  }
5
6  // all true
7  isNumeric(3);
8  isNumeric('3');
9
10 // all false
11 isNumeric(NaN);
12 isNumeric(Infinity);
```

---

[15]www.ecma-international.org/ecma-262/5.1/#sec-4.3.11
[16]http://wiki.ecmascript.org/doku.php?id=harmony%3Atypeof_null

The addition of parseFloat when determining whether a value is NaN is required for properly evaluating a null value. In other words, if maybeNumber is null and we leave out the parseFloat(), isNaN() will evaluate to false and the null value will erroneously be declared "numeric".

Arrays

In all browsers, determining whether a value is an array is trivial, but modern browser support for this determination is exceptionally elegant. For that, we have Array.isArray():

```
1  // both are true
2  Array.isArray([]);
3  Array.isArray(new Array());
4
5  // both are false
6  Array.isArray(3);
7  Array.isArray({});
```

The JavaScript Array object was given an isArray() method in ECMAScript-262 5.1.[17] And jQuery has included a similar convenience method for quite some time: $.isArray():

```
1  // both are true
2  $.isArray([]);
3  $.isArray(new Array());
4
5  // both are false
6  $.isArray(3);
7  $.isArray({});
```

But all versions of jQuery since 2.0 delegate directly to the native Array.isArray() in *all* cases. In other words, $.isArray() is just an alias for Array.isArray(). Older version of jQuery also delegated to Array.isArray(), but only conditionally. If Array.isArray() was not available (which would be the case in an ancient browser) jQuery's type method was used to determine if value was an 'array.' But *we* can duplicate the same behavior and support all browsers without jQuery, even ancient ones:

```
1  function isArray(value) {
2    return Array.isArray
3    ? Array.isArray(value)
4    : Object.prototype.toString.call(value) === '[object Array]';
5  }
6
7  // both are true
8  isArray([]);
9  isArray(new Array());
10
11  // both are false
12  isArray(3);
13  isArray({});
```

---

[17]www.ecma-international.org/ecma-262/5.1/#sec-15.4.3.2

Keep in mind the preceding code is only useful if you plan on supporting very old browsers, such as Internet Explorer 8. Otherwise, `Array.isArray()` covers all possible cases. But let's look closer at a portion of the example above anyway, specifically `Object.prototype.toString.call(value)`. You may be wondering why we don't simply use typeof here. Somewhat surprisingly, typeof `[]` and typeof new `Array()` produce a result of "object". This is technically true—an `Array` is a type of `Object` since it inherits from `Object. prototype`, a type value of "object" is a little less specific than expected. Of course, a more effective result would be "array". But, sadly, this is not the case.

It's often helpful to think of JavaScript arrays as objects with a few convenience methods. This is, more or less, the truth. Diving deeper into arrays, you'll see that array element access follows the same pattern as object property access. For example, to access the third element in an array: `myArray[2]`. And to access a property named 2 in an object: `myObject[2]`. Arrays are mostly just objects with some convenience methods and a `length` property, and typeof reflects this reality. By calling the `toString()` method available on the `Object` prototype using the `call()` method, which allows us to change the context of the call of `toString()` to the array literal, we are able to see the "true" type of our array. Don't worry if you are confused about the call method. I cover that near the end of this chapter.

Objects

An object is not a primitive data type, partly because objects are mutable and primitive data types are generally *immutable* across most programming languages. But the object type in JavaScript is the base type for *all* non-primitive values. Functions are objects, and arrays are objects too! More on those two value types soon.

In JavaScript, an object is just a "collection" of key/value properties. Keys can be strings, or integers (which are converted to strings), or even Symbols (if the browser supports this primitive data type). *Anything* is a valid property value, even another object.

jQuery's type API method can certainly tell us when a value is an object, just as the native typeof keyword. But remember from the earlier sections that typeof null === 'object' *and* typeof [] === 'object'. These values are identified instead as "null" and "array" by `$.type()`, and it's possible that this is the behavior you desire and expect. So, how can we create a simple cross-browser function that will identify any "real" object as an object, leaving out the "array object"? This can be accomplished as follows:

```
1  function isObject(value) {
2    return value !== null &&
3      Object.prototype.toString.call(value) === '[object Object]';
4  }
5
6  // both are true
7  isObject({});
8  isObject(new Object());
9
10 // both are false
11 isObject(null);
12 isObject([]);
```

In addition to `$.type()`, jQuery has a couple more interesting methods used to identify specific kinds of JavaScript objects. One is `$.isPlainObject()`, which is supposed to determine if a specific value is either an object literal (`{}`) or a base `Object` instance (new `Object()`). jQuery's type() method is not appropriate in this case, as it will identify DOM elements as objects (which *is* technically correct). But even though isPlainObject() is useful in theory, it is a determination that I have rarely needed to make across my entire career. Also, jQuery's documentation for isPlainObject() warns that the method is potentially unreliable and may provide unexpected results in some browsers. For these reasons, I'm not going to focus further on this particular API method. Suffice it to say that, if you need to reliably determine if a value is an object literal, you may find that reframing your problem is a better route to pursue.

jQuery's isEmptyObject() is another interesting method, with more practical use cases. It's not uncommon to find yourself in a situation where you are passed an object and need to determine whether the object includes any properties at all. Perhaps an "empty" object indicates that no data is available when querying an API. jQuery's isEmptyObject() method fulfills this need:

```
1  // true
2  $.isEmptyObject({});
3
4  // false
5  $.isEmptyObject({name: 'Ray'});
```

And there *is* a simple (though not as elegant) solution to make the same determination without jQuery, for all browsers. Peering at jQuery's implementation of isPlainObject(), we can extract this logic and create a tiny reusable function for our own project, without pulling in an entire library:

```
1  function isEmptyObject(value) {
2    for (property in value) {
3      return false;
4    }
5    return true;
6  }
7
8  // true
9  isEmptyObject({});
10
11  // false
12  isEmptyObject({name: 'Ray'});
```

Functions

Functions are, with one specific exception, really easy to identify with or without jQuery. jQuery provides two API methods that will allow you to determine whether a JavaScript value is a function or not. One is $.type(), which I've demonstrated several times already in this section. Another is $.isFunction(), which simply delegates to $.type(), effectively making it an alias:

```
1  // all true
2  $.isFunction(function() {});
3  $.type(function() {}) === 'function';
4  $.isFunction(Object.prototype.toString);
5  $.isFunction(document.body.getAttribute);
6
7  // all false
8  $.isFunction({});
9  $.type({}) === 'function';
10 $.isFunction(3);
```

The standard typeof operator in JavaScript produces the exact same results:

```
1  // all true
2  typeof function() {} === 'function';
3  typeof Object.prototype.toString === 'function';
```

```
4  typeof document.body.getAttribute === 'function';
5
6  // all false
7  typeof {} === 'function';
8  typeof 3 === 'function';
```

Even JavaScript classes are identified as "functions" by both jQuery and the typeof operator. This is not entirely surprising since there is no "class" type in JavaScript. ECMAScript 2015 classes are nothing more than "syntactic sugar"—an easier way to create an object that inherits from another object.

jQuery really doesn't perform any magic to determine if a value is a function. This is true to the extent that an unexpected result is produced when attempting to identify web API functions in ancient browsers both with *and* without jQuery. Earlier versions of Internet Explorer (version 8 and older) misreported standard web API functions, such as those defined on the Element and Window interfaces, as objects. For example, in Internet Explorer 8, $.isFunction(document.body.getAttribute) is false, as is typeof document.body.getAttribute === 'function'. Clearly this *is* a function, but IE appears to consider it an "object". This is not completely incorrect—after all, functions *are* objects. They inherit from Object.prototype. They are sometimes even called "function objects."

Making JavaScript Objects Bend to Your Will

As you learned in the last section, all non-primitive values in JavaScript inherit from Object. This makes Object the most important type of value to understand when working with complex data. And once you are able to identify a value as an Object—something you learned in the previous section—it's helpful to understand how to copy, parse, and create objects without the help of any third-party code. Here, I show you how jQuery allows you to perform various important and useful operations on objects *and* how you can achieve the exact same results just by using the standard methods provided by JavaScript. In most cases, these "native" solutions will be equally or similarly elegant when compared with jQuery's API. But of course, some operations will admittedly show the elegance of jQuery. Still, even covering the native solutions that seem less ideal compared to a library-based solution has great value. All code in this section will allow you to gain more insight into JavaScript, and this will in turn give you more confidence and make you a stronger and more capable developer. After all, this *is* the primary goal of *Beyond jQuery*.

Iterating over Keys and Values

Let's start out with an object that contains a number of properties:

```
1  var user = {
2    name: 'Ray Nicholus',
3    address: '1313 Mockingbird Lane',
4    city: 'Mockingbird Heights',
5    state: 'California'
6  };
```

. . . and we have an HTML form that needs to receive these values:

```
1  <form>
2    <input name='name'>
3    <input name='address'>
4    <input name='city'>
5    <input name='state'>
6  </form>
```

As you can see, each form field has a matching property in our initial object. This particular object might be supplied by an AJAX call, and we must simply take the resulting object data and fill in the form with the matching values. Assume you know nothing about the form or object ahead of time, other than the object will have properties that match name attributes on form fields, and these form fields may be updated using their value property. This requires that we do the following:

- Loop over the properties in the object

- Set the value for the matching <input> to equal the object property's value

You already learned how to work with HTML elements in previous chapters. Here, I show you how to loop over the properties of an object so you can easily solve this problem without jQuery. But first, let's look at the solution *with* jQuery:

```
1  $.each(user, function(property, value) {
2     $('form [name="' + property + '"]').val(value);
3  });
```

We can solve this problem very easily without jQuery for modern browsers and IE8:

```
1  for (var property in user) {
2     var value = user[property];
3     document.querySelector('FORM [name="' + property + '"]').value = value;
4  }
```

We're using a standard for...in loop, something that has *always* been part of the language. The only reason our code is "limited" to Internet Explorer 8 and newer is due to the use of querySelector, but this seems like a reasonable accommodation. Note that, in this case, we can be sure that our object only contains properties defined on *that* object, and not any properties defined on an inherited object. But if that is a concern, and you only want to retrieve properties that belong exclusively to this user object, you will need to make use of an additional check, and your code will look like this:

```
1  for (var property in user) {
2     if (user.hasOwnProperty(property)) {
3        var value = user[property];
4        document.querySelector('FORM [name="' + property + '"]').value = value;
5     }
6  }
```

The hasOwnProperty() method, present on every Object, tells us if a given property belongs exclusively to the source object. It has been part of the language since the 3rd edition of the ECMAScript specification, so it's quite safe to use in all browsers. Again, this is not something we *need* to use in our case, but you might find it useful in alternate circumstances.

You might be asking yourself, "Why didn't I have to use hasOwnProperty() in the jQuery example earlier?" And the answer is: you do! jQuery's each() API method does *not* call hasOwnProperty() when iterating through the properties of an object. It was determined that call is simply too expensive[18] to use in the library in all cases, and the work required to add this "enhancement" to the existing method implementation was too substantial. It's unfortunate that the documentation page for $.each() does not alert users to the fact that they *may* have to use hasOwnProperty() themselves.

---

[18]https://bugs.jquery.com/ticket/5499

JavaScript provides another standard way to iterate over object properties, with an added benefit: no need for hasOwnProperty() (ever):

```
1  Object.keys(user).forEach(function(property) {
2    var value = user[property];
3    document.querySelector('FORM [name="' + property + '"]').value = value;
4  });
```

The preceding code uses Object.keys(), a method that turns all properties in an object into an array. This method was added to Object in ECMAScript 5.1,[19] and is available in all modern browsers. We are then utilizing the forEach() method available on all Array objects. More on this property in the next section, but it too is supported in all modern browsers. True, this is still one more line than the jQuery solution (I told you, stop worrying about lines of code!), but it eliminates the need to ever invoke hasOwnProperty(), which does potentially end up saving some code (if you still care about that sort of thing).

Copying and Merging Objects

Extending the preceding example a bit, suppose we have two mostly different sets of information about the same user, and we need to combine one of them into the other to form a single object that contains all user data. Our two objects look like this:

```
1  var userLocation = {
2    name: 'Ray Nicholus',
3    address: '1313 Mockingbird Lane',
4    city: 'Mockingbird Heights',
5    state: 'California'
6  };
7
8  var userPersonal = {
9    name: 'Ray Nicholus',
10   sex: 'male',
11   age: 35
12 };
```

What we want is *one* object—user—that contains all properties from the userLocation and userPersonal objects. The combined object will need to look like this:

```
1  var user = {
2    name: 'Ray Nicholus',
3    address: '1313 Mockingbird Lane',
4    city: 'Mockingbird Heights',
5    state: 'California',
6    sex: 'male',
7    age: 35
8  };
```

jQuery provides a single API method to handle this quite effectively - $.extend():

```
1  var user = $.extend(userLocation, userPersonal);
```

---

[19]www.ecma-international.org/ecma-262/5.1/#sec-15.2.3.14

So now we have a *single* user object with properties from both initial user objects. The ability to merge two objects is possible without jQuery as well (unsurprisingly—why else would I have started to describe object merging otherwise?) While there is a very elegant method, similar to jQuery's extend() (which I will demonstrate very soon), wide browser support (at the current time) is only possible with a more long-winded solution. In effect, we must write our own poor man's extend() method to support all browsers:

```
1  function extend(first, second) {
2    for (var secondProp in second) {
3      var secondVal = second[secondProp];
4      first[secondProp] = secondVal;
5    }
6    return first;
7  }
8
9  var user = extend(userLocation, userPersonal);
```

Another, much simpler approach requires Object.assign(), which was first added to the language in ECMAScript 2015:[20]

```
1  var user = Object.assign(userLocation, userPersonal);
```

Object.assign() is great, but no version of Internet Explorer supports it. Until Internet Explorer 11 is completely eclipsed by Microsoft Edge, you'll need to rely on a polyfill to provide access to this language feature in all browsers. Not to worry, though, there are several very small polyfills that will suffice.

One valid concern with all of the preceding code examples (jQuery and non-jQuery) is that the first object, userLocation, is modified with the properties from userPersonal. The returned value for $.extend(), our custom extend() method, *and* Object.assign() is the *first* object passed to each function. So how can we create a *new* object that contains the two merged user objects without modifying either object? Simple: we need to create a copy of the first object and then merge the second object into that copy.

With jQuery's extend method, we can simply declare the first parameter (the "target" object) to be an empty object. Since $.extend() takes a variable number of parameters, we can specify the two initial user objects as the subsequent parameters:

```
1  var user = $.extend({}, userLocation, userPersonal);
```

The custom extend function we wrote earlier can be used to produce the exact same result. Remember, we need to create a copy of the first user object and then merge the second object into this copy:

```
1  var user = extend(extend({}, userLocation), userPersonal);
```

The nested extend() call results in a copy of userLocation as the first parameter to the outer extend, which is exactly what we need to do to create a brand new object based on the two original user objects.

The newest addition to JavaScript, Object.assign(), tackles this problem with the same elegance and simplicity as jQuery's extend:

```
1  var user = Object.assign({}, userLocation, userPersonal);
```

---

[20]www.ecma-international.org/ecma-262/6.0/#sec-object.assign

Solving Problems with Arrays

Similar to the previous section on objects, you'll learn how to copy, parse, and create *arrays* in this section. Remember that arrays *are* objects. That is, they inherit all methods/properties defined on Object. prototype.[21] But the Array object defines some unique methods of its own, such as forEach(), map(), concat(), indexOf(), find(), and many, many more. I'll introduce you to a number of these methods and demonstrate how *you* can duplicate the results from some popular array-specific jQuery API methods.

Iterating over Array Items

Without having any scientific data to back up this assertion (or the motivation to search for such statistics), I would say that, from my own experience as a developer, iterating over items in an array is one of the most common and basic patterns present in software projects. As expected, jQuery has a single method that iterates over arrays (and objects too)—$.each():

```
1  var languages = ['C', 'JavaScript', 'Go'];
2
3  $.each(languages, function(index, language) {
4    // ...
5  });
```

That loop will execute three times, once for each array element. index will be, for each iteration: 0, 1, and 2 (respectively). Similarly, the language value will be "C", "JavaScript", and "Go". You're likely familiar with jQuery, so none of this is particularly surprising. And perhaps you already know how to iterate over array elements without jQuery too. But maybe you aren't familiar with the most modern method of array iteration, and you may not know about one particular type of looping mechanism that you should *not* use when dealing with arrays. I address all of this next.

Many developers will likely make use of a traditional for loop when attempting to iterate over *anything*. Especially if you have working experience in C/C++ or a C-influenced language, such as Java, PHP, or Perl (to name a few). The code required to iterate over our languages array using a C-loop would look something like this (for all browsers):

```
1  var languages = ['C', 'JavaScript', 'Go'];
2
3  for (var index = 0; index < languages.length; index++) {
4    var language = languages[index];
5    // ...
6  }
```

Another advantage of the preceding loop (in addition to familiarity) is browser support. C-loops have always been supported in JavaScript. But clearly this approach is not as elegant as jQuery's each() method. There's some seemingly unnecessary boilerplate in our "native" solution. Luckily, ECMAScript 5 defines a new method on Array.prototype: forEach().[22] It behaves exactly like jQuery's each(), with a more appealing API:

```
1  var languages = ['C', 'JavaScript', 'Go'];
2
3  languages.forEach(function(language) {
4    // ...
5  });
```

---

[21]www.ecma-international.org/ecma-262/6.0/#sec-properties-of-the-object-prototype-object
[22]www.ecma-international.org/ecma-262/5.1/#sec-15.4.4.18

Can you spot the two improvements that forEach() offers over $.each()?

1. More intuitive syntax. Instead of passing the array into a utility function, you can call the loop method directly on the array.

2. The "current item" argument is the *first* argument passed to the callback function. This is *usually* what you are most interested in anyway. Sometimes, the array index is unimportant.

Both of these improvements also eliminate redundant code and make the loop more readable. But perhaps you are wondering, "Why not just use a for . . . in loop?" Certainly, that was a reasonably elegant solution in the previous section when dealing with objects. But there is a hidden danger when using a for . . . in loop when attempting to iterative over Array elements. The order of the elements traversed by a for . . . in loop is not guaranteed. In other words, it is conceivable that your for . . . in loop may encounter the second item before the first, for example. This may lead to unexpected results in your code if order is important, and this is a reasonable assumption since arrays are used to store data in a specific order. Another issue: for . . . in loops will include *all* properties that belong to the target object (in this case, an array object). So, if a custom property is added to the Array instance, this will be unexpectedly included among the index values. In short, don't use a for . . . in loop to iterate over arrays. There are many other safer choices.

An even more modern native looping mechanism, which works for modern browsers except for IE, is the for . . . of loop, first defined in ECMAScript 6:[23]

```
1  var languages = ['C', 'JavaScript', 'Go'];
2
3  for (var language of languages) {
4      // ...
5  }
```

In this case, each element in the languages array *will* be encountered in the expected order. This is due to the fact that for . . . of loops call a special iterator method that exists on Array.prototype. This iterator method was also first defined in ES6,[24] and is present on other iterable types, including Set, Map, and even NodeList (returned by querySelectorAll()).

Locating Specific Items

Being able to loop through the items in an array opens up the door to other possibilities, such as filtering and searching. All the methods discussed in this chapter—both jQuery and non-jQuery—are simply wrappers around a traditional loop. But these more focused functions make searching and filtering arrays more intuitive.

As luck would have it, jQuery has dedicated two of its own API methods to searching and filtering. First, let's talk about $.inArray(), which is a method that returns the index of a matching element (or –1 if no match can be located). Consider the following array:

```
1  var names = [
2      'Joe',
3      'Jane',
4      'Jen',
5      'Jim',
6      'Bill',
7      'Beth'
8  ];
```

---

[23]www.ecma-international.org/ecma-262/6.0/#sec-for-in-and-for-of-statements
[24]www.ecma-international.org/ecma-262/6.0/#sec-symbol.iterator

If we wanted to locate the position of 'Jen', we could do so quite easily using jQuery's inArray() method:

```
1  // returns 2
2  $.inArray('Jen', names);
```

Without jQuery, there is no elegant way to search an array in *ancient browsers* without writing your own helper function, for example:

```
1  function inArray(value, array) {
2    var foundIndex = -1;
3    for (var index = 0; index < array.length; index++) {
4      if (array[index] === value) {
5        foundIndex = index;
6        break;
7      }
8    }
9    return foundIndex;
10 }
11
12 // returns 2
13 inArray('Jen', names);
```

Luckily, modern browsers have it a bit easier with ES5's indexOf() method on Array.prototype:[25]

```
1  // returns 2
2  names.indexOf('Jen');
```

Just like Array.prototype.forEach(), indexOf() provides an even more elegant interface over jQuery's $.inArray() and solves the exact same problem. But modern browser support for arrays goes much further than indexOf(). Suppose you aren't looking for a specific value, but you need to gather some information about your array. Say you want to know if at least one value in the names array starts with the letter "B". Array.prototype.some() allows you to pass a function to test elements of the array. As soon as the condition is met, the method returns true. Otherwise, false is returned once all array items are exhausted:

```
1  // returns true
2  names.some(function(name) {
3    return name[0] === 'B';
4  });
```

Notice how we're able to treat the string literal as an array. ECMAScript 5 first standardized this behavior, which is available on all modern browsers. But a string is not a *real* array, it's a "pseudo-array." More on that later. Similarly, Array.prototype.every() will return true if each and every array item matches the passed test function. This is also an ECMAScript 5 method, supported in all modern browsers.

ECMAScript 2015 provides Array.prototype.findIndex()[26] and Array.prototype.find()[27]. The former will return the index of the array item that matches the passed test function, and the latter will return the actual matching array item, for modern desktop browsers except IE and some mobile browsers:

```
1  // returns 4
2  names.findIndex(function(name) {
```

[25]www.ecma-international.org/ecma-262/5.1/#sec-15.4.4.14
[26]www.ecma-international.org/ecma-262/6.0/#sec-array.prototype.findIndex
[27]www.ecma-international.org/ecma-262/6.0/#sec-array.prototype.find

```
3    return name[0] === 'B';
4  });
5
6  // returns "Bill"
7  names.find(function(name) {
8    return name[0] === 'B';
9  });
```

find() and findIndex() have somewhat limited browser support as of mid-2016. In an already crowded group of array methods, ECMAScript 2016 provides yet another way to determine if a specific element exists in an array. We can use Array.prototype.includes()[28] to even more elegantly determine if one or more array items are "Bill", for modern desktop browsers except IE and Edge, and all mobile browsers except IE:

```
1  // returns true
2  names.includes("Bill");
```

Many of these new methods are arguably unnecessary and only really save a line or two of code, but their presence illustrates the rapid growth of the language in response to libraries like jQuery.

The other array-specific API method provided by jQuery is $.grep(), which searches an array and returns all items that match a test function. Using our names array, you can use $.grep() to locate all items that are exactly three characters long:

```
1  // returns ["Joe", "Jen", "Jim"]
2  $.grep(names, function(name) {
3    return name.length === 3;
4  });
```

ECMAScript 5 provides a Array.prototype.filter() to solve the same exact problem in modern browsers:

```
1  // returns ["Joe", "Jen", "Jim"]
2  names.filter(function(name) {
3    return name.length === 3;
4  });
```

Although many of these utility functions have been present in jQuery since version 1.0, JavaScript has come a long way since then. Not only does the language provide native implementations for these jQuery functions, it even provides additional methods that offer *more* functionality than anything present in jQuery's API.

Managing Pseudo-arrays

In JavaScript, there are *real* arrays:

```
1  var realArray = ['a', 'b', 'c'];
```

---

[28]https://tc39.github.io/ecma262/#sec-array.prototype.includes

. . . and "pseudo-arrays":

```
1  var pseudoArray = {
2    0: 'a',
3    1: 'b',
4    2: 'c',
5    length: 3
6  };
```

There are some *native* pseudo-arrays as well, such as NodeList,[29] HTMLCollection,[30] and FileList,[31] to name a few. Pseudo-arrays are not *real* arrays since they are not on the same prototype chain as Array. That is, they inherit nothing from Array.prototype because they are *not* arrays. In fact, they are just plain old objects. But, due to their length property, you can treat them as an array, in some respects. For example, you may iterate over their "elements" using a C-loop, just as you would any *real* array.

When dealing with a pseudo-array in an ancient browser, the fact that it doesn't inherit from Array.prototype probably doesn't matter much, since you'll need to iterate over the items using a traditional for loop anyway. But, suppose you are using a modern browser, and you want to make this object that looks very much like an array *act* like an array. Perhaps you want to use forEach(), or map(), or filter(), or any of the other array methods I've already covered in this section. Or maybe you need to pass it to an API method that expects a *real* array.

You can convert a pseudo-array to a *real* array in jQuery using $.makeArray();

```
1  var realArray = $.makeArray(pseudoArray);
2
3  // now you can call all methods available on Array.prototype:
4  realArray.forEach(function(element, index) {
5    // ...
6  });
```

If you'd like to transform a pseudo-array to a *real* array without jQuery for modern browsers, you can use this trick:

```
1  var realArray = [].slice.call(pseudoArray);
2
3  // now you can call all methods available on Array.prototype:
4  realArray.forEach(function(element, index) {
5    // ...
6  });
```

A real-world-scenario might require you to select a bunch of elements and iterate over them, or even gather those that meet specific criteria. Imagine selecting all text inputs and excluding those that are empty:

```
1  var textInputs = document.querySelectorAll('INPUT[type="text"]');
2  var textInputsArray = [].slice.call(textInputs);
3  var nonEmptyFields = textInputsArray.filter(
4    function(input) {
5      return input.value.length > 0;
6    }
7  );
```

---

[29]https://developer.mozilla.org/en-US/docs/Web/API/NodeList
[30]https://developer.mozilla.org/en-US/docs/Web/API/HTMLCollection
[31]https://developer.mozilla.org/en-US/docs/Web/API/FileList

Why does this work? The slice() method on Array.prototype only expects the object it is operating on to have numeric properties along with a length property. So, by changing the context of the call to slice() to the pseudo-array, we end up getting a *real* array in exchange. This also works since Array. prototype.slice(), when called with no parameters, simply returns a new Array.

The preceding "trick" seems like more of a hack, even though it reliably works cross-browser. Starting with ECMAScript 2015, we have an official method on the Array object that will convert a pseudo-array into a real array: Array.from():

```
1  var realArray = Array.from(pseudoArray);
2
3  // now you can call all methods available on Array.prototype:
4  realArray.forEach(function(element, index) {
5    // ...
6  });
```

Less hacky, but unfortunately this method is not supported in Internet Explorer or most mobile browsers. This will become less of an issue over time. In the meantime, the cross-browser code demonstrated earlier is effective and simple if you want to work with pseudo-arrays without using jQuery.

Mapping and Merging

Here, look at this array of names:

```
1  var names = [
2    'ray',
3    'kat',
4    'mark',
5    'emily'
6  ];
```

Do you notice anything *wrong* with these names? Names are proper nouns in English, and, as such, should begin with a capital letter, but all of the names in our array start with a lowercase letter. Perhaps these names are not meant for display. One way to fix this involves creating a new array with the proper case for each name. jQuery's map() function allows us to do just that—create a new array based on an existing one:

```
1  // properNames will contain properly-cased names after execution
2  var properNames = $.map(names, function(name) {
3    return name[0].toUpperCase() + name.slice(1);
4  });
```

In ancient browsers, we must create a new empty array, use a C-loop to iterate over the values of the names array, and push each properly cased name onto the new properNames array. This isn't difficult, but it would be nice if a more elegant solution were available (without using jQuery). ECMAScript 5 gave us a native solution: Array.prototype.map():[32]

```
1  // properNames will contain properly-cased names after execution
2  var properNames = names.map(function(name) {
3    return name[0].toUpperCase() + name.slice(1);
4  });
```

---

[32]www.ecma-international.org/ecma-262/5.1/#sec-15.4.4.19

Mapping one array to a new array is obviously useful, but what if we want to *combine* two arrays? As usual, jQuery offers one method for this specific purpose: the aptly named merge(). Let's use jQuery's merge() method to combine two arrays of users. Each of these arrays represents a set of users from a different system, and we want to account for each set in a *single* array.

The two arrays look something like this:

```
1  var users1 = [
2    {name: 'Ray'},
3    {name: 'Kat'},
4    {name: 'Mark'}
5  ];
6
7  var users2 = [
8    {name: 'Emily'},
9    {name: 'Joe'},
10   {name: 'Huang'}
11 ];
```

And our jQuery code is as follows:

```
1  // users1 will contain all users1 user and
2  // all users2 users after this completes
3  $.merge(users1, users2);
```

Now we have a single array with both sets of users, but we've also modified one of the original arrays (users1). We might not want to do this. Instead, it is probably wiser to create a *new* array that merges the contents of users1 and users2. Although $.merge() wasn't built with this specific scenario in mind, it is still possible, though the solution isn't particularly elegant:

```
1  // users3 will contain all users1 user and
2  // all users2 users after this completes
3  var users3 = $.merge($.merge([], users1), users2);
```

You can alternatively merge two arrays into a new array by using the native Array.prototype.concat() method:

```
1  // users3 will contain all users1 user and
2  // all users2 users after this completes
3  var users3 = users1.concat(users2);
```

Not only is that *far* easier than using jQuery, it's also supported in *all* browsers. But let's say, for the sake of argument, you really do want to merge all items from users2 into users1. In this specific (and probably uncommon) scenario, jQuery's merge() method wins in terms of simplicity, but you can still accomplish this without too much trouble using nothing but the tools provided by the TC39 group:[33]

```
1  // users1 will contain all users1 user and
2  // all users2 users after this completes
3  users2.forEach(function(user) {
4    users1.push(user);
5  });
```

---

[33]www.ecma-international.org/memento/TC39.htm

We can make the preceding code work in ancient browsers too by using a standard C-loop instead of Array.prototype.forEach().

But there's another option! ECMAScript 2015 defines a new "spread" operator[34] that can be used to (among other things) combine two arrays, for browsers except IE:

```
1   // users3 will contain all users1 user and
2   // all users2 users after this completes
3   var users3 = [...users1, ...users2];
```

The preceding is functionally equivalent to our earlier use of Array.prototype.concat(). The users3 array contains the values of both of the other users arrays, and no changes are made to users1 or users2.

Useful Function Tricks

There are a number of interesting ways to make JavaScript arrays and objects solve problems for you and meet the requirements of your project. We've already walked through many such examples in the preceding sections. I've covered generic Objects, and Array objects, but I have yet to cover one more important Object type: functions! That's right, JavaScript functions are objects too.

In this final section, you will learn how to create new functions, change the context of existing functions, and even create a new function that calls an old function with a set of default arguments. jQuery provides *some* support for all of this, but, as usual, all of the power required to work with functions effectively exists in the underlying language (JavaScript).

A Word about JavaScript Context

There are many important concepts that JavaScript and front-end developers must understand in order to be effective. Although my intent is not to cover *all* of these concepts in this book, I've already demonstrated quite a few. In this section, I focus on yet another important language feature: context.

In JavaScript, *context* dictates the value of the this keyword at any given time during execution of code. That's a pretty simple explanation for an often confused and misunderstood concept. One common error involves conflating scope and context, or ignorance of the differences between scope and context. Suffice it to say, scope and context are two completely different concepts. Whereas context deals with this, scope describes which variables are accessible at a particular point. Up until ECMAScript 2015, JavaScript only supported function scope. Now, with the introduction of the const and let keywords, block scope is finally available as well.

I think the best way to explain context is through code examples. Next, I'll illustrate three separate and common scenarios where the value of this differs. This is not meant to be a complete and exhaustive discussion of context, but a bit of information to remove some of the complexity from the subject and allow you to gain a better overall understanding.

In this first example, the value of this, inside the function, will be the "global" object. In the browser, this global object is window, and on the server (with Node.js) the value is the global object.

```
1   function printThis() {
2       console.log(this);
3   }
4
5   printThis();
```

---

[34]www.ecma-international.org/ecma-262/6.0/#sec-array-initializer

That code will log the window or global object to the console. But there's a bit of a catch. If this code is executed in "strict" mode, the value of this will be undefined. To execute the same code in strict mode, all we need to do is add the "use strict" pragma to the top of our printThis() function:

```
1  function printThis() {
2    'use strict';
3    console.log(this);
4  }
5
6  printThis();
```

And now, undefined is logged to the console. Strict mode was first introduced in ECMAScript 5.[35] While I don't intend to talk much more about this in this book, suffice it to say that strict mode attempts to guard against some potentially dangerous coding errors, such as relying on the value of this inside of a standalone function or attempting to override an arguments pseudo-array. Browser support for strict mode is limited to modern browsers, with the exception of Internet Explorer 9.

A second example of context in JavaScript involves executing a function that is a property of an object. What do you think will be printed to the console in the following code fragment?

```
1  var person = {
2    name: 'Ray',
3    printName: function() {
4      console.log(this.name);
5    }
6  }
7
8  person.printName();
```

If you guessed "Ray" you're correct. When a function belongs to an object, the context of that function is bound to the parent object. Strict mode does not change the context in this scenario. In some respects, this is no different than the previous example. Since all "orphan" functions belong to the global or window object, it stands to reason that the context of these functions would be bound to the window/global object, at least for the sake of consistency.

A third and final example of context relates to constructor functions. A *constructor function* represents an object that can be created using the new keyword. Consider the following constructor function and some code that constructs a new instance of the associated object. Perhaps you can guess what will be printed to the console:

```
1  var Person = function(name) {
2    console.log(name + ' lives in the ' + this.country);
3  };
4  Person.prototype.country = 'United States';
5
6  var rayPerson = new Person('Ray');
```

Spoiler alert: executing the preceding code will print "Ray lives in the United States" to the console. But why? Person is an "orphan" function, isn't it? Well, yes, it is, and if we removed the new keyword from the last line, our code fragment would end with var rayPerson = Person('Ray') and this.country would

---

[35]www.ecma-international.org/ecma-262/5.1/#sec-10.1.1

be undefined (unless of course some other code added a country property to the window/global object beforehand). When a function is "constructed," the context of that function is bound to the corresponding object. In this case, that is the Person object, which has a country property on its prototype chain.

One other question you may have regarding this constructor function: why is the first letter in the constructor function name capitalized? This is completely unrelated to scope, but still a fair question. By convention, constructor function names are capitalized. When this convention is followed consistently, it becomes easier for developers to distinguish between objects that *should* be constructed using the new keyword and those that should not be constructed. If an object that is meant to be created using new is not created this way, unexpected behavior will likely occur.

Creating a New Function from an Old One

Knowing the particulars of how context is assigned to a function is useful, but these are not hard-and-fast rules. No, not at all. Context can be arbitrarily specified for any function. First, you can create a new function from an existing function *and* initialize that new function using an alternate context. jQuery provides $.proxy() for this specific purpose:

```
1  var person = {
2    name: 'Ray',
3    handleClick: function() {
4      console.log(this.name + ' was clicked');
5    }
6  }
7
8  $('#my-person').click(
9    $.proxy(person.handleClick, person)
10 );
```

When the element (presumably a <button>) with an ID of "my-person" is clicked, "Ray was clicked" will be printed to the console. If we remove the $.proxy() call, the result will be "undefined was clicked" instead. But why? Shouldn't the handleClick() function, which belongs to the person object, receive person as its context by default? Yes, by default it will, but handleClick() is no ordinary function—it's an event handler. And the browser auto-magically sets the context for all event handlers to the target element. In this case, that would be the "clicked" element, and this is *not* what we want. So, we need to create a *new* function that uses the person object as its context so we can log the name of the person when handling the click event. jQuery's proxy() API method provides a way to accomplish this, as you saw earlier.

jQuery's proxy() method was amazingly useful and elegant before ECMAScript 5 came along and created the Function.prototype.bind() method.[36] Before support for bind(), a mind-bending polyfill was required to achieve the same behavior, or you could simply pull in jQuery and move on to coding up your project. Luckily, all modern browsers support bind(), and the preceding example can be duplicated without jQuery, and without the indirection of a wrapper, for modern browsers:

```
1  var person = {
2    name: 'Ray',
3    handleClick: function() {
4      console.log(this.name + ' was clicked');
5    }
6  };
```

---

[36]www.ecma-international.org/ecma-262/5.1/#sec-15.3.4.5

```
 7
 8  document.getElementById('my-person').addEventListener(
 9    'click',
10    person.handleClick.bind(person)
11  );
```

Fantastic—we can change the context of our event handlers to match the object holding these functions, mirroring our expectations for functions properties bound to objects. But what if we need to do more? What if we need to supply specific arguments to this event handler when the handler function is bound? Suppose the handle also needs to know some specifics about its environment outside of the object it is bound to. In our case, the person.handleClick() function also needs to have a handle on the current logged-in user. With jQuery's proxy() function, we can fulfill this new requirement simply by passing the user information as an additional parameter, after the context argument:

```
 1  var person = {
 2    name: 'Ray',
 3    handleClick: function(user) {
 4      console.log(this.name + ' was clicked by ' + user);
 5    }
 6  };
 7
 8  $('#my-person').click(
 9    $.proxy(person.handleClick, person, 'Kat')
10  );
```

We can do this using Function.prototype.bind() too!

```
 1  var person = {
 2    name: 'Ray',
 3    handleClick: function(user) {
 4      console.log(this.name + ' was clicked by ' + user);
 5    }
 6  };
 7
 8  document.getElementById('my-person').addEventListener(
 9    'click',
10    person.handleClick.bind(person, 'Kat')
11  );
```

Again, just as with the $.proxy() example, the preceding code will print "Ray was clicked by Kat" to the console. I suspect that some of you are wondering what happened to the Event object parameter that is usually passed as the first argument to an event handler function. Well, it's still there, and it *is* passed by the browser to our event handler. Remember the new function we created with bind? We insisted that our new function receive an argument of "Kat." This will always be the *first* argument received by our new function, making the Event object second in line. Had we passed two new arguments as part of our call to bind(), Event would have been the *third* argument instead. jQuery's proxy() method works the same way.

Calling an Existing Function with a New Context

There *is* an alternative to creating an entirely new function with an altered context and additional arguments. Instead, you may prefer to invoke the original function on demand and specify a new context (and optionally arguments) at the time of invocation. jQuery does not provide any methods to accomplish this, which is likely due to the fact that this behavior has been supported natively by JavaScript since the early days of the language.

The first version of JavaScript included `Function.prototype.call()`, which allows an arbitrary function to be called with an alternate context. Let's rewrite the first vanilla JavaScript `person` event handler that used `bind` with `call` instead:

```
1   var person = {
2     name: 'Ray',
3     handleClick: function() {
4       console.log(this.name + ' was clicked');
5     }
6   };
7
8   document.getElementById('my-person').addEventListener(
9     'click',
10    function() {
11      person.handleClick.call(person);
12    }
13  );
```

Instead of creating a new function based off of the `person.handleClick()` function, we're providing a function to `addEventListener()` that, when executed by a click action, invokes `person.handleClick()` function with a context of `person`. The result is the same as our previous `bind` example, but the approach is a bit different. Before `bind` was introduced, using `call` in this manner was an alternative to using a polyfill or pulling in jQuery to make use of `$.proxy()`.

The `call()` method also provides a way to supply additional arguments to the target function, just like `bind()`. So, we can rewrite the second `bind()` example using `call()` as well:

```
1   var person = {
2     name: 'Ray',
3     handleClick: function(user) {
4       console.log(this.name + ' was clicked by ' + user);
5     }
6   };
7
8   document.getElementById('my-person').addEventListener(
9     'click',
10    function() {
11      person.handleClick.call(person, 'Kat');
12    }
13  );
```

The call() method, like bind(), accepts a new context as the first parameter, and a set of comma-separated initial arguments to pass to the target function. This comma-separated list becomes the arguments pseudo-array made available to the target function. In our example, the argument passed to the initial event handler function is completely ignored (the Event object)—it is *not* passed on to the handleClick() function. This is another way in which call() differs from bind(). In cases where a single known argument needs to passed through to the target function, this is ideal. But if an intermediate function must act as a simple proxy for a target function, the requirement to pass a comma-separated list of arguments becomes a limitation.

Imagine a function that is designed to log function calls. It doesn't want or need to know much about the target function. Its job is simple: intercept the function call, log it, and then pass control to the target function. To properly accomplish this feat, we must be able to pass the entire arguments pseudo-array on to the target function. For this, we must use Function.protoype.apply(), which allows us to pass an array or array-like object in addition to the context of the target function:

```
1   var person = {
2     name: 'Ray',
3     handleClick: function(user) {
4       console.log(this.name + ' was clicked by ' + user);
5     }
6   };
7
8   function logFunctionCall(targetFunction) {
9     // We need to pass only the "original" arguments, which means
10    // we have to slice off the first one passed to this function,
11    // and remember `arguments` is a pseudo-array!
12    var originalArguments = [].slice.call(arguments, 1);
13
14    console.log('Calling ' + targetFunction.toString() +
15      ' with ' + originalArguments);
16
17    targetFunction.apply(this, originalArguments);
18  }
19
20  document.getElementById('my-person').addEventListener(
21    'click',
22    logFunctionCall.bind(person, person.handleClick, 'Kat')
23  );
```

In our original event handler, to keep things simple, we're using bind() to call our intermediate logging function. The context of the log() function will be the person object. This will make it easier for the log() function to blindly invoke the target function with the desired context. And of course, we need to supply the current user's name to the handleClick() function, so that is passed to the log() function, along with a "reference" to the handleClick() function.

When the logFunctionCall() function is invoked as part of handling the click event, the target function source and and target arguments are logged to the console, and then the target function is called with whatever arguments were supplied to the original calling function. In this case, this will ensure the user name "Kat" and the MouseEvent object instance representing the click event are all passed to the person.handleClick() function. And since logFunctionCall's context is already bound to the person object, we can use this as the desired context when invoking the target function.

This last example is a bit more complex than some of the previous, but it illustrates a non-trivial and real-world use of the powerful API that is natively available to us as web developers. You can assert full control over functions, arrays, objects, and primitives without the help of any libraries. A simple understanding of the language is all that is required!

CHAPTER 13

■ ■ ■

Going Forward

It's been fun, but, sadly, *Beyond jQuery* has to end eventually. A lot of time and research has been put into demonstrating to you that there are viable alternatives to jQuery present in the browser and in JavaScript itself. In fact, even *I* stumbled upon some new knowledge while putting this book together. And even if you do decide to rely on a familiar and convenient option, such as jQuery, you now have a much better understanding of how this particular abstraction functions. This knowledge will not only prepare you for your next project, it will also help you to troubleshoot performance or behavior issues you run into on existing projects that are still tied to jQuery.

As I pointed out in the opening chapters of the book, we are all software developers, and web developers, and JavaScript developers, not jQuery, or Zepto, or AngularJS, or (insert your favorite library or framework here) developers. Libraries come and go, but the web and the language that holds it all together will live on for much longer.

What shall we do with all this newfound knowledge? Well, I know what I'm going to do, but do you? For some, it may be obvious what your next course of action is. For others, not so much. It might not be clear what your options are, or how you should proceed with current and future projects. Should you change anything at all? And what about any questions you might have that are not answered in this book? How do you stay current with the constantly evolving landscape?

This final chapter offers some suggestions and guidance for life after *Beyond jQuery*.

Now What?

If you learned even half as much about JavaScript and the web API reading this book as I did writing it, you probably have a lot to think about. There are quite a few choices you could make, and a number of different reactions you might have in response to the content and tone of this book. Realistically, I think there are four common paths forward for readers. While some may pick one of these paths, others may find that this section outlines four successive stages that follow completion of this book.

Option/Stage 1: Ignore Everything

Perhaps you are still defiant, even after reading the entire book (or maybe you just skimmed it). The language and DOM API are ugly. jQuery is still the best choice. Well, we are all entitled to our own opinions. And there is nothing wrong with using jQuery, as long as the choice isn't made in ignorance of the alternatives. Unless this is merely the first stage in a process that ends in enlightenment, it is unlikely that much else will change your mind. I can only hope that you at least benefitted from this book in some small way. Maybe you learned a new CSS selector, or gained a better understanding of promises. Regardless, if *Beyond jQuery* provided you with some new knowledge and made you a stronger developer, then I'm certainly happy.

© Ray Nicholus 2016
R. Nicholus, *Beyond jQuery*, DOI 10.1007/978-1-4842-2235-5_13

Option/Stage 2: Rip jQuery Out of All Your Projects

Some readers may have the urge to take an opposite approach to Option 1. Instead of a laissez-faire attitude, you may decide to take on major refactors of all of your active (and inactive) projects. Your mantra may be "Remove all of the jQuery, replace with vanilla JS." I can certainly respect this point of view (I felt this way myself at one point), but I would suggest you step back, take a deep breath, and think about the consequences of this decision for a while first. Does your project have a comprehensive set of automated tests? Do you have a fair amount of free time on your hands? Is there nothing else more important for you to do instead? If the answer to one or more of these questions is no, then I would suggest you not rock the boat and make a lot of unnecessary changes to an existing codebase—unless at least one of the following are true:

- The project is fairly small.

- You don't really have any (or many) users, and this is more of an academic exercise to get you started down the vanilla JS path.

- A major refactor is already underway for other reasons, or you have one planned.

- After profiling your project, your current use of jQuery is causing notable performance issues.

If any of those describes your situation, happy coding, and best of luck to you! *Beyond jQuery* will serve as a useful reference during your quest.

Option/Stage 3: Rock Back and Forth in a Corner, Crying

"I can't or shouldn't use jQuery anymore?!" For many, jQuery has been a core component in every web project throughout their entire career. The thought of giving up such a reliable and familiar helper can be devastating to some. But fear not, you do not have to abandon jQuery, as I've already mentioned several times throughout the book, unless you really want to. So if you'd prefer to ween yourself off and slowly move over to closer-to-the-metal solutions, bit by bit, feel free to do that instead. jQuery (probably) isn't going anywhere. Let this phase be a short bump in the road as you move on the the final and most important step in the post-reading process.

Option/Stage 4: Decide to Be More Discerning Going Forward

If you end up (or start) here, then I've accomplished one of the goals I set out to reach with this book. It is not just a guide for those looking to move beyond a specific library—the intent is also for you to begin thinking more critically about libraries, frameworks, and your browser-side dependencies in general. Personally, I've found this way of thinking prevents me (though not necessarily those around me) from unnecessarily complicating dependency trees in new projects. This state of mind helps me be more frugal, more careful, and forces me to spend more time thinking, and less time coding. I'm not sure this is something that can be taught, but perhaps, with enough inculcation, you can adopt this state of mind yourself.

The Future of Web Development

It is, of course, impossible to definitively predict the future of software development, especially since the technology evolves and common workflows pivot so quickly and often. Still it's fun to think about what our world might look like at some distant point from now. As you ponder (and live though) the future of web development, I think it's important to keep a solid set of best practices in mind. And you cannot simply follow a set of practices because someone tells you to do so. You must believe in them yourself.

Some will say that "best practices" evolve over time, and this is true to some extent. Although it is important to have a set of established goals and guidelines when developing a complex project, there are few hard-and-fast rules, and context is key when deciding what best practices are most appropriate. There may be many reasons to abandon established best practices. Once you have decided to abide by a specific set of guidelines, it's important not to discard them simply out of convenience (or laziness). It will be easy to cut corners "just this once," especially with the dizzying array of options that you will face as the software technology landscape progresses at the current breakneck pace. Here are some established "best practices" that I like to follow, a few of which are mentioned in this book:

- Maintain a separation of concerns, not necessarily between HTML, CSS, and JavaScript, but in terms of behavior and roles. Though I will admit this particular best practice has a wide array of interpretations. For example, does React violate this principle? Is vue.js a better choice since it maintains a clearer separation between HTML, CSS, and JavaScript? Speaking strictly in the context of code, concerns don't *necessarily* need to be divided in terms of files. Although I do believe that this particular example illustrates that, this is perhaps a larger debate for another book.

- Develop small, focused components that do one thing, and do it well.

- Keep dependencies light and focused. Use external dependencies sparingly. And be discerning.

- Explore the code base of any dependency before relying on it. Is it well designed? Well maintained? Well tested? Do the developers of that dependency subscribe to the same set of best practices?

- When using dependencies, favor shims and polyfills over libraries and frameworks. That is not to say that all libraries and frameworks are bad and should be avoided, but I tend to favor smaller and more focused ones.

- Write automated tests wherever and whenever feasible. This will make refactoring less risky and painful. Some developers maintain that Test Driven Development is the only way to write tests, but I disagree. TDD can be overwhelming, and is not appropriate in all cases, based on my experience. What is important is that you write reliable and comprehensive tests, not necessarily how you write them.

Of course, there are others, but that represents a list of the most notable best practices that I follow, and they have served me well. But why have I dedicated so much of a section titled "The Future of Web Development" to a discussion of best practices? Simple: I feel it is important to have a set of guiding principles to keep you on course as you navigate a constantly changing set of new technologies.

As I've mentioned a number of times throughout this chapter (and book), web technology seems to be changing and growing at an unbelievable pace. I myself find it difficult to stay on top of the latest advancements. But often the advancements we focus on are limited to libraries and frameworks. These are usually the most "interesting" aspects of our evolving industry. Just as web and JavaScript specifications are the building blocks that allow jQuery to work its magic, the same is true of all of the newest flashy libraries and framework. As standards evolve, libraries and frameworks are able to evolve in turn. The future of the Web lies in the W3C, WHATWG, and ECMAScript specifications. Follow the newest libraries and frameworks, but keep just as close an eye on standards. The additions to existing specs and the birth of new ones will give you and others the ability to create more powerful, efficient, and performant solutions to complex problems.

Further Reading and Reference

Learning never stops, especially in our industry. *Beyond jQuery* can and should be a new reference for you whenever you're looking for a refresher on DOM manipulation, Ajax requests, JavaScript in general, or any of the other many topics covered here. But this book can't be your only reference. It was never meant to be an exhaustive source for all things web and JavaScript. The focus of this book has always been on the areas of the web API and the language that overlap with jQuery. This allowed for a large range of material to be discussed, but there are admittedly other topics that had to be left out as a result.

For everything that is not covered in this book, there are a set of resources that come with my full recommendation as I rely on all of them quite heavily myself. Some of the following are geared toward keeping your knowledge of web development and JavaScript up-to-date as well, something that a book cannot offer. For each recommended resource, I explain any notable limitations and strengths.

The Official Web and Language Specs

The specs themselves—WHATWG,[1] W3C,[2] and ECMA-262[3]—wield the most information in terms of the the web API and JavaScript. They contain an incredible amount of detail and can be seen as the source of truth for all of the native APIs discussed in this book. I wrote about each of these standards documents in Chapter 3. Unfortunately, these documents are also a bit hard to digest for most. If you truly want to understand every minute detail of a particular method or property, and are willing and able to spend time deciphering the abstruse language in these documents, then the official specs are an ideal resource. Otherwise, there are more appropriate choices.

The TC39 group, responsible for curating the JavaScript specification, maintains a GitHub organization.[4] There, they record their meeting notes, agendas, and proposals. It's a great place to keep up on the very latest progress on ECMA-262, and sometimes the proposals and meeting notes are a bit easier to follow than the official standards documents themselves. My favorite reference in this organization is the README.md file[5] inside of the proposals repository.[6] There, you can see the latest progress of each proposal, from stage 1 to 3. This document even links to a list of stage 0 proposals, which provides insight into possibilities regarding the distant future of the language.

Mozilla Developer Network

The clearest and most concise alternative to the official standards documents is, without a doubt, Mozilla Developer Network.[7] This is often my first reference choice if I am looking for a details about a specific web API or JavaScript method. In addition to easy-to-parse language and code examples, MDN also includes a browser support matrix for almost every interface. And for API items that are not well supported cross-browser, MDN often includes code for a polyfill that you can simply drop into your project. If you really want to take a peek at the underlying specification document, each page includes a table that details when a particular feature was first introduced along with links to the official documents. Mozilla Developer Network is considered by many (me included) to be the best comprehensive reference for web developers available today.

---

[1]http://whatwg.org
[2]www.w3.org
[3]www.ecma-international.org/publications/standards/Ecma-262.htm
[4]https://github.com/tc39
[5]https://github.com/tc39/proposals/blob/master/README.md
[6]https://github.com/tc39/proposals
[7]https://developer.mozilla.org/en-US/

Caniuse.com

If you're instead looking for more details regarding browser support for a specific feature, a group of related features, or even a group of unrelated features, caniuse.com is the ultimate resource. For any specific interface or feature, caniuse.com describes browser support in the form of a table, with a separate column for each popular browser. Support for each feature is tracked all the way back to include ancient browsers (even Internet Explorer 6). Exceptional cases are noted in the table as well. Take the FileReader API as an example—caniuse includes notes that link to an article (written by me)[8] that describes critical bugs introduced into the implementation of the API in iOS 8. Each feature tracks these types of issues and other related resources, such as a link to the MDN page, the specification document, browser-specific support documents, and even important browser-specific implementation notes. For example, on the SVG favicons support table, a note indicates that Firefox requires the MIME-type of the served resource to be "image/svg+xml."

Caniuse also allows you to group information by browser, feature category, and type of browser (desktop, mobile, and so on). A neat feature renders the support table as a bar graph that determines the height of each browser version bar under a particular browser based on the relative usage of each browser version. And this relative browser version data can be region specific as well, if desired. Although I prefer MDN for an understandable explanation of web and JavaScript features, caniuse is unmatched in terms of browser support information.

Stack Overflow

Most of us have already spent a fair amount of time on Stack Overflow. After all, it seems most software development questions, when typed into your search engine of choice, reveal Stack Overflow at the top of the results list. SO is a no-nonsense question and answer site, with a set of strict rules and a dedicated community hell-bent on enforcing these rules. This level of purity and perfection that the SO community maintains often frustrates new or casual contributors, but it also makes the site an amazingly effective resource for all things programming.

Even seemingly picayune topics are represented on Stack Overflow, such as this question, "What is the best comment in source code you have ever encountered?"[9] But be warned, new questions of this nature are frowned upon these days. Still, if you are (amazingly) unable to find an existing answer to your unusual programming question on Stack Overflow, the enormous community is available to answer your well-formed query. This is particularly true for JavaScript related questions, as "javascript" is the most used tag on the site.

Twitter

In terms of keeping up-to-date with the latest advancements in web development, Twitter is my number one resource. I don't personally follow many developers on Twitter, but I still manage to almost drown in the seemingly endless flow of interesting discussions, news about new web and JavaScript features, and notable libraries that make the future of the web seem more like the present. Twitter is an often-overlooked medium for broadcasting and absorbing bite-sized software-related information. And some of the more interesting web-dev-related discussions happen on Twitter, in my experience. It's not critical to simply follow the most influential or prolific developers. If you are able to locate a handful of engineers that are willing to share interesting opinions and articles, you'll find that your sphere of knowledge can grow quite rapidly.

Whichever resource you choose to keep up-to-date, or to explore existing APIs, the most important goal is to keep learning. The first step is to move *Beyond jQuery*, but don't just stop there. Comfort is a sign of stagnation. If you become set in your ways, are unwilling keep an open mind, and refuse to consider moving beyond your current set of tools and processes, you will stop growing as a software developer.

---

[8]http://blog.fineuploader.com/2014/09/10/ios8-presents-serious-issues-that-prevent-file-uploading/
[9]http://stackoverflow.com/questions/184618/what-is-the-best-comment-in-source-code-you-have-ever-encountered

Index

© Ray Nicholus 2016
R. Nicholus, *Beyond jQuery*, DOI 10.1007/978-1-4842-2235-5

Get the eBook for only $5!

Why limit yourself?

Now you can take the weightless companion with you wherever you go and access your content on your PC, phone, tablet, or reader.

Since you've purchased this print book, we're happy to offer you the eBook in all 3 formats for just $5.

Convenient and fully searchable, the PDF version enables you to easily find and copy code—or perform examples by quickly toggling between instructions and applications. The MOBI format is ideal for your Kindle, while the ePUB can be utilized on a variety of mobile devices.

To learn more, go to www.apress.com/companion or contact support@apress.com.

All Apress eBooks are subject to copyright. All rights are reserved by the Publisher, whether the whole or part of the material is concerned, specifically the rights of translation, reprinting, reuse of illustrations, recitation, broadcasting, reproduction on microfilms or in any other physical way, and transmission or information storage and retrieval, electronic adaptation, computer software, or by similar or dissimilar methodology now known or hereafter developed. Exempted from this legal reservation are brief excerpts in connection with reviews or scholarly analysis or material supplied specifically for the purpose of being entered and executed on a computer system, for exclusive use by the purchaser of the work. Duplication of this publication or parts thereof is permitted only under the provisions of the Copyright Law of the Publisher's location, in its current version, and permission for use must always be obtained from Springer. Permissions for use may be obtained through RightsLink at the Copyright Clearance Center. Violations are liable to prosecution under the respective Copyright Law.

Printed in the United States
By Bookmasters

Printed in the United States
By Bookmasters